More Praise for *Big Topics*

"In exquisite detail, derived from astonishing memory, and articulated in vivid multisensory language, Nancy Thurston takes us as companions along every twist and turn of her spiritual journey. To accept Thurston's offer of companionship for this very wild ride is to be catapulted into one's own adventure of spiritual discovery and discernment."

—David Schlafer
Episcopal priest, homiletics professor and author of *Your Way with God's Word*

"This is the story of a bold journey to self-knowledge. It is also a tale of how to find and to bind together with partners in sustainable service to a vision for building a new world. Caution: the habits of heart, mind, and practice presented in this book could be habit forming."

—Laurie Emrich
Lead Partner, National Progressive Leadership Campus

"*Big Topics at Midnight* gives us an incredibly clear and simple architecture for white people—and those who care about white people—to move away from generations of racism past and to imagine and build a different future. Food for thought and dialogue for years to come."

—Cynthia R. Renfro
Philanthropy Executive

"A woman of privilege, Thurston embarks on a sacred pilgrimage to unshackle the chains of race, class, and gender that have kept her a prisoner within her own myopic world. Her process of unfettering herself has social implications for anyone living in the United States, where the legacy of slavery, the power of money, and the category of gender still profoundly shape our lives. Insightful and powerful! Our country needs more Thurstons who will tell the truth of our past and present-day realities."

—AJ Johnston, M.Div.
Executive Director of Mindful Peacebuilding

"This book is revealing and fun. In a time when more and more of us want to know about our ancestors to better understand ourselves, Nancy encourages us to go deeper by superbly weaving her own stories in and out of those of her ancestors. I applaud her adventurous research."

—Holly Fulton
DeWolf descendant, participant in *Traces of the Trade*
and board member of Coming to the Table

"*Big Topics at Midnight* is a book of questing, questioning, growing and connecting."

—Jennifer Ladd
Jennifer Ladd Consulting and co-founder of Class Action

"How do we speak up when we know something isn't socially just? Nancy Thurston gives us a road map to delve deeply into these topics *and* to heal ourselves right along with her. A must read for those who need to be part of the change. This is a book I'll be recommending to all of my clients."

—Olivia Boyce-Abel
Founder and principal, Boyce-Abel Associates & Family Lands Consulting

"Nancy's willingness to explore the voices within and to follow the leading of the Spirit in her choices is a powerful witness for those who seek transformation in the world for the sake of our children."

—Rose Feerick
Director of Harvest Time and mother of two boys

Big Topics
at Midnight

To Christina
You taught me how to write a book
and held the rim with love and patience

To Ann
You taught me how to remember
my birthright — my connection to
Earth.

Thank you. Blessings,

Nancy
August 2012

Big Topics
at Midnight

A Texas Girl Wakes Up to Race,
Class, Gender and Herself

Nancy M. Thurston

ROSEGATEPRESS

Ten percent of the proceeds from the sale of this book will be donated to
Be Present, Inc., Community Wholeness Venture and Harvest Time.

Published by
Rosegate Press
4341 NE Halsey #18
Portland, OR 97213
www.rosegatepress.com

Cover and book design by Lubosh Cech, okodesignstudio.com

Front cover photo by Arthur Tipps
Back cover photo by Lubosh Cech
Book illustrations by Khara Scott-Bey and Mary Sue Tipps Mathys

"Economic Injustice: Fire Burning in the Bones," (an excerpt) by Nancy Thurston in
Preaching as Prophetic Calling: Sermons that Work XII, ed. Roger Alling and David J.
Schlafer, ©2004. Used by permission from Church Publishing Incorporated.

Thurston, Nancy M. (Nancy Mathys), 1954–

    Big topics at midnight : a Texas girl wakes up to race, class, gender
    and herself / Nancy M. Thurston.—1st ed.—Portland, Ore. :
    Rosegate Press, c2012.

    xx, 400 p., lc22.9 cm.

    ISBN: 978-0-9854510-1-1
    Includes bibliographical references and index.

    1. Thurston, Nancy M. (Nancy Mathys), 1954– 2. Racism—
    Psychological aspects. 3. Social classes—Psychological aspects.
    4. Money—Psychological aspects. 5. Sexism—Psychological
    aspects. 6. Social justice. 7. Spirituality. 8. Spiritual formation.
    9. Equality. 10. Spiritual biography. I. Title.

BL73.T487 A3 2012   2012909291
155.9092–dc23   1211

First Edition
Printed in the United States of America

MIX
Paper from
responsible sources
FSC® C014174

Dedication

My ancestors and I dedicate this book to
Paul and Laura. May you and other young
adults and children around the globe
today, as well as your children, benefit
from my generation's work to create the
transformation we long for. Blessings as you
live your own lives fully, wildly and boldly.

Acknowledgments

Lillie Allen, Margherita Vacchiano, LaVerne Robinson and so many in the network of Be Present, Inc. have been such wonderful teachers, mentors and friends on the path toward knowing myself outside the distress of my oppression, listening in a present and conscious state and learning how to build sustainable relationships, true alliances and collective leadership. That's a mouthful, but it is the heart of living in my own skin and in the world.

Rose Feerick, the only co-director (ever trusting that the other co-director will manifest one day soon) of Harvest Time, has taught me so much about living an incarnational and mystical faith, bringing my heart in line with all of my life—money included. Plus, Rose, you are an incredible friend.

Alease Bess, director of Community Wholeness Venture, standing in the gap with me, on the phone or washing my feet, has taught me how to follow God in all things. Our friendship is full of miracles everywhere, even in the mess.

Howard Thurston, the man who has loved me since I was sixteen, allowed his life to become much more public than he ever would have chosen and picked up all the daily chores that I've dropped in these seven years of writing. I love you.

Howard, a civil/structural engineer, reminded me that hidden details are critical to keep the whole building—or book—standing strong and beautiful. The behind the scenes beauty was provided by:

- family, including, but not limited to Howard, Paul, Laura, Brent, Martha, Hannah and Red, my favorite great uncle who died just before this book was finished

- the irreplaceable records and letters created and saved by my mom and her father and organized by my dad
- homiletics mentor David Schlafer
- Earthmothers and healers Candice Covington, Rosemary Beam, Kim Cottrell, Tami Kent, Beth Yohalem-Ilsley, Lindsey George, Susan Allen, Rebecca Reese, Sohi McCaw, Nan Narboe, Andrea Mathieson, to name a few
- editors in the early phases of the book Jacqueline Sowell, Molly Thurston Parker and final draft copyeditor Ann Eames
- book cover and page layout designer Lubosh Cech of Oko Design Studio
- photographers, including Noa Mohlabane, Judy Bork and Great Uncle Arthur Tipps, who took my childhood photo used on the book's cover
- web designer Jason Parker
- the detail-gifted Lydia Marsalli and Lila Isbell
- friends and communities too numerous to mention
- all of the trees from which the paper came for writing and publishing this book

Jen Violi, Khara Scott-Bey and Christina Baldwin were on my creative support team. More about their work is found near the back of the book.

Then there's the tulip tree outside my window, the neighborhood crows, the migrating finches, the roses ... but that list gets a little long.

All of these and more have supported my exploration of waking up at the midnight hour. Thank you to all who have added to the beauty of my life and this book of my heart.

Contents

Nancy's Family Tree

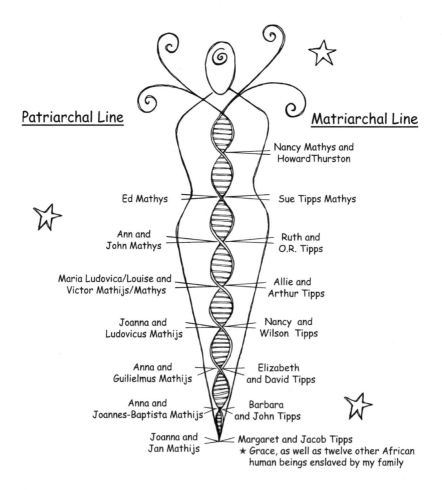

Patriarchal Line

Matriarchal Line

Nancy Mathys and Howard Thurston

Ed Mathys — Sue Tipps Mathys

Ann and John Mathys — Ruth and O.R. Tipps

Maria Ludovica/Louise and Victor Mathijs/Mathys — Allie and Arthur Tipps

Joanna and Ludovicus Mathijs — Nancy and Wilson Tipps

Anna and Guilielmus Mathijs — Elizabeth and David Tipps

Anna and Joannes-Baptista Mathijs — Barbara and John Tipps

Joanna and Jan Mathijs — Margaret and Jacob Tipps
★ Grace, as well as twelve other African human beings enslaved by my family

Unlike my mother Sue's genealogical charts, this one does not have the full names of all ancestors.

Introduction

Cynthia spoke and the bottom fell out of my world. I hadn't flown across the country for this. But even as I struggled to find my footing, I knew that I didn't want to go back to sleep, blind to life outside my little neighborhood and experience.

A year before this moment I'd attended Be Present, Inc.'s 2002 National Conference on Power & Class on the recommendation of Jenny Ladd, a woman I'd talked to for ten minutes. I arrived in Atlanta and entered a large room with lively music pulsing through the air, cloths of every color covering the walls and strands of tiny lights twinkling all around. In the midst of it all were a hundred strangers, from children to grey-haired elders, with skin from black to mocha to pink. I'd never been in a group this diverse, and it looked more like the world than my lifetime of neighborhoods.

I had no idea that my life would soon be shaken to the core.

At the dining room table during lunch, three black women told stories about growing up in the Boston housing projects—stories of conflict between Irish immigrants and black residents—of police graft and despair. Yet, these women had birthed drama programs for young people to explore their lives and creatively envision justice in the inner city. A white woman spoke of her lifelong work of community organizing, which led her to form a new style of foundation that addressed the roots of racial and economic injustice.

Fascinated, I listened carefully. I was, nonetheless, embarrassed that I'd only been a volunteer, never an activist or organizer.

Later, in the conference sessions, I heard anecdotes of the pain of not being able to pay an electric bill shared alongside stories of guilt about inheriting millions of dollars. For the first time I heard about DWB—driving while black—which increased one's chances of being pulled over by the police. People spoke openly about their own personal experiences with class and race, their joys and their struggles.

I wanted to know more. Returning a year later to begin an eighteen-month training on the issues of race, gender, power and class, I met Cynthia Renfro, another attendee. Cynthia and I visited as we walked back and forth between the dining hall and the meeting room. A shy woman, Cynthia had sparkling, mischievous eyes, a head full of hundreds of thin dreadlocks and Caribbean brown skin.

As we began to share our experiences within the circle, Cynthia told a story about her mother, Pat. Her parents had moved from the West Coast to Dallas, Texas, in 1965. One morning shortly after she arrived, Pat took the week's dirty clothes to a laundromat, as she'd done many times before. A hand-printed WHITES ONLY sign propped up in the window confused her. "Why in the world would they want me to wash only white clothes?" she wondered. Mystified, she balanced the basket of dirty laundry on her hip and proceeded inside to wash all of her clothes, colors and whites. A few hours later as she was hanging up her dresses, she gasped. The sign, she realized, referred to her skin color and not the clothes.

I didn't hear another word of Cynthia's story.

Dallas, Texas ...

1965 ...

I lived in Texas in 1965.

Had there been WHITES ONLY signs in my hometown too? I hadn't thought Texas was caught up in this "Deep South" style of racism. Were there signs in the windows of Walgreens or the Blue Star Inn Restaurant? I had no idea.

I was in fifth grade in 1965. My heart sank when I realized that I, sweet and thoughtful as I was at eleven years old, hadn't noticed that anyone was excluded from my schools, neighborhoods, businesses or church. Sequestered in my white-skinned world, all signs I noticed pointed the way to freedom.

I was stunned. I didn't know where to turn as Cynthia's story careened through me. LaVerne Robinson, one of the trainers, gently touched my arm and asked what was happening. I burst into tears.

If I hadn't noticed that, what else hadn't I seen? Cynthia's story ripped my life wide open.

I was frantic. Part of me wanted to tie the loose ends back together again, nice and neat, and get on with life. The deepest part of me, though, knew that some of my old, limiting blind spots had just been exposed.

Growing up within upper middle class neighborhoods filled with white people, I'd been oblivious to how segregated my life and the world around me was. Now I wanted to make sense of the convoluted ways skin color, gender and money had impacted history, the nation's and mine.

When I looked back at history, signs in windows were only one part of a larger system of racism that still held strong in my hometown during my adolescence. Once I noticed, I was furious. Things I'd heard at the Be Present conference also let me know that this sort of prejudice wasn't just a thing of the past. I wrestled with anger and shame that other white-skinned or rich or privileged or Christian or Native Texan people—my people—could have been, and still be, so asleep to the injustice all around us.

Had my ancestors been any different? My mother, Mary "Sue" Tipps Mathys, was drawn to genealogy after the death of her father, O.R. Tipps. She studied census records, wills, ship passenger manifests, church records and land deeds. Mom's main interest, however, was in the stories beneath these bits of fact. As I read over her files, my disgust with historical figures in general shifted to disdain for my own ancestors.

Surrounded, it seemed, by others caught in prejudice, I also wanted to look inwardly. What else hadn't I noticed growing up? Searching for things to help jog my memory, I rummaged through my basement keepsake boxes and found small, keyed diaries, scrapbooks, school annuals and photographs.

As I started to wake up to myself, my ancestors beckoned me in a new way. Since they had all died and I wasn't prone to communication across the veil of death, I had to suspend my skepticism in order to hear what they had to say. I returned to Mom's genealogical research, brought family stories to mind, let my imagination go and listened with my heart. Then I went to my computer and wrote down what I heard, using their voices.

My female ancestors "spoke" first, one at a time, beginning with my grandmothers Ann Cahoon Mathys and Ruth Owen Tipps, followed by my mother. Seven generations of Tipps grandmothers spoke to me, from my mother back to Margaret Grount who married Jacob Tipps, son of our family's original immigrant, Lorenz. Grace, the only one of thirteen slaves of Margaret and Jacob Tipps whose name made it through the generations, also had her say. Later, my father, Ed Mathys, and grandfathers, O.R. Tipps and John Mathys, told me tidbits about their lives.

I was shocked at the power of the stories that emerged as each ancestor spoke in her or his unique voice. A number of them demanded to be included in this book. I'd learned the futility of arguing with some of these people while they were alive, so I thought it best just to honor their requests. Their stories weave in and out of my own.

Are their stories true? All of them referenced documented moments of their lives, but each went beyond these details. Some might call their stories tall tales. Regardless, I heard their words as truth stronger than facts.

Beyond my ancestors, two other "voices" showed up and wouldn't be ignored. One was the first full moon of 1986, shining brightly the night my daughter, Laura Anne, was born. The other was Hectate, my own combination of the goddess Hecate and my wise inner guide with an attitude the size of Texas.

What I heard influenced how I looked at my life, reminding me that I was part of a much greater whole. With them at my side and over my shoulders, I looked back at my own life and began to write.

I followed the chronology of my life, attempting to speak from my perspective along the way. As I awakened, I circled back to things that had happened to me, and then braided them back into my life. I told my story as honestly as I could, but the "facts" of my own life were filtered through my memory and understanding, and I changed a few names and details to protect the privacy of others. As with the stories from my ancestors, I sought to touch a truth beyond the facts.

During this process, I walked beyond the edges of my homogeneous lifetime of neighborhoods and outside the periphery of "my people" and my generation. I walked beyond anger and shame to transformation. I wanted to live in the global world, the natural world, while also keeping future generations in mind. My exploration became a sacred pilgrimage of learning to adapt my behavior, language and assumptions to become congruent with my awakening sight. My faith and integrity demanded nothing less.

Blending personal chronicle, historical research and ancestral voices into one book became a huge undertaking, but the world called for diverse languages and bold actions. Wars and rumors of wars cascaded one after another. Oil spilled into delicate oceans and bays. Personal, national and international debt shot sky high. The wealth gap grew wider each year. Fear and anxiety escalated among young and old alike. The earth and human societies quaked at this eleventh hour, unsure whether the future would bring continued destruction or something new.

As I awakened to the truth and texture of life, I began to see the gifts, support and joy all around me, just waiting to be noticed. I wanted to be part of what Joanna Macy called the "Great Turning" of our world toward a "life-sustaining civilization."[1]

Maybe I was an activist after all.

Once Cynthia's story shook me awake, I felt irresistibly drawn to begin, putting one step in front of the other on this pilgrimage. Ann Cahoon Mathys, my paternal grandmother, had graduated with her master's degree in physical education in 1915. Ahead of her time, she paved the way for me to follow.

Tucked into her photo album was a picture taken while she was teaching physical education to young college coeds in Riverside, California. For a May Day celebration, the men and women stood in a circle around a central pole topped with long cloth streamers. Each person held the end of a single ribbon. Under and over, over and under, women and men moved around the circle, slowly intertwining their strands around the pole.

I felt Grandma's spirit as my writing braided the many colored ribbons of diversity. I loved the idea of grandmother and granddaughter dancing together, plaiting beauty across the tears in the fabric of the world. Together we twirled, hoping beyond hope that our dance across the generations would serve those yet to come.

May it be so.

Maypole Dance, circa 1917

1

This Little World of Mine

My family had roots deep into the earth. Mom's dad, O.R. Tipps, grew up on a farm where the soil struggled to produce enough to feed a family of twelve. O.R. spent much of his adult life interested in the field grass that fed his grazing cattle, while his sister Kate cultivated beautiful flowers and his sister Allie Mae tended her abundant backyard garden. John Mathys, Dad's father, was a seeds man who grew beautiful flowers and bushes in his yard and became vice president of the Garden and Home Seed Division of Northrup King Seed Company.

My parents, Sue Tipps and Ed Mathys, fell in love in Wichita Falls, Texas—the land of big "blue skies" and "golden opportunities."[1] The sky kissed the land's ranches covered with grass and cattle and farms growing cotton, corn and wheat. Beneath it all, oil had collected in porous rock far underground.

North central Texas was a land of extremes. Weather included droughts and thunderstorms, blistering summer heat and frigid winter cold and wind that either blew head-on or swirled in a funnel cloud. We considered ourselves part of ruggedly independent West Texas, the home of self-made men. Christian churches dotted the town from edge to edge. Sheppard Air Force Base grounded the military firmly into the land. Everywhere Mom and Dad went around town—neighborhood barbeques and family reunions, work and church, stores and the public swimming pool—they saw smiling faces on other white-skinned families.

President Eisenhower promised that the 1950s would be a decade of peace, prosperity and progress. We'd won World War II, but our soldiers were still fighting in Korea, and our military supported the French in their war against North Vietnam. Here at home, Senator McCarthy led the battle against communism while Mom got so big with me growing in her belly that she was almost ready to pop.

Mom and Dad were a typical American couple; they had one car and owned a two-bedroom, one-bath home close to the average 1950s house size of eleven hundred square feet.[2] Dad went to work as a geologist at Shell Oil Company every morning, and Mom stayed home.

My family held extremes, just like the land around us. Dad was a Yankee (he'd spent most of his growing up years in Minnesota) while Mom was a native Texan. He was quiet; she was bold. He liked her independence. She liked his calm, even ways. Dad's father had come to this country as a baby, while Mom's family had lived here for ten generations. Dad insisted that his income alone pay for the family's living expenses, while Mom's family insisted on financing the young couple's first home and giving them annual gifts of money to build their "nest egg."

One year, eight months, and seven days after their wedding, Mom went to the Wichita Falls City Hospital in the throes of labor. Dad and his mother-in-law, Ruth, paced back and forth in the waiting room until the doctor delivered me at 9:17 a.m. on May 12, 1954. I held my family's differences within my body as clearly as I held their names: "Nancy" after Aunt Nancy Jane who'd died too young, and "Ann" after Dad's mother, all tied up neatly with the family name "Mathys." I was the first grandchild, and everyone was excited.

When I turned two, people smiled as I experimented with my new word: "NO." Everyone said I was really cute. One day Mom and Dad told me I was going to be a big sister. Mom's tummy kept growing, and when she was really big, I got the chickenpox and went across town to my grandparents' house to get better. When I got back home a week later, I was scared because Mom looked completely different. Her tummy was flatter, and she had a little bitty baby, my new brother, Glenn.

At home, we had lots of books, a radio and record player but no television. Disneyland opened, and I dreamed about going there sometime. New toys, just waiting for my friends and me when we got old enough, included Lego blocks and Barbie dolls, the latter rumored to be modeled after German sex toys. The polio vaccine was developed twelve years after that disease took the life of Aunt Nancy Jane Tipps.

Around the time of my three finger birthday, I got really good at dancing and singing. I kept asking Mom and Dad to twirl around with me whenever they were sitting down and doing nothing. They were usually too tired.

Once, after he finally got home from work, I eagerly tapped on the newspaper Dad was reading. I wanted to tell him about the doggie I saw that afternoon over at Sandy's house.

Dad yelled, "Stop it!"

I ran off, surprised that he got so mad at such a little thing.

A few days later, I decided to get his attention in a different way. Almost every afternoon around 5:30 Mom warned me to be quiet when Dad first got home from a hard day at the office. That was silly. I knew that a little spin around the living room would be more fun than sitting in his chair.

So that day, just as Dad was getting ready to sit down, I sang a little louder than usual and leapt up on the footstool. When I spun around, I saw Dad's face, red and furious at me.

"Hush!" he hollered. "Can't I have a little peace and quiet around here?"

I stopped in horror. I never wanted to have Dad mad at me again. The next evening when he came home, I gave him a gentle hug and then went to play in another part of the house. I never again bothered him

Nancy, 1957

when he was reading the newspaper after he got home from the office. I tried to be real quiet instead. Then he smiled at me. I liked that.

Mom's parents also wanted a cute, well-behaved granddaughter, so I was good around them just like I was around Dad. Even Mom got mad if I danced or sang or wanted to talk for too long, especially when we had company or she was on the telephone. At church we learned about being good little boys and girls. I felt so safe and secure when the grownups were proud of me.

Dad docked a bright red rowboat in our backyard. It looked silly there, so far away from the lake, until he filled it with sand, and the rowboat became the best sandbox ever. In our neighborhood-under-construction, the trees were newly planted and too small to climb. I loved having the bright yellow Caterpillar tractors around, building home after home. All day long men drove these huge machines back and forth. One evening after they had gone home for the day, Dad lifted me up onto the tractor. It felt wild and bold to be a girl sitting up so high in the driver's seat.

While my Catholic friends saved their pennies and nickels to save "pagan babies" from the mission fields of China, India or Africa—whatever that meant—I gave no thought to people around the world. In our family, we were to serve through the right use of our intelligence and diligence and by exhibiting leadership in our daily life and work.

As far as I could see, our great country was filled with wonderful little neighborhoods just like mine. The soil seemed pure and rich. America was a beacon of freedom, and we needed to let our little light shine all the way around the world.

Ed Mathys, age 36, 1957

Wichita Falls, Texas

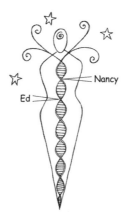

For me, who grew so tall,
I always felt small.

As a boy
at home, in my room,
or out on the lake
this "lefty" was free.

Stuttering or not,
I could be me.

I grew up
and left solitude behind
for a career.
Work, not play, was the way of men.

Geology degree in hand
newly hired in Texas
I went on my fifth date – ever.
Sue was strong and independent,
just like I wanted to be.

Two years after our marriage,
your birth filled the house with laughter.
For you, I faithfully provided,
staying in a job I didn't enjoy.

You slept.
You smiled.
You captured our hearts.

Then
after your third birthday,
you became like your mother:
headstrong, quick thinking, willful.
You and Sue
sparked with your own power.
I felt upstaged,
jealous.

It was too much.
I was outnumbered.

I was tall
and felt short.
You were short
and acted tall.

Something had to change.

Ed and Nancy, 1957

Sue Mathys, age 28, 1954

Wichita Falls, Texas

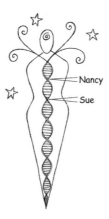

"You have no talent," my junior high school art teacher told me. Mother com-
miserated. O.R. thought art was extraneous anyway. Only my sister, Nancy
Jane, disagreed. She told me all of the things she liked about my drawing,
then said, "You're a good artist." But Nancy Jane sugar-coated most things,
so I didn't pay any attention to her. I believed the teacher, quit art and took
Greek instead.

Fifteen years later, my baby Nancy's birth brought me back to art. I
needed something other than mothering to feel like a whole woman again.
When Nancy was three months old, I signed up for a class at the art museum,
and Mother agreed to babysit. When the demands of parenting were too
difficult, I imagined myself sketching things I saw around the room, yard or
even the grocery store. On the hard days, it got me through. I was so excited
when the sun finally came up that morning.

Sitting in the front of the class, I was completely focused on my drawing when the teacher stopped to ask me how long I had been working
with pen and ink. She saw my talent, my potential and was surprised that
I was a novice.

When I returned home after my class, I kept my sketches hidden until

Sue and Nancy, 1954

after Mother left. Even after all of these years, I was afraid she'd be critical. As she drove off, I spread my drawings out on the floor and picked up Nancy. I sat surrounded by the creations that had flowed through me. Nancy ripped through my body and into my heart in ways that simultaneously astounded and exhausted me. Today, my art brought me back to myself.

I will never limit Nancy's life to sharpening her intellect and building her moral fiber. Her childhood will be different than mine. She will grow up surrounded by art and creativity. I imagine a group of her girlfriends painting, putting on plays with costumes they assembled, making puppets for little performances or publishing neighborhood newspapers.

Today I know that my sister Nancy Jane was right after all. I am talented, and art matters to me and to my baby.

Drawing by Sue

2

Grandparents Set the Table

I called Ann and John Mathys Grandma and Grandpa. They retired to Monterey, California, when I was three. For all but one of the next fourteen summers, Dad would drive Mom, my brother and me across Texas, New Mexico, Arizona and California for a visit.

O.R. and Ruth Tipps had more unusual grandparent names. O.R. decided that his name was good enough for children as well as adults. That was that. The naming of my grandmother Ruth, however, was in honor of a fruit.

Before I was old enough to join the family at the dining table, Ruth would feed me mashed up bananas. I'd clap my hands in glee as I squished them between my fingers and let their sweet taste fill my mouth. When I began to speak, I called my Tipps grandmother the most wonderful name I could imagine. My baby-talk word for bananas sounded like Mano, and the name stuck. When my brother and three boy cousins were born, they followed my lead.

Unbeknownst to me, bananas were hot the year I was born. A small country in Central America was filled to the brim with United Fruit banana plantations. Under the rule of Dictator Jorge Ubico, United Fruit had gained control of almost half of Guatemala's land.

This golden arrangement was threatened in 1951. Jacobo Árbenz Guzmán became Guatemala's President in an election celebrated as a model of democracy. Despite this fact, United Fruit launched a giant campaign headed by the "father of public relations," Edward Bernays, and tricked our nation into believing Guatemala's new government was communist.[1]

A few months before I began to squish bananas around my mouth, US propaganda and military action resulted in the exile of this democratically elected president and the installation of US backed Colonel Carlos Castillo Armas.[2] Guatemala's new government protected United Fruit's banana plantations and orchestrated the displacement, torture and murder of millions of Guatemalan Mayan Indians.

I didn't know we were fighting to make our world safe for bananas. I was just content sitting on Mano's lap.

When I learned my table manners, I was invited to sit with the rest of the family for dinner. At home, my family ate together every night, but I particularly enjoyed dinners with my grandparents.

After we moved away from Wichita Falls, our visits to O.R. and Mano involved a boring one hundred and forty three mile drive every few months. I always hoped that our visits would include a Sunday, as that was the day we ate like Western royalty: barbequed two-inch thick steaks fresh from O.R.'s cattle ranch, seasoned perfectly with Lawry's salt and Worcestershire sauce and cooked medium rare, along-side baked potatoes (oiled with Crisco and lightly salted), green beans flavored with leftover bacon fat, iced tea (unsweetened) and a tossed green salad.

O.R. held court by his Portable Kitchen—a cast aluminum barbeque pit in the backyard—telling anyone interested how to determine when the steaks were perfectly done. In the bright yellow kitchen, Mano set everything needed for the table out on the counter—bumpy white milk-glass tumblers, beige pottery plates and silverware. As I set the table, I looked out the window. Past the white, iron rocking chairs on the covered porch, I could see the bright green lawn with Mano's shrubbery and flowers along the fence.

As soon as the steaks were done, we all sat around the kitchen table. The blessing was quick, and always offered by O.R., "Dear Lord, bless this food for our bodies and us to thy service. In Christ's name we pray. Amen."

When it was time for us to head home, O.R. would fill a Styrofoam chest with a variety of cuts of beef and send us on our way. Mano stood silently by his side and waved. Seemed like she'd learned to be good and quiet, just like me.

During our annual summer trips to California, I loved to wander through Grandpa's garden. He grew award-winning flowers, bringing home blue ribbons from the Monterey County Fair for his dinner-plate-sized dahlias. During his tenure as vice president of Northrup King, the company developed hybrid dahlias and Transvaal daisies. They were the pride and joy of his garden. Out behind the garage he had a compost bin, the only one I'd ever seen. Smoldering beside the bin, he burned old leaves, twigs, weeds and dead branches he'd cleaned out of the garden. Grandpa's yard seemed so exotic, so old-worldish.

Though the beauty of the garden amazed me, Grandpa's real interest wasn't gardening. While he showed off his garden, he told me about the hybrid seeds, herbicide and pesticide advances made by Northrup King, and politics. Not interested in plant science or world affairs, I preferred wandering between the old oak tree and the flowers, pretending I was in my own secret garden.

Late each afternoon, Mom would call for me to come inside to take a quick bath and put on a dress. At the stroke of five, cleaned and looking good, I would join the adults who were already sipping their bourbons in the living room.

I felt like a queen there. Oriental rugs covered the floors. A grand piano stood in the corner. When no one was around, I played "The Battle Hymn of the Republic" and "Exodus"—my entire repertoire—which filled the space with beautiful sound. Hummel figurines and fine glass statues, collected on my grandparents' overseas trips, were neatly arranged on the shelves. Grandpa would bring my brother and me ginger ale and serve pretzels or nuts. We'd sit on the couch looking out over the lawn, gardens and the Del Monte golf course while we enjoyed our cocktail hour.

When dinner was ready, we moved into the next room and gathered around their huge wooden dining table. Food was served on blue and white china plates, and we ate with sterling silverware. At least once every visit Grandma and Grandpa served us locally grown artichokes. Since we never ate them at home in Texas, dipping hot leaves into mayonnaise felt like a fancy culinary experience.

After our week's visit we would say goodbye to Grandpa and Grandma and begin our fifteen hundred-mile drive home. I loved their home and the Monterey Bay and was glad we would be back the following year.

On Mano's lap when I was a baby, or at the tables of both grandparents as a young girl, I was blissfully unaware of how the food we enjoyed might affect people around the world. I merely knew that we ate delicious meals in the warm circle of family.

Ruth Owen (Tipps), age 15, 1915

Hereford, Texas

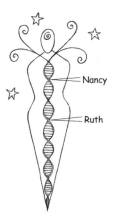

I was an aunt seven times before I was born. From the very beginning I felt different than my siblings. I wondered if I had been plucked up from a nearby orphanage and dropped into the middle of my family. I pondered that for years, but asked Mother only once.

"Was I adopted?"

She threw back her head and roared with laughter. "You *must* be joking!"

I never knew if this meant "yes" or "no." It is only from the distance of many years that I understood her laughter. Why in the world would she adopt her fourteenth child?

Feeding our big family would have been enough, but it seemed like we often had a guest or two—especially traveling Baptist preachers or evangelists. They came to our dining table like bears to honey. I must confess that my proudest meal was one that started in a snit. After washing the last dish from a big Sunday meal, a traveling preacher turned up at our door, hungry, as usual. Rather than sending him on his way, Mother invited him in and sent my brother Hope and me back to the kitchen to prepare a plate for him. An hour previously, we had picked the lunch chicken carcass clean, ready to be boiled for broth. Hope and I plopped that bare carcass on a platter and stuffed it to the ribs with leftover dressing. While it heated up, we made fresh gravy. I thought I was going to pop with excitement when we presented our feast to the preacher, even though we knew full well that we'd have extra chores and Mother's wrath to face later.

The preacher man, his good manners solid on that holy day, didn't miss a beat. "Ah shor' do like dressin'," he proclaimed as he picked up his fork and started in.

My workload increased as my older sisters married and left home. Mother loved for all of us to stay clean and freshly pressed. And she was particularly finicky about her own clothes. In this dusty land, that translated into two outfits for each of us and three or four different dresses for her each day. With such a big family, my sisters and I spent hours each week bent over a boiling wash tub, dipping clothes in hot starch, hanging wash on the line, then heating and reheating the iron so that everything was neatly pressed.

Owen Family (minus three siblings), 1925. Ruth—back row, third from right.

After Mother had to learn to sew the hard way, she taught all of us girls to sew. Shortly after their wedding, Daddy had told Mother to make him a new pair of pants. She'd grown up in a Southern plantation family and had never touched a needle. What she lacked in skill, she possessed in ingenuity. Mother took his best pair of trousers, ripped out the seams and used the pants as a pattern. Then she sewed both the old and the new pair up again. Under her tutelage, I learned to turn a beautiful stitch, expanding my creativity beyond the kitchen sink and wash tub. Someday I hope I'll get an opportunity to explore other talents outside the four walls of my home.

John Mathys, age 9 months, 1892

On a boat to America

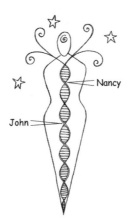

The first time I sat up on my own was in the middle of my grandparents' garden at the edge of St. Joris Weert, Belgium.

Opa and Oma brought me to their garden for our final good-bye. My grandparents knelt down on the dirt path between curly vines with wide leaves and short, tiny-leafed bushes and sat me on the ground. I wobbled at first, before catching my balance enough to look around. I reached out to touch a small green bumpy thing on the vines growing up trellises that seemed to touch the sky. In the distance, bright red balls hung in clumps, and a short bush was thick and green. White flowers lined the edges of the garden. The colors, the smells, and the soft dirt under my legs made me giggle.

Tears streamed down Oma's face. She knew that soon my parents and I would sail out of her life to a place so far away it might as well be the moon. In the short time that remained, she wanted me to feel the soil of the land that birthed me and had supported our family for longer than anyone could remember. She wanted me to know the delight of all things that grew. We would soon be thousands of miles apart, but still nourished by the same earth.

Opa and Oma introduced me to each and every planting bed and vegetable as if they were dear, well-loved relatives. They also told me little stories about Oma's grandparents and great-grandparents whose love saturated this garden so long ago. Once the stories stilled, Opa pinched a bit of dirt and put it in my hand. It was gritty but tasty.

Oma picked me up and held me close, sobbing openly. Her tears dripping on my face were soon replaced by ocean spray mixed with Moeder's tears. One sunny fall afternoon in the year 1892, Moeder, Vader and I peered into the waving crowd lining the shore as our boat pulled away from the dock. Slowly we moved further and further out to sea until I lost sight of Opa and Oma. Moeder never saw her beloved Flanders homeland or family again.

3

Jesus Went Before Us

Just after I completed kindergarten, all of us Shell Oil Company families moved a little further west. When we arrived in Abilene, Texas, in June of 1960, Jesus was everywhere, and so were Christian morals.

The Baptists, Methodists and Church of Christ folks all had universities in town. Dancing wasn't allowed in the schools; prayer followed the national anthem at every football game and stores closed on Sunday. My dad had to drive just outside the county line to Pinkies Liquor Store to get his hooch, Jim Beam bourbon, for my parents' single drink every night at cocktail hour. Dad drank his watching the TV news. Mom drank hers in the kitchen fixing dinner.

The week before first grade started, Mom and I walked over to Sam Houston Elementary School. We carefully checked each classroom until I found my name on Miss Allen's door. She was nice and told me just what to bring on the first day: wide-lined red Big Chief tablet, three fat pencils (all sharpened), a yellow box of eight crayons and a pair of little round-tipped scissors.

Mom told me to be a good girl, and I was. I followed Miss Allen's rules explicitly. I put my supplies into my desk. I sat quietly. I always raised my hand when I had a question. If I had to go to the bathroom in the middle of the morning, I held it until just before recess. When I wrote in my Big Chief tablet, I tried really hard to print neatly, with the big letters staying within the solid lines and little letters touching, but not crossing, the dotted line in the middle. Miss Allen's Texas twang was, I assumed, a bastion of good English. Following Miss Allen's lead, I corrected the way I said certain words by replacing "get" with "git" and "wash" with "warsh." Mom wasn't too happy about that part, but she wasn't a teacher, so how could she understand?

Later in the year, Miss Allen told Mom that I'd always make good grades in school because I wanted to please the teacher so much. I beamed. Mom looked a little concerned.

For Christmas I got a Nurse Nancy kit. I used the scientific instruments to help heal my dolly Chatty Cathy and favorite stuffed animal Duckie. Once I even did surgery using a little strainer over Cathy's mouth to put her to sleep with ether before I took out her appendix. She came through the operation without any problems.

Despite all my efforts, sometimes I got into trouble. After school one day I took my Nurse Nancy kit over to Gina's house. We decided to play doctor on her front porch. We spread her Felix the Cat towel out on a wooden bench. Gina was going to operate on me first, so I took off my clothes and lay very still. Using my red stethoscope, she checked my heart, which was beating just fine. When I was ready, she put me to sleep with a shot. She was about to cut into my belly to fix my stomach when the front door flew open.

"What in heaven's name are you two girls doing?" Gina's mom shouted. "Nancy, put your clothes back on this instant. You two should be ashamed of yourselves, acting like this in the front yard!"

I was ashamed, but I didn't understand why. Adults could be confusing sometimes.

At school, we learned important things about the world. In second grade we made a pilgrim village in a sand table with neat rows of plastic ears of yellow corn made of those pokey things you stick into the end of an ear of real sweet corn. Some of us made pilgrim homes, and others made teepees for nearby Indian camps. My teacher said that the Indian

Nancy, 1960

people lived in simple ways but didn't believe in God. She explained that they were peaceful most of the time, but occasionally they scalped settlers. Once, we went on a field trip to a Comanche village at the Methodist College. College students dressed up like Indians and made arts and crafts. Far as I knew, though, Indians didn't live around our place anymore. At least I'd never seen any.

Except for our annual drive to California, I spent the lazy days of summer with either Prudy or Diane, my two neighborhood girlfriends. One August day in 1962, Prudy and I spent the morning at the community pool before we escaped the stifling afternoon heat in her cool house. We sprawled across her bed and wiggled around until our skinny legs pointed up the wall.

As we gazed at our feet, Prudy sighed. She asked, "What was there before the world was created? What was there before God?"

I wasn't sure it was okay to wonder about a time before God. I pondered the vast expanse of space, unable to imagine an empty void before everything, even God. Sometimes life in this neighborhood seemed so small, such a tiny part of the world.

When fall came around again, I turned my thoughts to learning important third grade things. Right in the middle of our science lesson, my teacher, Mrs. Sharp, said something that seemed to me even more dangerous than Prudy's question about the universe. My head hurt just thinking about it, and it gave me a tummy ache. As soon as the final bell rang, I left my girlfriends behind and ran home.

As soon as I burst in the door, I started hollering for Mom. She didn't answer. I found her in her art studio—also known as the laundry room—searching for just the right colored glass tile for her huge mosaic about a chicken and an egg.

She didn't turn around until I caught my breath and began to explain the crisis. "Is it true that women and men have the same number of ribs? That's what my teacher said, but it is not what the Bible says!"

Her irritated expression broke into a smile.

"Yes, women and men have the same number of ribs. The Bible isn't like a history or science book full of facts. The Bible tells why God created the world, not how he created it."

Her answer was as shocking as the time she told me the Easter Bunny didn't exist.

She continued, "When the church was young, there were lots of ways to understand Jesus and the life of faith. Then they began to call meetings or councils of priests and bishops to decide what was true and what was false. Whatever they decided about the Bible or faith was then declared to be God's truth. Today some churches believe that every word in the Bible is God's true word. Those people believe that the Adam and Eve story really happened. We don't."

As Mom talked and I listened, halfway around the world Pope John Paul XXIII had called together a modern day council, Vatican II, "to let some fresh air into the Church." Their work opened a doorway for dialogue and collaboration between the Catholics and Protestants.

Mom's explanations of long ago councils and edicts may have made perfect sense to her, yet they troubled me. I couldn't even ask Dad after work because he never went to church and wouldn't know about Bible stuff.

I was left to work it out on my own. If my Sunday School teachers were wrong about women being made from one of Adam's ribs, what else had they taught, and I believed, that was wrong? Fears that maybe God didn't have the whole world in his hands haunted me. A few nights after my discussion with Mom, I had a dream:

One Sunday morning at dawn, I was walking alone down a city street. I turned a corner and caught a glimpse of my church—the Leaning Tower of Pisa. The tall thin church leaned to the right. I entered the huge doors and found myself in a well-lit space, open from floor to ceiling. Sunday School classrooms formed the perimeter of the tower. An elegant circular staircase wound its way from where I stood, past all the classroom doors, up to the ceiling. Attached to the center of the ceiling was a large gold ring holding the corner of a floor-to-ceiling red velvet drape.

I was transfixed by this exquisite drape. As I walked up the stairs, I couldn't take my eyes off the soft red folds. Finally, about two-thirds of the way up, I couldn't stand it any longer. I had to touch this cloth. I reached out over the banister, but I still couldn't touch it. I stretched a little farther. Almost. I lunged even farther and finally touched the plush cloth.

Unfortunately, I'd reached a little too far and fell over the banister. Clinging tightly to the drape, I hung suspended for a moment before the corner ripped out of the gold ring.

Suddenly, I was falling, falling, falling toward the marble floor below, clinging tightly to the swirling red drape.

I woke with a start. In dreamland, it had all started so wonderfully. The red velvet drape was the most beautiful thing I'd ever seen, and I was captivated by it. When I finally grasped the cloth, however, I started falling. The sharp contrast between the longing and the tumbling scared me. Since I was certain to hurt myself, or worse, at the end of my dream's fall, it seemed that God couldn't have been present in that strange church after all.

This dream kept returning. Sometimes I'd have it twice in a week, and then it might be months before it popped up again. Every time the dream came, I woke up afraid. I'd hurry down the hall to slip in bed beside Mom, safe and secure again.

Real church made a lot more sense to me than dreams. I tried hard to be a good Christian girl—acting nice and reading the *Living Bible* I kept at my bedside. We didn't pray a blessing before our meals. Mom, who grew up Methodist like me, used to pray before dinner when she was a girl. Maybe the reason we didn't pray together was because Dad didn't want to pray anymore since he'd quit going to his church, the Episcopal one, when he was a teenager.

At school, we all said the Pledge of Allegiance and a prayer each morning, and then turned to our schoolwork. Being Christian, like being American, was just what we all were.

Jesus was everywhere, including my heart. In Sunday School we sang, "Leaning, leaning, safe and secure from all alarms."[1] I had nothing to fear, safe and secure in the everlasting arms of Jesus. Loving God was as natural as loving my mother and father. I liked having Jesus around but wished he would help me understand my dreams and teach me how to stop getting scared.

Barbara Tipps, age 20, 1815

Near Short Creek, North Carolina

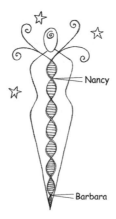

Ever'body's left. Sheets cleaned. Blood washed away. Mary Lou sucklin' at my breast. She's beautiful. She's a gift.

She sure was a painful gift to git, though, bein' alone and all. Her daddy's dead.

Last summer, it was hard to know what scared me most—stories of savage attacks over apiece in Mississippi Territory or John leavin' to fight in the War of 1812. He held back when the first men left. With four childr'n under six, I sure enough needed him. Our thirty-five-acres 'long Short Creek needed clearin', crops put in, and mud packed 'tween the logs where winter winds blow in.

Last fall, the savages attacked folks nearby. We prayed, and it seemed like John should join up with the West Tennessee Militia for six months. His regiment was followin' Andrew Jackson. Jackson was a name we knew 'round here. John and the other men was ordered to march to New Orleans. That sounded like a mighty important mission. As it turned out, the men was marched long hours with barely nothin' to eat. By the time they made it, they was half dead. Jackson didn't care. He ordered them to start fightin' right then and there.

Jackson won the battle to save New Orleans. A battle fought two weeks after the war ended. A battle fought two days after John died. Jackson a hero. Me, a widow.

When the soldiers come to tell me that dark January afternoon, I wanted to curl up and die. There I was, twenty, pregnant and a widow with four childr'n underfoot and a half workin' farm. Worked from sunup to sun down with my pa and brothers' help, then cried myself to sleep. Jackson's fight for freedom cost my family way too much.

Belly kept growin'. Babies don't pay no attention to sadness.

But tonight, my labor's done. Mary Lou and the little sliver of a moon shinin' outside my window call me back to life.

4

Land of the Free

Mom was the first-born son. Her father, O.R. Tipps, had wanted a boy, yet had three daughters. Mom felt that O.R. was okay with her being a smart and interested-in-knowledge sort of girl, as opposed, I presumed, to being a "typical" girl.

Mom informed me, "Women who have only daughters are not as interesting as women who've had at least one son." Though she had a lot of women friends, Mom once said that she preferred the company of men. In addition, Mom's sister Martha said she was grateful she'd had three sons, as she had "no idea how to raise a girl."

Ouch. All this focus on boys being preferred to girls hurt my feelings. I liked being a girl. As unsentimental as Mom could be, I loved my relationship with her and wanted to have a daughter one day so that I could have that too.

For generations Tipps and Mathys women had avoided the pitfalls of sexism by being exceptional women. We strove to be intelligent, responsible, hard workers so no one could accuse us of being emotional or shallow. It must have worked, because in the early 1900s a group of boys passed by several of my great-aunts, then young teenagers. One boy taunted them saying, "There are those Tipps girls who think they are smarter than everyone else." Years later, when Great Aunt Kate told the story she always added, "And the truth was, we were!"

Tipps women also looked out for each other. If I needed to complain about school, or talk about problems with a friend, Mom was always there for me. Moreover, she let me know that I needed to be careful about what I shared with Dad, since we didn't want to upset him with our little troubles.

While our family had opinions about whether girls or boys were better, opinions about skin color didn't seem to be much of an issue in our household since no one talked about it. One night in 1962, the TV was on during dinner. The newscasters mentioned a question on the latest Gallup Poll: "Do you think the Negro children in your community have the same opportunities as white children to get a good education, or not?" Eighty-six percent of Southern white adults believed that they did.[1] I assumed the adults knew what they were talking about since I'd never seen any sign of unequal opportunities.

I had no idea where black people lived. The only ones I knew worked as maids like Beatrice who came to clean our home once a week. She seemed okay with her life.

Just before the end of third grade, I celebrated my ninth birthday. My favorite gift was a Brownie instamatic camera. From the time I got up the next morning, I began taking pictures: two pictures of things in my room; one of my brother; three in the backyard; two of my friend Diane; and two of my dog Tippy.

I poked my head inside the front door and hollered, "Beatrice, can you come out for a sec? I want to take your picture on my new camera."

She followed me out to our front lawn and stood in the sun right in front of the pink, wispy blossoms on the Mimosa tree. I looked at my watch to note that I took this eleventh picture of my first roll of film at 12:15.

"Smile!" I encouraged as I snapped her photo. "Thanks, Beatrice," I said as I turned and headed across the street to take photo number twelve of Mrs. Sheer, Diane's mother.

I had no idea that seven hundred and seventy-seven miles away people in Selma, Alabama, were still reeling from memories of the previous month's Bloody Sunday. Six hundred people had set out from there on a march to Montgomery to gain voting rights for black Americans. They were met with swinging billy clubs and clouds of tear gas in a violent attack by state and local police.

Simultaneously, in Washington, DC, the Civil Rights Act was stuck in the House of Representatives. Howard W. Smith, a Capitol Hill Democrat from Virginia, adamantly opposed to civil rights, described "this nefarious bill" as "full of booby traps as a dog is full of fleas."[2]

While government battles were underway, Aunt Martha married and graduated with her journalism degree. She moved back to Wichita Falls, excited because the *Wichita Falls Herald and News* editor had told her she could have a job when she finished school.

Instead, when she went to see the editor, he explained, "We already have two women reporters in the news department and that's enough." The newspaper hired a young man without a journalism degree. Apparently not everyone agreed with our family that smart women were as good as men.

Aunt Martha was really mad that day. I didn't understand why, so I played in my room when she came over to talk to Mom.

Far away in Washington this bill for civil rights also became a women's rights bill. In the summer of 1964, Title VII of the Civil Rights Act outlawed employment discrimination based on race, color, religion, sex or national origin.

The reaction to this new law was swift. The *New York Times* referred to it as the "bunny law," wondering what might happen if a man applied to the Playboy Club for the position of a "bunny."[3] Three days after the Senate vote, two carloads of Mississippi KKK members murdered three men who were working for a voter registration drive. Racist and sexist prejudice and violence continued to erupt across the nation.

I didn't know anything about that stuff.

But I knew that something big was happening in my world—Don. He sat next to me in fourth grade, first row, third chair back, next to the counter. A week before Christmas vacation I slipped a book of Lifesavers into his locker and waited to see if he would give me a gift. He didn't. But my heart went all pitter-patter whenever he was around, and he smiled at me a lot. Near Valentine's Day we traded tokens of our love. I gave him my heart-shaped, silver-colored necklace, encircled with faux diamonds around an engraved *Nancy*; he gave me his gold-colored bracelet engraved with *Don*. I don't remember that we ever talked much.

The world felt tranquil and dreamy while Don and I were in love. But romance or not, we needed to be prepared for disasters. We all learned how to hide under our desks and protect ourselves in case of a tornado or nuclear bomb explosion. I liked knowing what to do in case life got out of hand.

In between school, church and watching TV, I was an author. Prudy and I did our part to keep our neighborhood well informed through our own newspaper, *The Avondale Press*. We'd go door to door asking for neighborhood news, then write up our report alongside good jokes. Mom helped us mimeograph it using this strange jello-like stuff in a metal box. We'd return to the streets to sell the paper for a nickel. I also wrote a novel dedicated to my uncle Jack Mathys who was recovering from a heart attack. The mystery, *The Charming Miss Clark with Terror in Her Eyes*, surely made him feel better.

In 1965, just after I finished fifth grade, I left Prudy and Don behind when we moved further west to Midland, Texas. Midland didn't have any Christian universities, so you could dance in the schools.

I found a new neighborhood girlfriend, Lauri Leaverton. She and I did all sorts of things together. We established a Herman's Hermits fan club—and remained the only two members. We practiced kissing by hugging our own knees and smooching our kneecaps; however, we never figured out what to do with our noses during a real kiss.

We bemoaned how dumb we felt once we entered San Jacinto Junior High school down the block. Together we worried over every zit and every pooch of fat that made us look ugly. We fought, and then made up a few hours later.

In addition to playing together, Lauri and I were both smart and liked school. Especially science. Especially Coach Brown, the cute teacher who taught seventh grade biology. In preparation for a project in his class, I had a guy friend kill a chicken for me. I boiled the dead chicken whole, picked off all of the meat and skin, and then glued the skeleton back together again. It was exciting to do such a big project. I got the best grade in all of Coach Brown's classes, and I loved seeing how all of the bones fit together.

Nancy, 1963

In eighth grade earth science I was fascinated by the differences between the rocks in the collection all lined up on the shelf beside the wall of windows. Mica flaked off in shiny black sheets while granite was hard and sparkled.

Each morning before school I made sure my dress was long enough so I wouldn't get in trouble with the principal. Our skirts were supposed to touch the floor if we knelt on the ground; I never saw anyone asked to kneel, but I didn't want to risk an accusation. I memorized worthless things like the name and county seat of the two hundred and fifty-four counties in Texas. We did jumping jacks in salmon-colored jumpsuits in the girls gym to the tune of "Oh, I'd love to be an Oscar Mayer wiener ... 'cause if I were an Oscar Mayer wiener, everyone would be in love in with me." I didn't feel like everyone was in love with me. I felt smart when I wrote a good paper, then dumb whenever I found out I'd misspelled too many words. I felt great in my green dress, but ugly in my blue pedal pushers.

April 4, 1968 started like any other day. I got up early enough to put on my makeup and slip into my outfit: a flower-print, empire waist dress, finished with girdle and hose. After lunch, I hurried, like I always did, to my history class. Just as the teacher picked up her piece of chalk, the principal interrupted on the loud speaker.

"Boys and girls, I have an announcement to make." He paused for a moment, then continued, "Martin Luther King, Jr. has been shot."

I gasped. I didn't know too much about Dr. King, but I knew he'd been working hard for civil rights. No one said anything at first. The silence was shattered when the boy behind me cheered. I was horrified he was so prejudiced.

I cringed inside, but said nothing. I had no idea what to say. Even if I had spoken, I doubted he would change. And if I opened my mouth, what would my friends think of me? Maybe they agreed with that boy—I had no idea since we'd never talked about things like race or protests before.

Our teacher was silent too. We never talked about the assassination in class.

Apparently King was successful with civil rights because that next summer Midland schools got everything ready to begin integration in the 1968–1969 school year. Fourteen years after *Brown v. Board of Education* and I were born, Midland desegregated the public schools through busing. When the school year began in September 1968, my friends and I were bused to the newly built Edison Freshman School on the other side of the tracks. For all the other years, though, most of the busing brought black students to schools on my side of town.

I hadn't known that Carver Junior and Senior High Schools, the black schools, were just a few miles away from Midland High School, across the tracks and down a dirt road. When the school board was talking about desegregating the schools in order not to lose federal funding, the Carver faculty and community had requested that Carver remain open as a freshman school rather than building Edison.[4] The request was denied.

Carver schools closed and the students bused out of the neighborhood. This marked an abrupt end of the community that had gathered there for years. No one told us white students anything about those details.

Many assumed that the black students weren't as smart as we were. I never thought about it one way or the other. Regardless, we were never told that one year two Carver students earned the highest scores on the citywide, end-of-the-year exam to determine each school's graduating class valedictorian and salutatorian.[5]

The 1960s resulted in sweeping changes across the nation, but the roots of the issues remained largely unnoticed. Sitting in my freshman high school seventh period English class, I often gazed out the windows looking at the buses lining up at the curb. In those moments, I never stopped to wonder if their presence signified anything other than a long ride home.

Ruth Tipps, age 25, 1925

Quitaque, Texas

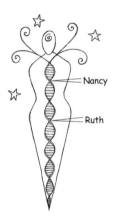

The day I graduated from Chickashaw Teacher's College, I could see change on the horizon. I was the first of my sisters to go off to college. When I graduated with my teacher's certificate, I left family and Oklahoma behind and took a job in Texas.

For a few years, I escaped the washing tub and kitchen chores when I headed to West Texas for my first (and last) teaching job. Quitaque wasn't any exotic place, but it was away from family. I was tired of being told how much my eyes were like Effie Bell's, my nose like Aunt Mary's, and my laugh like Dot's. In my new home I would just be me, Ruth, a competent teacher.

It was icing on the cake that Mrs. Bess at the boardinghouse served me at mealtimes before and after work. Except for those few years, I have spent my whole life feeding anyone and everyone who sat at my table.

I fell in love with the man who hired me. Both O.R. Tipps and I came to school early and left late. I had to prepare for my classes; he was school superintendent. O.R. took his job seriously and was a strong supporter of us teachers as well as the students. I liked his vision, his strength of character, and the passion with which he lived his life.

I was delighted by his attention, but the thing that really captured my heart was his love of books. He was the only man I'd ever met who loved books as much as I did. He'd memorized much of what he'd read. My heart melted when he looked into my eyes and recited, "Lay thy sheaf adown and come, Share my harvest and my home."[1]

O.R. Tipps asked for my hand in marriage under the bright light of the full moon.

After our wedding, O.R. told people that he "took off two days for the entire occasion." I didn't like the curt sound of that, but his assessment was true. We drove to Chickasha, Oklahoma, for our marriage, then turned around and drove back to Quitaque. On the return trip, our car tire kept going flat again and again. O.R. would pull off to the side of the road and patch it without complaint. I was impressed with the patience of my new husband.

Little did I know how much patience would be required of me in the years to come as O.R. continued his practice of going to work early and staying late.

O.R. and Ruth's wedding, 1925

5

Budding Love

I didn't know anything about sexual preference—I never had any choice in the matter. As if by magic, my heart had throbbed when I sat next to Don in fourth grade. Three years later, Lauri and I were both interested in David, the cute violin player. Suddenly I wasn't sure if Lauri was my friend or my competition.

Our family never talked about the ins and outs of relationships with friends or boyfriends. Mom was more concerned that I act in "mature" ways in all aspects of my life. O.R.'s advice was included in a letter he wrote me: "We hear a lot of talk about 'teenagers' and their mixed-up ideas. ... I think your good training, your fine mind, and your ambition to become a fine person will see you through each and every problem that confronts girls at that age."[1]

I tried not to get too tangled up in teen-aged roller-coaster emotions and focused instead on being responsible. In ninth grade, I submitted an article that was published in my church's teen newsletter. It included the following observation:

> *A subject that has been talked about quite a bit recently is how today's teenagers are going to the dogs, birds, horses, et cetera. ... True, there have always been some "nutty" groups, such as flappers, jitterbuggers, and hippies, but they are in the minority. Most teenagers have always been willing and ready to help others.*[2]

The bad girls of the 1920s, called flappers, wore short skirts the same length as mine, just below the knee, and we shared short haircuts. They voted, something I planned to do one day. We parted ways, however, with the flappers' open conversation about sex and publicly making out, though the lack of increase in pregnancy rates showed that sexual liberation of the 1920s didn't necessarily include intercourse. In addition, these wild women smoked, just like my mother.

Flappers smoking was the result of a well-crafted advertising campaign to manipulate the desires of women and to counter public bias against female smokers. The president of the American Tobacco Company hired public relations genius Edward Bernays to craft a marketing plan. Bernays hired famous women to march in the 1929 New York City Easter Parade. As instructed, at a prearranged place in the route, these elegant women simultaneously pulled out hidden matches and cigarettes. The *New York Times* headlines captured Bernays' spin on this act—"Group of Girls Puff Cigarettes as a Gesture of 'Freedom.'"[3] Women, including flappers, started smoking and felt free. The cigarette companies' profits soared.

While I tried to avoid thinking about excessive gestures of freedom, my body marked its transition into womanhood with the onset of my first menstrual period. Without fanfare, Mom gave me pads, a belt and the *Very Personally Yours* pamphlet, written to remind me to keep smiling during my time of the month.

It also stressed the importance of focusing on my posture—"Build a firm graceful figure by practicing 'model' posture while you're still in your teens, and you'll never have to worry about that 'middle-age bulge.'

So ... walk, stand and sit 'tall,' chest high, chin and stomach pulled in."[4]

Mom told me that she assumed I wouldn't be one of those "hypochondriac" women who had excessive cramps or moodiness at my time of the month. She was also glad that raging hormones or a desire to become a bad girl of the 1960s didn't occur to me.

Women's liberation hadn't hit West Texas. Personally, I saw no need for it. I assumed I could do anything I wanted to. I had so much freedom that I already had too many conflicting messages in my head. My thoughts bounced back and forth, trying to integrate what I'd learned from books, girlfriends, school, magazines, church and movies. *I am independent; guys don't like strong-willed girls. I want to get married and have a husband take care of me; I want a career. Women can do anything; don't be too smart around boys since it will make them feel dumb. I am too fat, too emotional; I like to look beautiful for boys.*

I got confused trying to keep it all straight. Mostly, I tried not to think about it and ignored my inconsistencies. I knew I wanted to have a career and a family of my own someday. Mom had stayed home, but she was an artist who showed her work in local galleries and was very active in leadership in organizations like the Local Artists Association and the Midland Community Theatre. I was taught by example, not words, that a strong sense of personal independence would trump any cultural limitation. Being responsible, I wasn't about to dip my toes into jitterbugging, irresponsible sex or lazy society-women sorts of behaviors.

The TV news let me know that some women were burning their bras and fighting for rights. Others stepped into the halls of power. Attorney Barbara Jordan, a black woman, was appointed to the newly established Texas Senate in 1966, two years before my school integrated. She was, however, never mentioned in my social studies class.

School was fine, but I wished a boy would like me. Ever since my first kiss, a dreamy good-bye caress on my cheek after seventh grade, my hopes were high. Just before I turned sweet sixteen, my romantic luck changed. I opened my parent and brother-proof, locked jewelry box and removed my diary to record my first three dates.

Thurs, Feb 13, 1969

While I was watching Leave it to Beaver the phone rang.
"Hi Nancy! This is Bobby Conner."
Shock in the first degree!!!!!
"Can you go to the show with me Saturday?"

Nancy, 1969

I knew Bobby from my children's community theatre group, but I never dreamed he would ask me, a freshman, on a date. It was embarrassing to ask him, a senior, to call back so Mom and Dad could decide whether or not they would allow me to go on my first date. They talked about it for hours and hours. Finally they agreed, and Bobby and I set up the details for the following Saturday night.

We had a super time at the movies. He held my hand and stroked it while he made comments throughout the show.

Pure heaven ...

A few days later Bobby called to invite me to the Midland High School court coronation, a formal event, for our second date. Luckily I already had a long dress, but I spent the better part of the week planning the details of my make-up, earrings and shoes.

Saturday, February 22, 1969

Bobby arrived very near his promised 7:30. He looked even better in his pale yellow double-breasted suit. He even gave me a corsage.

When we got into the Midland auditorium a colored usher led us to our seats. The court was beautiful and there was even one colored couple in the court. It was good to see that integration happening so easily here.

Driving home around 9:30, we stopped at a stop sign. He turned and kissed me. It was firm and a little wet. Wonderful. He did this a few times before he drove into my driveway.

In a moment of insanity a few weeks later, I invited Bobby to come to a church dance. No one talked and almost no one danced.

After that miserable date I waited, week after week, for Bobby to call again. He didn't. I realized that he was looking for a steady girlfriend, and I was too young and not exactly what he wanted. In the middle of my pining, I got a call from another boy.

April 20, 1969

Ya know that freshman formal on May 10? Well Howard Thurston, a fellow viola player, asked me to go with him. He was just as nervous as I was when I asked Bobby to go to the church dance. I am going. I had hoped that I might go somewhere else with Bobby, but I probably won't get asked. I hope Howard and I have fun.

Howard's blue eyes, striking jaw and muscular body were hard to miss in my school's orchestra or on the football field. The two of us had shared a music stand while playing our violas at a Christmas program the year before. At Edison we'd had fun within our four-person freshman orchestra class. Lauri was jealous that Howard asked me out instead of her.

A few days before the freshman prom, I was ready to quit waiting for Bobby to call back. I worked out the last of my feelings about him in my diary.

May 7, 1969

I am just thankful for what Bobby did for me and am always indebted to him. Sure I want to date him again but I can only thank him and, most of all, God that I dated him as many times as I did and of what the experience did for me. I wish I could help him find the girl he is looking for in another way besides prayer. Oh well! Good-luck Bobby.

On the evening of May 10, wearing my one and only formal dress once again, I paced in my room waiting for Howard to arrive. After the awkward, chauffeured drive by his father to the school, we had fun despite one almost-disaster. When those who had helped decorate the gym for the dance were asked to stand, I shot up. Howard, being a gentleman, pulled my seat back few inches. He hadn't anticipated my shooting back down into my chair a few seconds later. Luckily, I caught the lip of the seat and didn't sprawl on the floor.

We laughed and danced and visited with friends. A few days later, I recorded this first date with Howard—*"We had a blast!"* I was a little disappointed when Howard said that he didn't want to date again until after he could drive, but I knew we'd see each other in classes at school.

I loved being a girl. I was smart and got good grades in school. I enjoyed the boys' attention, and cared about my clothes, haircut and curves. Why in the world would anyone want to burn their bras like those women's libbers or smoke like the flappers just to prove they were free? We girls could have it all just by being ourselves.

6

Stranger Prayer

Mom didn't believe in infant baptism. She wanted to wait for me to make my own decision. When my Sunday School classmates all began their preparation for confirmation, I joined in. Since confirmation had to follow baptism, I was the only one in my confirmation class of twenty-three to be baptized and confirmed on the same day.

Though I was partly just following along with my class, I also took this step, my public commitment to God and the Church, very seriously. Given that, it was disappointing that our Saturday morning preparation classes about becoming a Christian were so boring. The only interesting thing I remember was mention of a May 24, 1738 journal entry by the Methodist founder, John Wesley, where he recorded his body's reaction to his inner assurance that his faith was acceptable to God: "About a quarter before nine, ... I felt my heart strangely warmed."[1]

When the appointed morning finally arrived, we all appeared at church dressed in our best clothes. Standing at the altar rail, I was asked questions in preparation for being sprinkled with the waters of baptism, and then we all responded when it was time to receive the blessing of confirmation.

"Do you accept the freedom and power God gives you to resist evil, injustice and oppression in whatever forms they present themselves?"[2]

"I do," we replied in unison.

"According to the grace given to you, will you remain faithful members of Christ's holy Church and serve as Christ's representative in the world?"[3]

"I will."

I answered each question affirmatively, committed to honor my promise. Somewhere in the middle of it all, my heart felt warmed by the same Spirit I presumed had touched John Wesley two hundred years earlier. It was, however, a little more delicate a sensation than I'd expected.

Most of the time, Sunday School was boring, but once we got to listen to a record of the controversial musical *Jesus Christ Superstar*. I felt a little naughty but immensely enjoyed the mod rock rendition of the Gospel story. We also painted one wall of our classroom black and wrote inspirational sayings on it in colored chalk:

- You are what you do; you can't build a full life out of half-filled days
- In order to win friends one must sacrifice
- Freedom is nothing but a chance to do better

As much time as I spent in Sunday School and youth fellowship, however, my most potent spiritual heart-warming didn't happen there. One Wednesday morning near the end of my sophomore year, I arrived early to first period algebra. The girls behind me were talking excitedly about a prayer meeting they were having that night. I knew about prayer and I knew about meetings, but I'd never heard anyone so excited about them before. In a subtle and not-too-interested-so-I-won't-be-hurt-if-you-don't-include-me sort of way, I joined in the conversation. Sally was thrilled and quickly invited me to come to her home, just a few blocks from mine, at seven o'clock.

"Okay. Yes, I'll be there." Instantly I began to question my sanity. I didn't really know Sally and the other two girls. But I had committed myself. I was expectant, but didn't mention my plans to anyone.

After school, I stopped in my backyard to be alone for a while. Tippy, our dog and my loyal friend, came over and sat next to me as I leaned against the old elm tree. My playhouse over near the fence had been silent for many years. It seemed like just yesterday Lauri and I had spent hours reenacting the TV show *Bonanza*—with the addition of a girlfriend for Little Joe, of course. Yet in the same moment, those childish days seemed long ago. I was nervous and insecure about lots of things, including the prayer meeting, but I felt grown up at the same time.

I was glad that Mom was out running errands and had left a note saying dinner was on our own so I could avoid any conversation about my evening plans. Just before it was time to go, I took a shower, put on clean pedal pushers and a striped shirt and headed to the door. As I left, I told Dad I was going to a friend's house to study, trying to make it sound normal.

On the way to Sally's house, I fluctuated between believing that I must be crazy and basking in delicious anticipation. The evening sun made the fresh new leaves glow.

All three girls met me at the door, with the soft strains of praise music in the background. Sally's parents were nowhere in sight. The screen door banged behind us, and something about that felt dramatic and final.

I was ushered into the living room where one lamp glowed and candles flickered, and Sally invited me to sit down. The TV was silent in the corner. The girls' Bibles were open on the coffee table. I was embarrassed that I hadn't thought to bring mine.

Sally served us all glasses of iced tea before we started. Just after sitting down again, she turned her attention to the prayer meeting and began reading several Bible verses. As soon as she was done, Lucy began to pray in a loud voice.

I listened as I looked around the room. Sally's couch looked like

Mano's, and lots of paintings hung on the wall just like in my home. I was reassured by the ordinary surroundings. The Bible readings were long and the prayers rambling, but the spirit of welcome was palpable.

"Let's start the intercessory prayers now," Lucy announced and stood up.

We followed her lead.

"Each of us will get a chance to sit in the prayer chair. The rest of us will put our hands on the seated girl and pray as the Spirit leads," Lucy explained. She flicked her ponytail as she looked me straight in the eye and asked, "Would you like to be first?"

Gulp. "Yes," I replied, very quietly.

"Great!" she beamed. "Just sit here." I lowered myself into the high-backed dining chair and shut my eyes. I knew that prayer was always done with eyes closed.

Someone reached out and put her hand over my heart, right above my breasts. I gasped. The combination of her firm authority held with such a gentle loving touch startled me. Within seconds, her hand felt so hot that I peeked to make sure she wasn't using a heating pad or something.

The heat quickly spread from each girl's hand to my chest, back and the top of my head. As my body warmed, the prayers started.

Sally prayed, "Holy Spirit we pray for you to come down, to move mightily in this room and in Nancy's life." The prayers started in English but soon moved to an indecipherable language that sounded like gibberish. I had read about speaking in tongues but had never heard it before.

I might as well have been in an opium den. This was not how Methodists in my church prayed! I didn't know what the girls were saying or what I was supposed to do. Part of me wanted to bolt out the door and head for home as quickly as I could. The other part wanted to stay, wondering if I had just arrived home.

It didn't feel dangerous, so I sighed and tried to relax into the prayers. The warmth encircled my heart and felt like a hug on the inside. I felt more loved than I'd ever felt before—more than by Mom or Dad or any boyfriend I'd ever had. I felt so completely in my body and so full of God at the same moment. I'd thought I could only have it one way or the other.

My mind was quiet, but a gentle vibration traveled from my head to my toes. Time seemed to stand still. Is this what my Sunday School teachers meant when they talked about being loved by God?

Slowly the speaking quieted, and the girls' hands cooled and dropped away from my body. I opened my eyes.

They looked at me eagerly, perhaps hoping I would proclaim my praises, maybe even speak in tongues or testify to God's actions in my life. But I was mute. Words seemed so trivial to try to capture what had just happened, what was still unfolding.

"Come to the Open Bible Pentecostal church next Sunday," Lucy said. They continued to tell me all about their church, but I desperately wanted to be alone. Finally, all of the prayers were done, and they walked me to the door to say good-bye.

Stars filled the black sky overhead, and the sliver of a moon was just beginning its movement to become whole again. Usually afraid of the dark, I felt completely safe as I walked home slowly, savoring the afterglow of my encounter with God.

I stopped and leaned against a huge tree at the corner of my street. The tingling returned and my heart warmed again.

Slipping in the kitchen door, I pretended to get a snack. Luckily, my parents were in the middle of watching *The Beverly Hillbillies* on television, so a quick, "I think I'll head to bed. I'm tired," sufficed.

Once snuggled under the covers, I tried to understand what had happened. I had no idea. Speaking in tongues with the power of the Holy Spirit wasn't part of life at the First Methodist Church downtown or in my family. I felt no draw toward friendship with the girls or to their church, yet something had happened. I had fallen deeply in love with God.

What was I supposed to do now? My brain got tied up in knots trying to figure it out.

I decided to design a test, or "lay a fleece" as Gideon did in the Old Testament, to find out what God wanted me to do. The next day, in typing class at Midland High School, I sat in my usual place in the end chair of the front long table lined with typewriters.

I silently prayed, "God, if this Pentecostal path is true and this is to be my faith path, have me type this assignment perfectly."

When the timer went off, I had typed the exercise without mistakes. That answer was too terrifying.

I scrambled to figure out what to do next. I realized that it didn't make sense to base my religious future on a single test. Instead, I offered the same prayer with every exercise we did during that fifty-minute class. I typed better than I ever had, though occasionally I made a mistake.

My test didn't really help. While I couldn't imagine myself attending a Pentecostal church, something had happened to me. I didn't know what to do with that.

A few days later clarity came. But not through my mind, which was still panicked and working overtime. I heard God speak. Not in a booming voice. Not even in a still, small voice. My ears didn't hear anything, but my heart "heard" words I knew were from God: "That which is true will hold strong. That which is false will fall away. Just keep walking. It is fine to honor your limits and desires about how to worship me. I can be trusted to guide the way."

A few weeks later I spoke obliquely of my experience at Sally's to Mom and Rick, my boyfriend that school year. Mom dismissed it as nothing more than capricious emotions stirred up by the other girls. Rick warned me that I had been misled, since God hadn't spoken to people in tongues since the early church days. A few weeks later I wrote in my diary,

May 24, 1970

I was introduced to Pentecostal religion. At first I was real hung up on it but Mom and my boyfriend disapproved so strongly I gave it up.

In light of Mom and Rick's disapproval, I trivialized my experience of that evening of gibberish-sounding prayers. I rarely thought about it again.

The next fall my Sunday School class was in the middle of a Biblical conversation about Matthew 16:15-17 in which Peter calls Jesus "God's son." As my mouth said, "I think this passage means ... ," my inner voice asked, "Do you really believe that?"

My silent answer was immediate. No.

Without missing a beat, I continued speaking. I was skilled at looking composed no matter what was happening inside. I never mentioned the earthquake of doubt that shook the foundation of my faith in that moment. To vocalize those doubts seemed like heresy. Instead, I kept going to church but felt like a counterfeit Christian.

Since the belief that Jesus is God's son was central in the church, I assumed I was having a "crisis of faith." But for me, God felt like so much more than the daddy of Jesus; Jesus seemed like so much more than God's little boy.

I loved the image of Jesus as the Word made flesh, present at the

Nancy, 1970

beginning of all creation and through whom all things were made.[4] By contrast, describing the relationship of God and Jesus as father and son seemed bland. As soon as I inwardly questioned this belief, a floodgate of theological doubt opened, and I felt like a spiritual fraud. Ever faithful and still longing to find God, I kept going to Sunday School and youth group as if nothing had happened.

I was eager to turn my focus away from religious beliefs to the complexities of school. Studies were more demanding as I began my junior year, and I broke up with Rick. Slowly but surely, the memory of the explosion of the Spirit in a candlelit room with strangers began to fade.

7

Upperclassman

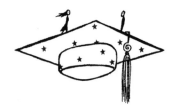

By the time I was a junior, my future was in sight. Only two more years of high school remained before the freedom of college.

Once a driver's license liberated my freshman prom date, Howard Thurston, from requiring his father as chauffeur, he finally asked me out for our second date. Soon Howard and I spent much of our spare time thinking about each other or doing something together.

During Howard's government class, he had plenty of time to write notes, which he'd slip inside my locker during breaks. By contrast, my honors government class was filled to the brim. We were assigned a research paper to explore some aspect of the US government. Searching for a subject, I read a book about a conspiracy plot behind President Kennedy's 1963 assassination. Conspiracy theories had been widely pooh-poohed in the media, and I felt like a flake to even read about one. At the same time,

I was horrified to discover evidence that implicated the government in the plot. Though the facts were convincing, that possibility was too ghastly to contemplate. I didn't want to be one of those people easily seduced by fearful schemes contrary to the official Warren Report.

I'd lived through a decade of one assassination after another—President Kennedy, Bobby Kennedy and Martin Luther King, Jr. Malcolm X's murder came and went without my noticing. At night the TV tallied the number of Vietnam soldiers who had died that day on the battlefield. I definitely didn't like thinking about conspiracies or war, so I decided to write about the pros and cons of the Electoral College instead. That was a controversy I could handle.

It took a few days, however, for me to shake off my agitation that what I'd read about President Kennedy's death might be true. In the middle of it all, Howard had the audacity to call me moody. The following morning my spirits had lifted. I laughed when I read the note he'd written the night before, then stuffed into my hall locker first thing in the morning.

> Dear Super Sunshine,
>   I certainly hope I didn't upset you by saying that girls were moody. That wasn't what I meant, but it was as close as I could come. I sort of meant that no two girls are alike, and it's difficult to understand them. I'm beginning to understand you, but I have to keep working at it! *Verstehe?*
>   I really have nothing to say, but I just wanted to tell you that in only 9 hours, 20 minutes, and 5 seconds I'll see you again!!!!!!!!!!!
>   *Sehr Liebe*[1]

Howard and I were definitely in love. We didn't express our love in daring ways like the 1920s flappers, but we had a strong connection and brought out the best in each other.

Despite the fact that I knew some teenagers around the country were sexually liberated, talking about sex wasn't something that we did in my

Howard, Nancy, and Tippy 1971

group of friends or family. The only advice I remember Mom giving me was, "You don't want to have sex for the first time in the back seat of a car." Maybe she had been worried about my tenth-grade boyfriend Rick's van, and it seemed like sage advice. I couldn't imagine rolling around in the backseat of a car, parked someplace out in public. Howard and I were once parked and kissing near a school, and a policeman came and shone his bright light in our car. That was embarrassing enough. Having sex in a car where we might be disturbed was out of the question.

Actually, it never occurred to me to have sex anywhere while I was in high school. I didn't hold any moralistic view about saving-myself-for-marriage or anything. No one I knew had had sex, or at least they never talked about it.

Besides, the important thing to me was preparing to go to college. As I couldn't imagine applying to college if I didn't know what I wanted to be when I grew up, I'd spent my junior year making my career choice. I loved biology, so that pointed to the medical field: lab technician (too many needles); nurse (too much yucky stuff like bed pans); doctor (too many demands and too much responsibility); or physical therapy. Physical therapy sounded like the best choice, even though I'd preferred volunteering as a candy striper on the hospital wards to assisting in a physical therapy clinic. Reassuring myself that my experience as a therapy professional would be different, I applied for early admission to Trinity University in San Antonio, Texas, and was accepted before Christmas of my senior year.

Trinity was affiliated with the Presbyterian Church, but it wasn't a church school. Though I assumed I'd go to church while I was there, I definitely wanted the freedom to choose to attend or not. A girl in my graduating class was going to Abilene Christian College and had to promise that she believed certain doctrines and would refrain from things like drinking – too many rules for me.

Dad wouldn't let me apply for a college loan because they had begun saving money for me to attend college since I was born. I was embarrassed that we had enough money to pay my way to school. It seemed like "normal" teens applied for financial aid, yet I felt normal too. I didn't want my friends to think I was different or assume that we were wealthy when we weren't. I preferred to believe that we lived regular lives like other people. It was just that we had a little extra money that my parents and Mano and O.R. had set aside when I was born so that I'd have college tuition available when I was eighteen.

With college all lined up, I was ready to enjoy my senior year. We had our class song to choose—"Precious and Few"[2]—and a prom to attend. In addition to the usual senior awards such as "Most Likely to Succeed," Midland High School had the tradition of also voting for the more avant-garde "Dubious Awards." Recorded in our school annual were winners in the categories of "Most Sarcastic," "Most Gullible," and the wanna be cowboy or rancher category of "Mr. and Miss Goatroper." In the glow of integration, we tried to be inclusive by adding two new categories: "Soul Brother and Soul Sister," and "Mr. and Miss Chicano." Good thing they were added, as all of the rest of the awards went to white students.

Despite the senior awards, prom and excitement, I admitted in my diary, *"I'll be glad when I graduate. I never thought I'd be the one to get sick of school, but I am. It's one hassle after another."*

On that same day, after a few pages of update on a few of my ex-boyfriends, many of whom *"grew up into fantastic people"* and were dating other girls, I worked my way around to Howard.

I really think Howard and I are in love. I know I've said that before, but this relationship is one of giving and taking. We can talk about anything, not hide our moods, be sloppy, be serious and funny.

That was the last entry in my golden diary. Howard and I were definitely in love, but we were heading to colleges two hundred and sixty-seven miles apart. We just needed to figure out how to put our relationship on hold for four years.

We talked about it and agreed; we would date other people while we were apart. Not to fall in love or anything. We both wanted to be able to enjoy the fullness of college, and to make absolutely positive that we were indeed the right partners for each other. Nothing else made sense.

Finally the big day arrived. Almost seven hundred graduates paraded across the football field, proud and hot in our purple and gold gowns. I graduated eighth in my class. As I walked onto the field that afternoon, I knew I was leaving my childhood behind.

I didn't get to stay in town for the weeks of after-graduation parties, however. As I received my diploma, my grandfather John Mathys had a stroke. A few days later my mother, father, brother and I flew out to Monterey, California, for his funeral. Since my grandmother Ann was already in a nursing home, we stayed for a month to work with my uncle's family dividing up their things and preparing to sell their house.

A couple of days after we returned home to Texas, my grandmother Ann Mathys died. I decided to stay home even though I would miss her funeral. The newspapers had just reported a plane crash, and I was too scared to fly again. Besides, it felt like I had honored both of my Mathys grandparents during Grandpa's funeral and the weeks we'd just spent in their home.

By the end of August, it was a relief to leave behind memories of death and the drama of high school and head off to college. As far as I could see, the horizons of my future and Howard's were expansive and bright.

Ann Cahoon (Mathys), age 23, 1913

Madison, Wisconsin

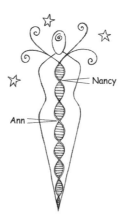

Games, dancing, and play strengthened my character and gave me such happiness as a young girl.[1] True, dancing was suspect in the holy halls of the Baptist church. But during home chore time, my feet tapped out rhythm after rhythm. I stretched my mind with books, promenaded in and out of school, and let my fingers tap out classical music on the piano keys.

After high school graduation, my girlfriends began to move to their soon-to-be-husbands' rhythms—jigs like Ruffy Tuffy and Little Man in a Fix.[a] Not me! I waltzed off to an ivory tower just for women, with golden library tables piled high with books. My heart skipped when I first saw Ellen Sabin, Milwaukee-Downer College President. I'd never seen a woman lead with such grace and wisdom—I wanted to be just like her.

As a student, I marched with many other Wisconsin suffragettes to change the rules so women could make their entrance into voting booths, halls of power, and ballrooms of worldly wisdom. We were bold young women with vision and a thirst for justice.

I wore a black flowing gown and received my diploma on a day I'll remember forever. Line dancing with all of the "Pomp and Circumstance" we could muster, we marched not to war but to the beat of our hearts and minds. I felt that we women of 1913 had what it took to change the world.

I packed my things and headed down the road a ways for graduate school. I imagined colorful spring ribbons tied to my ankles, purple dreams floating in my head, and yellow fire burning in my stomach as I strove onwards for more.

I glided into the University of Wisconsin to declare my graduate school major:

DANCE—
> Body wisdom,
>> Movement,
>>> Manners,
>>>> Anatomy:
>>>>> In short, wisdom and care of the body
>>>>> through movement

—and didn't blink an eye when I was told that no woman had ever performed those steps in these learned halls.

"I guess I'll take the lead then," I told them with a twinkle in my eye and a tapping of my toe.

And I did. It seemed that the whole world was open to me, free and unencumbered.

Ann, 1913

8

A Completely Free Woman

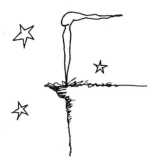

If you can overlook a little thing like complete financial dependence, I was a free woman when I left home for Trinity University in August of 1972. Sure I was ready to face the world all by myself, I moved into my dorm perched on the edge of a cliff.

Although only a whiff of the scent of civil rights and women's liberation had made it to Midland, I felt my world expand once I was on campus. Surely Trinity women would be free enough to wear whatever we wanted. Midland High had just begun to allow us girls to wear pants suits rather than dresses to school my senior year, and I wanted more autonomy than that!

Leaving behind the red, white and blue hallways of West Texas, I headed toward rooms filled with drugs, sex and rock and roll. I slipped into hip hugger jeans, halter-tops and leather moccasins. Being a modern woman, I stepped onto campus with a live-and-let-live attitude. I did not feel judgmental about others' actions and was glad that my new friends didn't criticize my limits.

In October of my freshman year, Trinity had a campus-wide fair and invited the dorms, fraternities and sororities to set up booths. The girls in my dorm decided to offer a massage parlor. We dragged six mattresses down the bluff to the site, set them up side-by-side in a tent and offered half-hour back massages.

I wore a heavy, long-sleeved, turtleneck sweater and, when it was my shift, sat on one of the mattresses waiting for a customer. Terry, my new dorm friend, was straddling a bare-chested boy on his stomach and giving him a back massage. She looked cute in her thin, cotton, peasant-style shirt, her long blonde hair loose and free.

I felt shy at the thought of giving a strange yet cute boy a massage. I was also excited at the thought of giving a strange yet cute boy a massage. My thoughts frequently seemed to go two directions at once.

I liked being close to the liberation that was sweeping the world, and I wanted to be a part of it all without having to stretch too far or take too many risks. Alcohol put me to sleep, so I rarely drank more than one or two drinks, but I liked the feeling of wild abandon that drinking offered. I did not want to smoke pot and was grateful no one pressured me to take a toke. Some friends experimented with sex, but I had a boyfriend at another campus, so I had a good excuse to abstain. Howard called occasionally, we wrote each other letters, and I saw him when we were home for the holidays.

The classroom and library were the places I felt most at home. To me, intellectual exploration was more intoxicating than rum and coke. I read about ideas and events I had never imagined before. New information filled my head as I researched themes to write and labs to complete. My class schedule provided the order I so craved.

I took only one religion class, where we explored Christianity and the modern world. For my mid-term paper I researched the story of the Presbyterian Church's involvement with radical, black activist Angela Davis. Davis publicly protested when three unarmed, black Soledad prisoners' deaths were deemed justified homicide while an armed, white guard's death was called murder.

Violence broke out during the middle of the murder trial. Though Davis was not present in the courtroom, one of the guns used was registered in her name. She was charged as an accomplice to conspiracy, kidnapping and homicide. An affiliate of the Presbyterian Church gave ten thousand dollars to her legal defense fund. I had never heard of a church involved with radicals, with racial justice issues or with someone who was a part of communist groups. Even though I didn't really like violence, I thought it was cool that a church could be so liberal and open-minded.

Nancy, 1973

Angela Davis was found not guilty and released from prison.

As if that topic wasn't bold enough for a religion class, we also studied the Bible from an academic standpoint. The teacher was a Christian who thought a lot like my mother. While both my teacher and Mom explored the intellectual and historical aspects of religion, he seemed much more liberal than Mom ever had. I discovered that many scholars believed that not all of the books of the Bible that were attributed to St. Paul were actually written by him. They didn't think Paul wrote the book of Timothy, for instance, with its appalling statements like, "Let a woman learn in silence with full submission. I permit no woman to teach or to have authority over a man, she is to keep silent."[1]

Focusing instead on the books scholars agreed Paul wrote, such as Galatians, I was moved by the inclusiveness of his words like, "There is no longer Jew or Greek, there is no longer slave or free, there is no longer male and female; for all of you are one in Christ Jesus."[2] I enjoyed proving my case that, despite popular opinion, Paul was really more feminist than sexist. I got an A+ on that paper.

Freedom rang inside and outside my classrooms. Some students streaked naked through streets—one obvious example of the many ways my peers were testing the limits. Although I was too embarrassed to look, I wondered if there wasn't something important about shaking up our country's shame about the human body. Personally, I felt risqué in a halter-top. My girlfriends talked of the excitement of their newfound sexual freedom, yet sometimes sadness and heartbreak permeated their tales. I felt daring enough drinking rum and cokes in our dorm room, but when the drinking age was lowered to nineteen a year later, we could also go to the bars. I felt so grown up sipping a Pimm's Cup, an exotic drink with a little umbrella or a plain old Lone Star beer.

Trinity was the most diverse place I'd ever lived. Students came from the East Coast, across Texas, Arizona and Oklahoma—all over the place. Since I wasn't hung up on things like race, I never noticed people of color at Trinity. All of my friends were white, but I presumed that was just a coincidence. The women around me seemed plenty liberated, so sexism seemed a thing of the past too.

I was oblivious to the fact that the courts were still debating whether women, married or not, should have equal access to credit and if employers could continue to pay women lower wages because they had traditionally received wages below the going market rate.[3] I was equally unmindful of the fact that opportunities were still unequal based on race and that the roots of prejudice hadn't changed with the advent of a few laws.

After having my own room in a household of four, dorm and college life was packed full of people. Nevertheless, I often felt lonely. Even though I was dating, I missed having my real boyfriend, Howard, close by. But my sadness wasn't just longing for my far-away sweetheart; I missed God's closeness too.

My high school fears of being a fraud in the church continued in the milieu of college, but I still felt drawn to go to church on Sunday mornings. Sometimes I went to a big Methodist church in town with a friend. That didn't do much for me. Later I tried a Unitarian church, the liberal church for intellectuals like me, but found it dry. When I started searching again, I went to the church service on campus. It was stuffy and boring.

My mind grew weary trying to figure out how to fill my emptiness, so I turned my focus to school. Thirsty to be well rounded, I took fun classes like bowling, but neither my empty heart nor my score improved by the end of that semester.

Since Howard and I had decided to date other people when we were apart, I accepted a date with Josh, a guy in my group of friends. Josh knew about my boyfriend and was cool with that. He respected my limits. We enjoyed each other. Life seemed simple.

Then Al called in the spring of my sophomore year. He was a muscular, tanned boy with a full head of black hair and a charming half smile. I had seen him at a few parties and thought he was cute. I was flattered when he called to ask me out to a formal debutante ball being held for a local friend of his. I had never heard of a debutante ball—a Southern tradition where a wealthy young woman (the debutante) was introduced into society—but it sounded elegant. Mom mailed me my high school formal dress. I felt a little outclassed at the dance, but Al and I had fun.

We dated a few more times that spring. One night we stopped at Al's off-campus home after a date and visited late into the night. A little after one a.m. he told me we either had to leave now or he needed to go move his car before two to avoid a parking ticket. I said I wasn't ready to go, so he moved the car. An hour later, I was ready to go. He was furious.

I was shocked that Al assumed that staying past two meant that I was staying for the night and, I presumed, having sex with him. That had never occurred to me. For the first time in my life I felt I put myself in a situation that could have easily turned into a date rape. Our relationship felt too complicated to continue, so I broke it off just before summer vacation.

Howard and I didn't see each other much over the summer due to his lifeguarding. Once my third and final year at Trinity started, my friends had busy lives of their own. One lived with her boyfriend in a home strewn with *Playboy* magazines. Another had a growing attachment to smoking pot. I missed Howard. I was alone many Friday or Saturday nights. For the most part, I kept busy with my studies and dreams of the future.

One afternoon in the middle of that year, Al called and asked me out again. The thought of spending some time with someone sounded wonderful. We'd had some good times together. Yet I didn't always feel safe with him. I vacillated ... yes ... no ... yes ... no ...

"Yes."

Loneliness felt worse than restarting a complicated relationship. Surely it would be fine if I were clear about my boundaries. Surely we could just have fun together even though it was hard to fully be myself around him.

One time Al had mentioned his heartbreak when past girlfriends had abandoned him. Not wanting to be another girl who hurt him, I tried to be very supportive.

Of course, I hadn't forgotten that I planned to marry Howard after college. I wished Howard had gone to Trinity, but pining for something that would never happen was a waste of time. Although liberation was about living in the moment, it was hard for me to do.

A month or so later, Al and I returned to my dorm room after dinner out. My roommate was gone for the night. We lay down on my bed and began kissing, just like we'd done many times before.

The next thing I remember was leaning against the door, heart pounding, after Al had left.

What had just happened? How did we go so far?

A night of troubled sleep followed. When I woke, my fear spiral continued. Although we didn't have textbook intercourse, I'd gone farther with Al than I had with any other man, and I was confused. I definitely didn't want that to happen, and yet it did. I wasn't that kind of girl. I loved Howard. What happened?

I didn't believe in grey areas; either I was a virgin, or I wasn't. Had I crossed the line out of virginity? Why had it happened with Al instead of Howard?

Al had pushed me much farther than I wanted to go, but I hadn't said "no." Was it my fault, then?

There was no way I could put together what had happened with what I knew about myself. My thoughts tumbled as I struggled to figure it all out. One possibility dawned on me. As far as I could see, being in love was the only acceptable explanation for why I would have gone that far. I began to consider that Al and I loved each other and last night was an expression of our love. Yet if that was true, why hadn't I realized it before?

I loved Howard. I wanted to marry him.

I had read that pregnancy could result from sperm swimming in from the outside, even when no intercourse occurred. Was it possible that I was pregnant?

After a few weeks of raging fears, my period was late. This was not unusual for me, but I was scared.

Sitting on the edge of a cold examination table at the campus clinic, I told a balding doctor, "I'm afraid I'm pregnant, but I didn't have sex."

I felt like such an idiot.

A few days later, the pregnancy test results came back negative. "However," he said, "since your periods have always been irregular, we should put you on the pill."

That sounded reasonable. I took the doctor's recommendation.

Since that night, I had been standoffish with Al. After a few attempts at being physically intimate again, he quit trying.

Nevertheless, not being pregnant didn't take away my unease about things going too far for me that one night. Even though I felt so freaked out, I reasoned, I must have wanted it to happen, or I would have said "no" very clearly and stopped everything.

Also, I didn't want to abandon Al as so many other girls had done.

My thoughts spun round and round.

I was an intelligent woman. I just needed to think a little harder and find the logical way to resolve my dilemma. My mind raced as my heart felt heavier by the day.

One bleak morning, an idea came. I had it! Since I apparently loved Al, yet didn't want to marry him, the least I could do was to give my body to him until I left campus in a few months. After that, I would give Howard, my beloved, the rest of my life.

After I had concocted this plan, the confusion and fear that had plagued me since that night began to calm.

Since this was the 1970s, and ours was a generation that espoused open and honest communication, I wanted to check out my decision with Howard. I wrote to him, laying out my plan, using strong, independent woman words—my native tongue. "I love Al, but I love you and want to spend the rest of my life with you. And I want to begin to make love to Al, but just until I leave Trinity. Yet I don't want to do anything to damage our future together. Are you okay with this?"

Howard replied in the return mail, clearly proclaiming his love for me and stating his trust that I would make the best choice.

Holding Howard's reply letter in my sweaty hands, all I knew was that I was still alone, left to make my own decision.

Mom was fond of saying that once we'd done something wrong, we needed to "step up and take our licks." I knew I'd gone too far with Al, so I must have done something wrong and now needed to take responsibility for my actions. The only way I knew how to do that was to follow my plan. Therefore, I told Al that I wanted to have sex with him until I left Trinity a few months later.

I carefully tried to tuck my emotions under the covers. If my decision was so right, why did I feel so wrong?

Al and I blended into the college scene like all of the other hooked-up couples. If I stopped and pondered too much, my emotions threatened to pull me down with guilt. The months proceeded in a blur. I felt like I was in a play, living someone else's life.

When the semester was over, I walked away from Trinity University and Al. I was ready to leave confusion behind and dive headfirst into my physical therapy program in Galveston, Texas.

Closer to Howard at this new school, I saw him regularly, and we began to rebuild our relationship. Regardless, what had happened during those last few months at Trinity was cloaked in silence. It seemed best to leave the past in the past.

Barbara Tipps, age 30, 1825

Near Short Creek, North Carolina

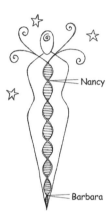

Yesterday, I stayed home from church and the picnic. I was plum tuckered out but told folks my stomach was sour. Weary to the bone, raisin' my family alone all them years since John died.

As soon as the childr'n left with Pa, I moved the old porch rockin' chair into a patch of shade and settled in. Birds singin' sounded like them church hymns. And the silence, Lordy be. The beauty of it all made my heart tingle. I ain't felt that peaceful in years.

I jumped to hear someone walkin' into the yard. I caught sight of Conner Bean, the sun shinin' off of his wavy yellow hair. Conner lived on a big plantation down the road a piece. I knew him from church and 'round town. Charmin' man. Handsome. People whispered 'bout him, though. 'Bout his slaves havin' mulatto babies.

"I noticed your family headin' towards church this mornin' without you. Wondered if that hullabaloo of a picnic seemed like jus' too much to you, too."

I smiled and nodded.

"A little walk on God's earth seemed more fittin' for the Sabbath. Mind if I sit here and rests a bit 'fore I head home?"

"Make yourself comfortable," I answered, pointin' at the chairs on the porch.

We visited. Mighty good talkin' to a grown man without bein' interrupted.

After a few minutes he leaned right over and kissed me. I declare, the heavens opened up. I kissed him back.

For the next few hours we touched and laughed and talked. His hands ran 'long me, touchin' places long parched. His kisses floated 'round my body. Took my breath away, 'specially after bein' dry as a bone for so long. No need to be quiet so's not to wake nobody. An hour or so 'fore the childr'n come back, Conner left. I felt like I'd been borned all over again. Never expected anythin' like that.

Ever'body might say I should be ashamed of myself, sinnin' on the Sabbath. Felt right, though. I figured even God would agree. I wasn't thinkin' 'bout marriage or nothin'. I'm not stupid—this bein' Conner after all.

Trouble is, this mornin' I had this light fluttery feelin' in my belly. Only felt this five times—when I was jus' pregnant with each of my childr'n. Sweet Jesus, what am I gonna do?

O.R. Tipps, age 33, 1933

Wichita Falls, Texas

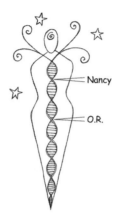

Unfortunately, immersing myself in law school at the University of Texas was not to be. I returned home for Christmas in 1923 and found out that my brother Kelly had a bad case of typhoid fever. I immediately insisted that my father have the rest of the family inoculated, but he refused. Years later I realized that Father probably felt he couldn't afford the vaccinations, but that turned out to be a very costly decision.

I only completed a few days of school before the telegram came. Kelly had recovered but Father, Mother, and sisters Hazel, Martha, and Allie Mae all caught this virulent type of typhoid fever at the same time. I left school and returned home to take charge. I did the best I could, but my father died. After I buried him, I came back to find Martha, my eighteen-year-old sister, dead. The doctors told me that my mother and Hazel would die that night. I made arrangements to bury Martha and got ambulances, against the local doctor's advice, and headed to Dallas with my mother, Hazel, and Allie Mae. I tried to admit them at Baylor Methodist Hospital, since we were all Methodists, but we were turned away because we had no money. The Catholic hospital across town took my family in without a dime and permitted me to pay the bill over a three-year period. In the care of fine doctors and nurses, all three recovered.

Judge O.R. Tipps,
circa 1932

After I got my family well, I was broke, had no job, and owed four thousand in hospital and medical bills. I leased a nearby field, put up hay, and saved seven hundred that summer, although I lost thirty pounds of weight in so doing.

Luckily, I got my old job back as Quitaque's superintendent of the schools that next fall, gave Hazel and Kate, two of my sisters, a job, and hired Ruth Owen as a second-grade teacher. Ruth and I married a year later. I bought a one-hundred-acre farm adjoining the town section and built a five-room house with barns for Mam and the younger boys, Kelly, Arthur, Chunk, and Red.

In 1926, I had paid all of my hospital and doctor bills, had my family settled again, and was determined to run for judge of Briscoe County as a way to get the law practice I wanted. When I won, I had access to a free office, a free library, salary as county judge, and plenty of time to study. I took the bar exams that first year and passed all subjects with an eighty-nine percent average.

I moved to Wichita Falls in 1933 with a new car, two daughters, Mary Sue and Nancy Jane, a wife, and eight hundred dollars. I had no business there and knew nobody. But I wasn't worried. After all I'd started out in the world with less than ten dollars when I ran away from home at sixteen and put myself through school. I opened my practice in oil and gas law and did some oil field financing on the side. I was confident in my abilities as a hard worker—just what was needed to live the American Dream.[a]

9

Wonders on the Inside

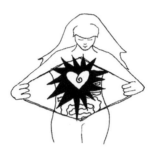

I walked away from Trinity University and left my "carefree" college days behind. Spending most of my time studying physical therapy at the University of Texas Medical Branch in Galveston, I never stopped to play in the warm waters of the Gulf of Mexico a few miles away.

Most of my classes intrigued me, but nothing compared to the inside view of the human body I was given in cadaver lab. Eager to share, one rainy Saturday morning I talked Howard, who was visiting, into coming to see this sight for himself. The formaldehyde overwhelmed him as we walked up the stairs, but he continued. He was ready to leave, though, as soon as I, all gloved and in my lab coat, asked him to hold the cadaver's arm so I could show him the branching nerves in the armpit. Luckily our love wasn't based on having similar interests.

Whether in dissection or in movement, the human body fascinated me. As I walked around town, I loved to watch people in motion: the smooth cadence of Howard's long-legged run; the ease of a child getting up and down off the ground; the laborious shuffle of a woman whose left leg and arm were stiff and twisted inward; the grace of a young woman arching her arm upward as she stocked the top shelf at Woolworth's five-and-dime.

Two weeks after my graduation, Howard and I married and soon moved to Boise, Idaho, for his structural engineering job. I worked at the Elk's Rehabilitation Hospital focusing primarily on patients who had suffered a stroke. While the science of dissection had illuminated the cold facts about muscles—where they originated and where they inserted, for

Nancy and Howard's wedding, 1976

instance—it did little to illuminate how movement, or its absence, affected one's life. Learning to walk again was an arduous process for many patients after a stroke, and I worked diligently to assist in that process. Yet learning to release their previously "normal" lives and walk into the unknown was the journey that most captured my imagination. I was thrilled that physical therapy was a profession that gave me extended periods of time with people as they learned to live within new parameters.

Members of my family were also adjusting to physical limitations. O.R.'s health had been deteriorating for several years. He had emphysema, and his labored breathing prevented him walking any distance. Mano's mind had begun to slip, and O.R. was agitated by her erratic behavior. In March of 1979, his body finally gave out. I flew to Texas to gather with relatives to celebrate the life of our family patriarch. Though I was often nervous around O.R., I loved and admired him. He'd lived a full life, but I missed him.

A few weeks after the funeral, a tornado tore through Wichita Falls. Many homes were destroyed. O.R. and Mano's home, where Mom had lived the year before she married and I had visited hundreds of times, was unharmed. In the wake of the storm, the house sold quickly, and Mano was moved into a nursing home near Mom and Dad in Houston.

In contrast to my patients in the rehabilitation center or my grandmother in the nursing home, I felt stable and secure. Howard and I had good jobs we enjoyed, friends in our neighborhood and church, a home mortgage in the form of a loan from my parents and a new VW Rabbit we owned free and clear.

All my satisfaction shifted one Sunday morning when, as usual, we went to church. Guest preacher Glenn Olds encouraged the congregation to listen prayerfully for calls in their lives. He hoped someone would feel led to apply for a job at a Methodist college in Alaska where he was president.

I had no interest in working in Alaska; nevertheless, his sermon stirred me up.

That afternoon I wasn't able to read or work in the garden or make dinner. My heart was reverberating with what felt like an insane warning: "Be careful! If you don't do something soon, you'll be forever trapped inside of the seductive American Dream."

The Spirit had blown through my body and overturned my contentment. What was wrong with the American Dream? I'd never wondered before. Yet after the sermon I knew that something was askew with the way I'd always imagined my life would unfold.

There hadn't been anything wrong with our moving up the ladder from living in an apartment to a rental house to a starter home, or our buying furniture, decorations and appliances. Progress and growth, I'd learned, were honorable life goals. But was "more" really better? What about those people who didn't have the resources to buy more? What about the poor? Was it okay for us to be getting good, professional salaries when others of equal intelligence hadn't had the same opportunities all their lives?

I didn't know what the inequities in our society had to do with us, yet continuing on the "normal path" suddenly felt dangerous.

I was certain that Howard would help me sort things out and return to normal. But something had shifted in his heart too. Though our new desire for something different made no logical sense, the invitation to our hearts was irresistible.

The jolt was big enough that we began exploring the possibility of joining the Peace Corps—the only bold, alternative work we knew about. That way we would live more simply and help other people in the process. Our only other idea was returning to graduate school for more training in some area of service.

When we shared our thoughts about doing something radically different with our friends, some of them shared that they had wondered about doing something bold before having children, also. The weird part, the warning about being careful of the American Dream, we kept to ourselves. I couldn't figure out any way to talk about fears that we would soon grow too attached to our secure lifestyle.

In order to make sure we didn't slip back, I decided we needed to publicly share our intent. When I wrote the next month's family letter—eight carbon copies mailed to extended family all over the country—I informed them that we were seriously considering joining the Peace Corps.

If O.R. had been alive, he would have called us immediately to demand we explain our rationale, but most of the recipients never commented on my proclamation. I presumed my parents received their copy of the letter just before they left to come to visit us. From our first hug at the airport, I waited for Mom's response. Dinner came and went, with no mention. The next day we wandered through the park and museum, but nothing was said. I feared a storm was brewing, but I was too afraid of Mom's thunder to bring it up myself.

After dinner on the third day of their visit, Mom launched her rebuttal. She fought long, hard and predictably against our joining the Peace Corps and adamantly held out for graduate school.

Miraculously, I stood my ground, listening and holding on to myself—a difficult task in the face of my mother in the throes of her I'm-right-on-this-one. As a teenager I hated the fact that she was usually right. Year after year, I had done as she directed even though I disliked being swayed by her opinion. But not now. Not here. This time, I was going to trust my own nudge. I wasn't budging.

Dad was silent until the hour grew late. Near midnight he spoke words that glimmered in the middle of the battle, "Follow your heart."

I was stunned to receive that affirmation from the man I knew had provided for our family through work he didn't enjoy.

In the weeks that followed my parents' visit, Howard and I talked about our options. Going off to a foreign country and trying to adjust to a different language, culture, habits and living space were light years out of our comfort zones. I also wasn't as interested in helping change something far away; I wanted to find a way to live differently in the middle of our lives here at home. The more we talked about it, the less we felt a draw to the Peace Corps.

In contrast, I loved the thought of returning to graduate school so I could teach physical therapy. Howard also contemplated university-level teaching. Logic challenged that returning to graduate school would merely entrench us further in the American Dream. I was afraid that our choosing graduate school was also a sign that I was already too attached to the comforts of American life. Nevertheless, we decided to follow our hearts and trust their wisdom. As my questions slowed, I felt a deep settling in my bones that I interpreted as God affirming our choice.

When we shared our decision with Mom, she believed that she'd "lost the battle but won the war." We knew, however, that even though we chose to go in the same direction Mom's unwavering finger had pointed, our decision flowed from our fledgling desire for justice and simplicity and not her reasoned arguments.

As we opened up to unseen guidance about the next step of our lives, something else shifted within my spirit. After years of seeking, searching and praying that my faith problem would end, I woke up one morning and realized that I no longer felt like a fraud in church. None of my beliefs had changed, but I knew I was Christian through and through. It wasn't a born-again experience worthy of fanfare. I just knew without a doubt that my questions had no detrimental effect on the power of my faith or my relationship with God. Ten years of feeling like an outsider in the church were over, and I was grateful.

Like the human body, life wasn't as simple as I'd thought as a young girl. An alarming nudge after church one Sunday shook up my comfortable life. Howard and I were about to follow spiritual guidance in ways that made no sense to my logical mind. In the middle of it all, I had fully returned home to Christianity. While dissecting the human body and the human spirit—the wonders on the inside of me—I discovered that life was rarely as reasonable as I wanted it to be.

Ed Mathys, age 57, 1979

Houston, Texas

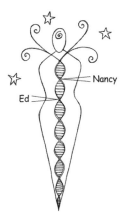

On that night in Boise
as you shared your dreams
and ideas,
I glimpsed a pattern.

Men in our family
have loved strong women,
and then
tried to tame them
again and again.

In Boise, I realized
I'm done
trying to be in charge.
Sue can march into wars
if she'd like. Not me.

Why did I think life was a contest?
That I'd shine brighter
if you faded
and became quiet like me?

If I step back in time
I see you were a normal three-year-old,
growing up.
Not a threat, just full of life.

If I could do it again ...

Actually, I did.
Twenty-two years after I squelched you,
I supported your desire
to do something wild.

It's never too late.

When you heard my heart,
the healing began.

Ed, 1976

Ann Cahoon (Mathys), age 23, 1914

Madison, Wisconsin

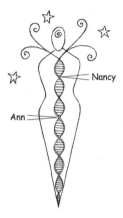

In the hallway outside of physiology class, I fell head over heels in love with John Mathys. He was everything my parents wanted for me—mixed with everything that horrified them.

We started by gazing into each other's eyes and soon became dance partners. We weren't wild enough for the Argentinean Tango, but one moonlit night at the spring dance gala we moved across the floor as one in the Waltz Tango. We didn't know everyone had stopped to watch us until the last note ended and the applause began. Yet that wasn't what made that dance memorable—John swept me off my feet.

My parents didn't care that he had won my heart. To them, John, like the Tango, was too wild. He drank beer. Worse than that, his father owned a tavern. And, worst of all, he was Catholic, a papist.

"Walk away," they warned.

They never stopped to notice that he was also intelligent, handsome, and had big dreams of his own. And, of course, he was a wonderful dance partner.

His parents were equally horrified that John had fallen in love with me—a Baptist, a "flighty dancer" and an "overly educated" Suffragette.

Our parents were united. "No marriage."

John and I held firm. We *will* marry, just as soon as we are ready.

Ann and John, 1916

10

The Fertile Years

Liberated or not, when we crossed into our mid-twenties, we caught the baby bug. We decided to focus on Howard finishing his master's degree first, then having a child, then returning to graduate school for me.

After several years of watching classes on video tapes, Howard needed to fulfill the final requirement for his degree: one semester on campus at the University of Idaho. To that end, we both arranged a six-month leave from our jobs. Howard signed up for his final semester of civil engineering courses while I took advantage of some of the offerings of the university.

Every part of campus life intrigued and excited me. I volunteered to join a crew of assistants in a human anatomy cadaver lab. I fell in love again with the exquisite human form through the postmortem gift of a woman's body. One day we peeled back her skin from her belly and removed the yellowish fat globules covering thin sheets of muscle. A strip of muscle, the rectus abdominis, ran up the center from pubic bone to the lower ribs. A deeper layer, the external abdominal oblique muscles, crisscrossed the stomach. These and other stomach muscles formed a thin, yet strong, wall to hold in all of her belly organs. Little wisps of white nerves poked in and around the muscles. I felt honored to introduce the lab students to the sublime inner structure of the body.

I also began to attend Thursday afternoon programs at the university's women's center. One month, six women gathered to discuss ancient societies led by women. Matriarchal societies, I learned, were generally egalitarian and peaceful. I couldn't even imagine such a civilization—long ago or now.

Another month, the women's center conversation focused on honoring our bodies. Everyone except me seemed very comfortable with this. The other women spoke about things that felt unspeakable in public: sex, vaginas, breasts and celebrating the powerful feminine. After that, I bought my first copy of the Boston Women's Collective's *Our Bodies, Ourselves*, a book packed with information about a woman's body, and hid it on an out-of-the-way bookshelf. I even bought a plastic speculum so I could, in the privacy of my own home, get acquainted with hidden parts of my female body.

Listening to the women talk about fighting for the passage of the Equal Rights Amendment and gender equality in organizations like National Aeronautics and Space Administration made me realize how complicated it still was to be a woman in today's world.

Simultaneously, my desire to teach physical therapy grew. I began to gather information about options for graduate school. Howard pondered the possibility of pursuing a PhD, also considering university teaching.

But first, we wanted a baby. Six months after we returned home to Boise from our semester away, I got pregnant, began to eat right, quit drinking beer, and read birthing and parenting books. Friends recommended Dr. Lock as a woman-centered doctor. On my first visit he mentioned his sixteen percent Cesarean section rate, but assured me that he fully supported natural birthing. I was confused by this contradiction and wondered if I should find another doctor. But since I couldn't point to any concrete problem with Dr. Lock, I continued as his patient and convinced myself that Howard's and my preparations would guarantee a natural birth.

My breasts grew. My ankles swelled. My abdominal muscles relaxed and stretched day-by-day, enlarging my baby's gestational home. People began to notice and reached out to touch my tight belly. I understood their desire to connect with the sacred miracle growing inside of me.

Paul Mathys Thurston arrived on October 5, 1982, four days early. I carefully recorded his birth in my journal,

The birthing experience, although it did not go as we had planned, was a great one.

My water broke at 3:00 in the morning of Monday, Oct 4. My contractions were mild. We stayed in bed and visited, talked of our dreams for the baby, and rested. ...

I laughed when the mail brought a letter from Stanford University responding to my inquiry about their master's of physical therapy program. It seemed like confirmation that baby and school were going to weave together beautifully. ...

By noon we were at the maternity ward. Dr. Lock was a real prince— though he disagreed with our choice to wait a bit longer he was very willing to go with our wishes without any pressure.

We paced the halls, looked in the nursery, checked out the post partum wing, and rested. My contractions were still very mild. They increased slightly in strength and frequency, but not enough.

By evening, I agreed to try Pitocin. After seven hours my contractions had strengthened, but I hadn't fully dilated. When my temperature began to spike, we agreed to a Cesarean. Paul was born at 3:38 in the morning of October 5. I recovered very quickly, determined not to let the surgery get me down.

I'd pushed aside my disappointment that the birthing hadn't gone as I'd wanted when I fell head over heels in love with our baby. It appeared to me that the red and yellow leaves twirled in the wind all month in celebration of Paul's birth. The changes in our lives and the season absorbed all of my attention, so regret about my Cesarean had no place to take hold.

This little one quickly figured out what he wanted and how he aimed

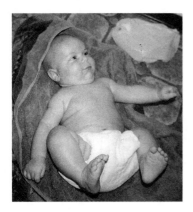

Paul, 1982

to get it. As exhausting as things were during a crying fit or yet another load of laundry, everything fell into place as soon as Paul curled up in my arms, soft and warm, with his tiny belly rising and falling with each breath.

John Mathys, age 22, 1914

St. Anthony, Idaho

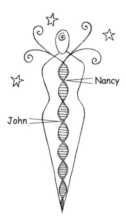

For most of my life I felt the call to return to the land of my birth. The summer before my senior year at University of Wisconsin, I sailed to Belgium. Oma and Opa had long since died, but aunts, uncles, and cousins gathered for a feast when I arrived back in St. Joris Weert. I walked around the town and stopped in Opa and Oma's garden, now tended by my cousin Clement Roelants. I only stayed a few days before Clement and I headed to Paris. We had the time of our lives, walking down those streets with our top hats and canes! By the time he returned to his home in St. Joris Weert and I to school in Madison, we were both filled with great memories.

We had no idea how quickly the tides would turn, especially for Clement. Last month Germany invaded Belgium. Letters from home have stopped coming. I know it is just a matter of time before Belgium is liberated, but it has been hard to continue to live my life free and safe while Europe is at war. Yet, what else can I do?

Immediately following graduation, I moved here to St. Anthony, Idaho, for my job as a handyman with Clark Seed Company. I had to start at the bottom and work my way up. The President hasn't had any experience with college boys before, and he wants to make sure I am a hard worker as well as book smart. I'll show him.

I have plans to help this company grow, marrying my scientific knowledge as a seeds man with Clark's solid agricultural expertise. Only a few garden seed growers across this nation maintain trial and breeding grounds where plants are tested, but that is what I hope to introduce here at Clark Seed.

I should make Assistant Manager in no time. Then I will send for Ann Cahoon. Never before or since have I met a woman like Ann—clear, intelligent, fascinated with life, and a dancer from her heart. By the time we get married, surely Belgium will be free once again.

Next year's harvest looms with great promise.

John, circa 1914

Ann Cahoon (Mathys), age 26, 1917

Manhattan, Kansas

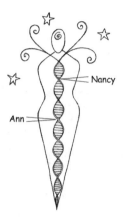

In June 1915, for the second time, I joined in a line dance of people in black robes and marched with "Pomp and Circumstance" in defense of knowledge and freedom. My love for John had grown, but we weren't yet ready to marry.

In everything except the Tango, I still took the lead. With my degrees in hand, I waltzed westward as Director of Health and Fitness Training at the Riverside California's Young Women's Christian Association. Bursting with confidence, the next year I moved to a land-locked ivory tower in Manhattan, Kansas. There I stood on my own two feet at the front of the class, teaching the rhythms of life to eager young women at Kansas State University.

Resolved to fight to give the students in my classes a little more freedom, I stood my ground in front of a room of stuffy Kansas legislators.

Calmly I explained to the men how difficult it was for women to exercise and dance in long skirts and long-sleeved blouses. I wondered if those gentlemen would be able to move in such an outfit. "Honorable men," I asked, "do you think that bloomers (with stockings, of course) and mid-length blouses (with high necklines, of course) would be acceptable for women who move in athletics and dance classes without excessively tempting the men around campus?"

Ann dancing Peter Pan, circa 1915

I wanted to scream, "Are men really that weak or stupid?" but didn't. I knew my manners, after all.

They overturned the law. For the first time, women at Kansas State University were given a few inches of freedom.

As much as I loved teaching, the yearning for my Tango partner never left my heart. I heard the song of my beloved from the land of the yellow stones, bubbly hot spots, and exploding geysers. John and I will marry, without family present, in thirty-six days. I want freedom. I want John. I want a family.

I hope I can have it all.

11

Birthing Myself

After Paul was tucked in his crib at night, Howard and I turned our attention to conversations about our next steps. Graduate school still seemed like an odd way to step outside the American Dream, but something about it felt right. Wanting to make the best decision possible, we made a pro/con list for my top two schools: Emory and Stanford. The Emory pro list was longer. Nevertheless, we chose Stanford. Our reasons were clear. First, we didn't want Paul to grow up with a Southern accent—embarrassing as that was to admit. Second, in the years since moving away from Texas, I'd grown critical of the Bible-belt conservatism I associated with the South. Third, my parents, planned to retire ninety miles south of Stanford in Monterey, California, and we wanted to be close enough to visit them regularly.

We hoped it was possible for both of us to remain faithful to our inner guidance and to make decisions based on what we wanted. In June of 1983,

Howard, nine-month old Paul and I headed off to Stanford University.

The Sunday after we arrived in California, we drove to the nearest Methodist church. I was at first rattled to find three grown men in sheets greeting us at the front door. They introduced themselves as the Old Testament characters Shadrach, Meshach and Abednego, ready to enter the fiery furnace in a special worship drama based on the first three chapters of Daniel. Excited to have found such a creative church, we soon became active members.

Families from all around the world filled Stanford's married student housing. I loved dancing with our Brazilian neighbors, visiting with our Japanese friends, and playing with the Israeli children at the sandbox. The wideness of the world felt just outside of my doorstep. Nevertheless, our closest friends—Dotty, Elizabeth, Bill and Ardath—were all white Americans.

When our neighbor Joan ranted and raved about the American actions in Nicaragua, it all seemed too complicated to understand what was really true. I refused to believe that we were undercutting a democratically elected president in order to protect economic interests of US based corporations, or selling arms to the violent opposition party, the Contras. Joan was often an alarmist, so I assumed her claims were exaggerated. Besides, global events were so overwhelming, and the information presented in the news so conflicting that I doubted I could ever understand enough about complex fields such as economics or politics to have an educated opinion about current events.

Howard was accepted into his Stanford PhD program a few months after mine started and began taking classes in January 1984. We found a part-time babysitter and worked around our two-school schedules. Our flexible days allowed lots of family playtime, especially since Howard did much of his homework around midnight after a short evening nap with Paul at bedtime.

This arrangement also meant that I could leave before dawn for our church's Wednesday covenant group meeting. The group had formed several years earlier after a workshop put on by members of the ecumenical Church of the Savior located in Washington, DC. Per their suggestion, our group agreed to deepen its spiritual journey through weekly meetings, daily silent prayer and spiritual reading. Each Wednesday, every member reported whether or not she or he had been faithful to all of these spiritual disciplines for each of the previous seven days. This structure was designed to support inner spiritual growth needed to equip Christians to engage in the work of justice in the world.

Once a week, the six of us arrived about the same time, nodded silently to each other, then slipped into our seats in the pastor's study for twenty minutes of silence. My whole body relaxed as I took a few deep breaths, my mind drifting between silence and thoughts.

Paul and his new friend Lucas played together yesterday. It was so sweet watching them go up and down the slide, running around the big field laughing.
Breathe. Let all thoughts go.
I'm not as far as I need to be in my report for Dr. Blood's class. I need to spend some time in the library this afternoon after class.
Breathe.
Morton Kelsey's book The Other Side of Silence *is startling. I don't understand what he is talking about, and yet his words touch something true beneath what I can comprehend. When we talk about the book in a few minutes I want to talk about how silence is supposed to help me detach from my old habits and be born again into a new life. How in the world does that happen?[1]*
Breathe.

Silence wasn't easy. When twenty minutes had passed, the week's leader rang the bell to bring us out of the quiet before inviting us to share our prayer concerns out loud. Once our prayers were complete, we each gave our accountability report.

"I was not faithful this past week," I told my friends one morning in March 1984.

I'd missed reading the scripture passage last Saturday. Answering affirmatively would have required that I had read the scripture passage and prayed silently every day of the week as well as read the assigned chapter of Kelsey's book. Obsessing on my lack of perfect faithfulness, I was nevertheless grateful to participate in a group that took our faith so seriously.

Thirsty for more, I joined an eight-week evening class on the ancient art of spiritual direction. A woman who had been part of the original Church of the Savior workshop but not part of the covenant group, Pam Bjorklund, was my assigned spiritual director for the duration of the class. Although we gathered at the church for class, we were instructed to meet during the week to practice what we were learning. Pam was a seasoned spiritual director, Jungian therapist and a young mother familiar with the demands of parenting.

One week during our session together, Pam pointed out an inconsistency. "I know your weekly accountability report is a central part of your covenant group, but there is something strange about stating 'I was not faithful' followed by page after page of the fruit of your walk with God. Your life is held in the context of your baby Paul, your husband Howard and school—all three things that you believe are part of God's plan for you. How do you reconcile that?"

I had no idea. I knew that my faith was deepening and broadening. I knew that my life was in a phase filled with demands. Yet, part of me believed that if I just tried a little harder I could do it all. Accountability felt important for a serious seeker.

"You sometimes act as if you are riding in a wagon pulled by six horses," Pam told me one day. "You're holding onto all of those reins for dear life, trying to get the horses to go just where you think they should go." She was right. Horses, or life, felt like they needed my full effort in order to keep moving in the right direction.

Pam and my early morning covenant group had worked for months to bring the Church of the Savior's Ministry of Money workshop to the Bay Area. Despite my busy schedule and even though I didn't know what to expect, I was eager to attend this weekend event.

Throughout the weeks prior, I worried about being separated from Paul for the three nights of the workshop. We'd never been apart at night. Alongside my worries, the process of writing my "money autobiography" intrigued me. It took me back to my childhood, remembering Dad meticulously updating his accounting sheets while Mom kept little stashes of "mad money," cash she earned from her art that she felt free to spend any way she wanted to. I wondered what Paul would remember of Howard's and my relationship with money when, in 2010, he would be my age.

When the workshop weekend arrived, I waved good-bye to Paul and Howard and drove down the road to a retreat center where fifty-four of us gathered. Don McClannen, founder and director of Ministry of Money, greeted us, saying,

> Since we believe money is the most demanding and consuming idol of all, we realize it will take major surgery of the total person to be converted into the world of freedom, health and gratitude – into being hilarious, contagious stewards. ... Our experience suggests that a companion or community is essential to help confront and console us in Bible study, prayer and sharing of these deep-seated emotions.[2]

Then Don broke down in tears. Just returned from one of their Trips of Reverse Mission to Haiti, he could talk of little except the moment of divine grace he had encountered while bathing a dying man at a Sisters of Charity home for the destitute. I'd never heard anyone hold together the idea of hilarious stewards and heart-wrenching poverty before. What would it mean to my little family if I took this stuff seriously?

Each time we gathered in the full group, I sat in the back and listened. Did Jesus really mean that "whoever has two coats must share with anyone who has none; and whoever had food must do likewise?"[3] What part of my warning about the American Dream had emerged from my visceral knowing that I couldn't serve both "God and wealth" in a society where money was considered a mark of success?[4]

Don's stories of impoverished people he knew in Haiti, India and Africa overwhelmed me. I wondered if I, too, would go on one of those trips someday. I struggled to understand how Don and the other presenters found the hope and joy they spoke about alongside their despair.

Each time we gathered in small groups, I cried. What was I supposed to do? How I lived, how I spent my money mattered not just in my local community, but around the world. What was being required of me? What joy would I find along the way?

In an instant, my cherished excuse that world events were too big for me to understand shattered. For the first time I heard, and knew in my bones, that the suffering in the world was related to my own life.

At the same time, I found a power in Christianity that I hadn't known existed— something outside the liberal/conservative duality. The type of spirituality I encountered in the workshop seemed to focus on the taproot of my faith tradition—radical in the best sense of the world. By comparison, my childhood religion seemed so tame, at least regarding those of us who were members. Through the Church of the Savior's ministries, I found a place within the Christian tradition where faith mattered in my daily decisions, where solidarity with strangers, especially those on the margins of life, was central, and where compassion replaced both niceness and judgment. I felt like I'd found my faith home.

Though Howard never attended a Ministry of Money workshop, weekly covenant group or spiritual direction, both of our lives were transformed as I shared the fruit of my explorations. Howard's, "Tell me all about it," would spark hours of conversation. We had different personalities; I moved with urgency and an eagerness to act while Howard held a cautious willingness to explore almost anything, if given enough time. The marriage of our different approaches to life led to a solidness as together we took one step and then another, from heading to graduate school to reexamining our donations to listening for God's guidance in the big and little decisions of our lives.

Within nine months of moving to Stanford, I was ready to birth a new spiritual part of myself. While my physical therapy studies explored the physical aspects of human life, my curiosity began to turn in the direction of the inner workings of the Spirit as it filled my flesh-and-blood body. Did the Spirit circulate through my heart, feeding every cell? How could I live from my own spirit, letting it mix with my breath when I spoke and powering my muscles when I moved? What was the difference between the voice of the Spirit that had guided us to Stanford and the clatter of mental gibberish? And how did I fit into the global body as one part of a complex web of interconnected systems? No scalpel was sharp enough to lay bare the answers to these questions. I understood many of the inner workings of the body, but the Spirit seemed mysterious and sometimes capricious.

Ironically, this move to return to graduate school had opened doorways that resulted in our lives changing just as wildly as they could have on the savannahs of Africa with the Peace Corps. I'd discovered the intersection between faith and money—how I worked with my own money and how my money related to people all around the world. Even though I'd rarely heard about it in church, I'd discovered the centrality of justice and equality within my own Christian tradition. I'd heard stories of people living in other parts of the world and felt my neighborhood expand.

Following the quiet guidance of Spirit, I discovered, opened far more doorways than my best thought out plan. Under the skin of my body and hidden from view in my spirit, something miraculous was afoot. I wasn't sure whether physical therapy or Christian spiritual formation would be the focus of my future work.

After the Ministry of Money workshop, I was also stretched by the book *In a Different Voice.* Author Carol Gilligan explored the ways that women's moral development and ethical decision-making were different than men's. That wouldn't have been a problem, except that men's process was considered "normal," leaving women's development labeled deficient.[5] Intrigued, I shared her ideas with Mom during one of her weekend visits. She dismissed Gilligan's research methods and conclusions as nonsense. I was hurt by her rebuff but didn't feel competent to defend what felt so true to me. Instead, I quickly changed the subject.

Conversations, school, covenant group, research, parenting and church were a lot to hold. Exhausting sometimes. A Tipps family reunion in Amarillo, Texas, offered a much-needed break from the intensity of school and our tightly packed married student-housing neighborhood. We decided that Howard and Paul would leave a few days earlier than my school schedule allowed and go first to visit his family in Midland.

The prospect of a few days of solitude sounded heavenly. Once Howard and Paul left, I fell asleep, peaceful and without a care in the world.

I woke with a start. Sometime in the dark of that July night, the supportive story I'd believed about Paul's birth cracked open. Twenty-one months after my son was born, I remembered what had really happened between the middle of the night on October 4, 1982 and 3:28 a.m. on October 5.

Forgotten details exploded in all directions. Memories flooded back. In the light of dawn, contractions of rage ripped me apart. This time, I was giving birth to myself. All alone. In my journal I wrote,

Paul's Birth Take Two

The pregnancy proceeded right on schedule, but apparently my natural birthing process is slower than "normal." Pitocin was prescribed to speed things up. Internal monitor readings captured the nurse's interest. She sat with her back to me.

Caught in grip after grip of strong artificial labor, I was preoccupied when the doctor returned to check me. "Nothing is happening; you're only eight cm. dilated," Dr. Lock decreed.

Soon he returned yelling at the nurse, "Why didn't you tell me she has a fever?"

Then to me,

"Nancy, you must have a c-section now. For the baby's sake."

What could I say? I politely thanked Dr. Lock for allowing me to follow my birthing desires for so long in the labor process.

My fabricated image of a supported birth was all I could let in while holding my newborn in my arms. Snuggling my nursing baby, I believed that I couldn't feel rage and feel love at the same time. I chose love and let my fury disappear into the fog.

A few days later I flew to meet Paul and Howard at the family reunion and again pushed my feelings out of sight. I smiled, ate potato salad and acted like the kind of smart, strong Tipps woman I was supposed to be. Throughout the following months, though, as my memory returned, I continued to write,

I almost erupted, just for a second, during my six-week post delivery check up.

"You need to be refitted for a diaphragm because you almost fully dilated during labor."

"Almost fully dilated" he says now … "nothing is happening" … then. But by the time I left the doctor's office, I let the thought float away.

Until I woke up alone one warm sunny morning in July with boiling blood and a furious, churning stomach. I felt tied up in knots and I wanted to scream (but, of course, I was too concerned that I might bother my neighbors to give voice to my cries). I didn't know how to let this churning out of my mind or body. I paced. I cried. I rehearsed again and again all I wish I'd said to my doctor.

In August, I ordered the hospital records that confirmed my fears. My "dangerous fever spike" that led to the insistence of an emergency C-section was a slight temperature increase, normal for birthing.

I also remembered that the anesthesiologist didn't talk to me at all as he stuck the needle in my back and proceeded to inject too much of the drug. I struggled to breathe. My blood pressure dropped to sixty over forty. I trembled uncontrollably. Howard feared I was dying.

Fury at my doctor morphed into a fierce anger at men. Emotions grabbed and squeezed and popped out about all of it—from the medical system's treatment of me to all the manipulation and harm that had been done to women over the centuries.

My rage mystified me. My logical brain listed all the reasons that my reaction was way out of proportion to what had happened to me. To me, a nice Christian girl, my fury felt like a crisis that needed to stop. Now. I had terrified myself.

Even as the volcano erupted within, I usually looked calm on the outside. I'd been working on that skill since I was three; so as far as I could tell, few, other than Howard and my covenant group, ever knew anything was wrong. From time to time, though, I slipped into a rant about the current state of obstetrics. Whenever I could, I shoved these big emotions away and focused on family and the schoolwork to be done. I poured out my feelings into the safety of my journal.

July 10

This has been a time of lowness—low self-esteem, grief with the birthing issue. ...

I still have the nagging problem with coping—healing my birth anger etc.—my heart aches for healing.

For a time, I went to see my spiritual director, Pam, on a weekly basis to sort through my experience. With Pam, I felt free enough to let my anger flow. I was certain if I could just understand what was happening inside me, I would know how to make it stop.

Anger seeped into other parts of my life: frustration with Paul's constant activity; disgust when Howard seemed to slack off with the chores; irritation when stores didn't give me good service. In nighttime dreams, I yelled at a moving company doing an inadequate job. My covenant group accountability reports were filled with gratitude right next to me feeling *"overwhelmed at working full time, finishing my master's research, parenting, and navigating my anger at the birthing issue."*

I struggled to put what happened to me personally into a bigger context. I tried to use it to practice letting go of control, an important spiritual journey lesson. I let my experience remind me that other women, especially poor women or people of color, had too often received inadequate or disrespectful treatment in medical clinics. I struggled to focus on my gratitude for young Paul and my own powerful birthing body.

Nevertheless, my life-long struggles with self-esteem only worsened as I waded through what I continued to refer to as "the birthing issue." I often felt inadequate and unlovable. I glimpsed a pattern larger than my doctor's violation of my birthing body—somewhere along the line, I'd absorbed disrespect of my own femininity.

As 1985 dawned, my emotional roller coaster cruised to a stop, almost as if the emotional frenzy had finished its ride within me. Grateful that the emotions had calmed, I never wanted to return to that level of rage again. I turned my focus to my young child, who was becoming more amusing by the day.

Meanwhile, we wanted to have another child, so finding a new obstetrician was critical. I interviewed several, including a woman, and walked away discouraged. A nurse from the Birthing Resource Center recommended I see Dr. Creevy, an obstetrician more in line with my values. During our first interview Dr. Creevy suggested I read Suzanne Arms' book *Immaculate Deception: A New Look at Women and Childbirth in America,* which exposed the lies behind the rising Cesarean rate in the US.[6] Clearly, Dr. Creevy and I saw eye-to-eye about birthing.

Now in the care of a doctor I trusted, I was ready to get pregnant again. Just at that moment, my last living grandparent, Mano, died. I was too engrossed in my master's research to fly to her funeral. It felt like she'd died years before when she faded into dementia, so I had few qualms about not gathering with family to honor her life and death.

In June, I graduated wearing Grandmother Ann Mathys's commencement gown covering my barely visible two-month pregnancy bump. We didn't know if our new little baby was a boy or girl, but we knew I'd be birthing again around January 9, 1986. This time, I was ready to trust my body to guide me through pregnancy and delivery.

Later that summer, a friend invited me join her at a lecture by Betty Friedan. Friedan founded the National Organization for Women (NOW) and wrote the groundbreaking work *The Feminine Mystique.* I'd always steered clear of feminists and feminist books, hers included, even though I believed in equality of the sexes. My few experiences with feminism had felt overwhelming—it too often had a hard edge (almost masculine), focused too much on anger at men and seemed to espouse that women should work, parent and volunteer all at once. I couldn't see how stepping into all of that could help me. Still, fresh from my encounter with the patriarchal birthing business, I was curious to hear her speak.

I'd known little about the history of NOW, so I checked out a few facts. In October 1966, the *National Organization for Women* held its organizing conference. Friedan penned their "statement of purpose" where she articulated the call for society to wake up to the fact that the inequality directed toward women was a problem for the whole culture to address, not just an individual's problem.[7]

I had experienced a small but painful thread of discrimination against women by my doctor when Paul was born, and it enraged me. Now, months later, I desperately clung to my newly returned peace. While I cared about addressing the patriarchal system that had affected my birthing event, Friedan's out-front anger and sharp edges were overwhelming. Listening to her, I quickly felt defensive about my decision to be a full time mom after my baby was born in January.

In the days that followed the lecture, I pushed the remaining whiffs of my hot emotions and Freidan's feminist ideas back into the shadows. Instead, I dove back into my studies, focused on my husband and friends, and enjoyed Paul's antics and my growing baby-to-be.

More comfortable with things of the spirit, I decided I was ready to talk to Mom about how my faith path had diverged from hers. Proclaiming my own spiritual path to Mother felt like a critical step of my independence.

One morning when we were alone in my parents' home, I broached the topic. I explained that my faith was no longer fed primarily by an intellectual understanding of the Christian tradition. I now approached my faith more mystically, interested in focusing on intuition rather than facts. I loved Eucharist, solitude and prayer, and I was more interested in truth behind the words of scripture and tradition than rational analysis. She listened respectfully.

I was grateful that this conversation was so unlike the one years before when I'd told her about my Pentecostal experience. I didn't need her approval, but I was glad for her respect. I was separate yet intimately connected to my mother, and I'd taken the next step of birthing myself as my own person.

Laura's Moon, January 25, 1986

The Sky

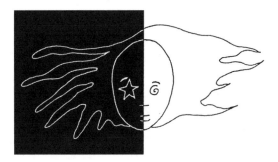

My Dearest Nancy,

Your body waited for my fullness
to herald this holy night of Laura's birth.
Nine months, two-and-a-half weeks
seemed too long to you,
but Laura was right on time.

You searched long and hard
to find a doctor to support you
this time 'round.
He let your body follow her own rhythm.

My tender beams light on your bed
on this birthing night,
illuminating my gifts to you.

You, like me, can reflect light
effortlessly. Without urgency.

Woman, lay down that load you've carried far too long.

Love your shadow.
Light and dark swirl lustrously together.

Join the universe
in a wild cycle of rhythms.
Our differences bring joy, not chaos.

Twenty-nine and a half days for me.
Twenty-four hours for your earth.
Three hundred-sixty five days for us both.
All part of the cycle of life.

Reflecting as the universe turns,
I can only be full and luscious
if I am also dark and hidden.
Join me in this miraculous
rhythm of creation.

Love and lunar blessings to you, dear mother,
The Woman in the Moon

P.S. Birthing is exhausting. May I offer you
some of my delectable cheese?

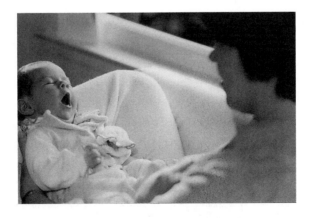

Laura and Nancy, 1986

12

Winter Solstice, 1986

Mom was a godsend. Despite her warning that she wasn't going to be one of those "over-involved" grandmothers—since she had a full life of her own—my parents' home became an oasis from the chaos of married student housing. Each month the four of us traveled ninety miles south for a visit. Mom carried Laura around the house so Howard and I could sit down to eat a meal. In the afternoons, Mom and four-year old Paul went on "Grand Adventures" around town. They walked up and down Fisherman's Wharf, looking at the harbor seals and bags of sea shells for sale and went on regular visits to the Monterey Bay Aquarium, stopping at the otter tank for the afternoon feeding.

After Thanksgiving, Mom and Paul decorated the first Christmas tree Laura had ever seen. Mom's gruff exterior melted as she enjoyed the antics of her young grandchildren.

That all came to a screeching halt around midnight of the winter solstice. The shrill phone woke me from a sound sleep.

"Nancy, Mom's gone," Dad said.

"Gone?" I asked. "What do you mean 'gone'?"

Almost a month before Laura's first birthday, and three days before Christmas, my mother was dead. She was putting the last stitches on holiday decorations when her heart stopped beating.

Christmas card designed and mailed
by Mom the week she died.

This woman who, thirty-two years earlier, had held me for nine months nestled under her heart, slipped out of her body on the darkest night of 1986. Paul insisted on going to the funeral home to see her body. Standing at the edge of her coffin, he asked that I lift the lower half of the lid so he could make sure that she would leave this earth with the feet that had led the two of them on so many wonderful adventures.

I held my full moon baby close to my broken heart as I ached for the loss of my own bright mama during that dark season of grief.

Ruth Tipps, age 49, 1949

Wichita Falls, Texas

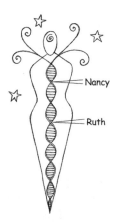

My life fell apart one September weekend in 1941.

I had finished Nancy Jane and Sue's school clothes a few weeks before. Nancy Jane was in fifth grade that year, while Sue was in high school. As dawn broke on Friday, September nineteenth, everything was running as usual. Nancy Jane came home from school sick that afternoon. She rapidly went downhill. Her face went slack and she had trouble swallowing. Then her breathing slowed way down. By Sunday afternoon, she was gone, a victim of Bulbar Polio.

Part of me died too, then and there.

O.R. pulled even deeper into his law practice. I knew, even if he didn't, that he was trying desperately to work his way out of grief. A few months later, I was pregnant again—excited and grieving at the same time. Newborn Martha came into our home just as Sue was preparing to leave for college. The grief from Nancy Jane's death softened some.

Luckily, over the years I found something to hold me on Friday and Sunday, the two days of the week that seemed filled with memories of her death. Monday, Tuesday, Wednesday, Thursday and Saturday made up my workweek. On those days I served the family from dawn to dusk (and later). But Friday and Sunday were special days when I felt closest to God and to myself.

Sunday, of course, was the day I spent in church. The other Sabbath day, the one closest to my heart, was Friday. After breakfast Friday mornings, I picked up my books and headed out the door. Twice a month I went to Storytelling League, and on the alternate weeks I met with the Literary Book Group. In both groups, I relished the love of stories that God had planted within me. On that day, unseen by family and untouched by daily chores, words came alive in my imagination.

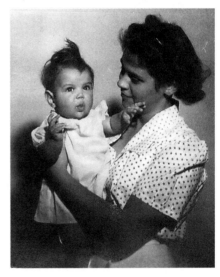

Martha and Sue, 1944

Sometimes I spent this day around a table with other women, our cups full of coffee, talking about the book we'd just read. Other times I performed for a women's club that was eager to hear my storytelling. Once I told stories in an orphanage and laughed remembering asking mother whether I was adopted. Wherever I was, the words came alive and captivated the listeners. Stories, I found, can heal like nothing else.

As Martha grew, she loved to hear me practice. Otherwise, I kept my storytelling experiences to myself, trusting that one day my family would discover the power I wielded each Friday.

13

Moving to the Frozen Edge
of the Earth

Moving to Fargo, North Dakota, sounded like moving to the frigid wilds at the edge of civilization. When Howard began his job search to teach at a university, I pictured lots of places. Fargo definitely wasn't one of them. In fact, for years I'd joked that he could move to North Dakota (a place he'd long dreamed of living) with his second wife after I was dead and gone. Nevertheless, when a civil engineering teaching position came available at North Dakota State University, we both knew this was to be our next home.

The California sun warmed our bare arms as we supervised the loading of our moving van in January 1988. A week later, we unloaded during a lull in a North Dakota blizzard. Twenty-five inches of swirling snow filled our driveway, and temperatures hovered near twenty degrees below zero.

Soon a neighbor with a snow blower came over to clear our driveway and our corner lot sidewalk—hospitality, Fargo style.

Three weeks later, I attended a class on women mystics at Communiversity—a month-long array of classes offered to the community by Concordia College. This program was intended to be an offering of light in the middle of the cold, dark month of February. After Sister Ruth Wirtzfeld completed her lecture, a small group of us gathered around to ask a few questions. Soon the conversation turned to plans of forming a prayer and study group to be held at the Presentation Prayer Center where Sister Ruth worked. I was invited. The wilds of North Dakota began to feel like home.

Each week this small group of women welcomed me. We studied spiritual exercises devised by the sixteenth century saint, Ignatius of Loyola, where we shared the fruit of stepping inside the assigned scripture story and allowing imagination and prayer to become one. From there we began to share the joys and struggles of our lives and experimented with different forms of prayer and creativity. Chris, one of the women in our circle, introduced the practice of continuous writing for ten minutes in response to the prompt of an unfinished sentence or a photograph. One evening she brought a picture of a woman riding a wild horse. I looked carefully, picked up my pen and began to write.

> *What a contrast! A woman, dressed to the hilt in a long dress and pantaloons, hair done up in the latest fashion, shoes pointed for fashion over comfort, with her groomed little doggie in tow, sitting delicately on a wild horse.*
>
> *The horse is bucking for all she's worth trying to tear down some of the woman's pretenses. To make her hair-do fall, shoes drop off, lace tear.*
>
> *But the amazing thing is that the woman is not only allowing it, she's enjoying it!*
>
> *What freedom—to take the best from both worlds, to be willing to let loose and risk letting go of the image you've worked so hard to develop.*
>
> *That freedom is beyond me now.*

The dog seems concerned that his mistress is off on a wild escapade. Does he fear she's lost her mind? Does he fear that she will desert him? There often seem to be people nipping at our heels when we want to break loose.

Am I like the little dog? Am I pulling others back from experiencing all sides of life?

Or am I like the horse, playfully bucking the system? Maybe sometimes the bucking is not so playful ...

Or like the woman willing to play dress-up but also eager to let loose, even if that's only on the inside of me now? The ride of their lives.

What is the ride of my life?

Wildness was easier for me to contemplate in writing than to experience in daily life. Being wild sounded so fierce and uncivilized and seemed incompatible with responsibility and politeness.

I missed Mom and her encouragement for me to let loose just a little bit. She'd urged me to do some writing or something to take time for

myself amid the demands of mothering young children. She'd nurtured my creativity and nudged me to go beyond my comfort zone—within "mature" limits, of course—but I needed to discover how to enjoy wildness on my own.

I worked occasionally in physical therapy clinics, mothered, and volunteered by coordinating and teaching adult

Thurston family, 1988

education at First United Methodist Church. The church held a prominent place in our family's life. Each Sunday morning I hurried everyone out the door. We began in worship together, before Paul and Laura headed off with all the children to their respective Sunday School classes. Sermons and the music touched my heart. While Howard served on the church council for a few years, I avoided those kinds of committees. More interested in study than church business, I gathered with thirteen other adults on Wednesday evenings for interesting, yet respectful and orderly discussions in a two-year *Disciple Bible Study* leadership class.

At the same time, the Spirit bucked in my life like the wild mare. I searched for something bolder, seeking out others who also wanted to dive into their own spiritual journeys. I participated in a yearlong visioning process at church with great hope. Yet when we presented the fruits of our work on a Sunday morning, very few people stepped forward to participate. As everyone was leaving the sanctuary after that service, my frustration exploded to Howard when I blurted out, "I guess we have a visionless congregation." His eyes widened in response, alerting me that many around us heard my wail. Trying to figure out how to manage a bucking Spirit and a desire to be tolerant wasn't an easy ride.

In addition to my busy church schedule, each week I returned to the small circle of women at the Presentation Prayer Center. Becky, Chris, Trudy, Julia and I went to our own Protestant churches on Sunday—Evangelical Free, ELCA Lutheran, United Church of Christ and Methodist—and were fed by Catholic mysticism when we gathered together at the Presentation Center.

We took a class on the Enneagram together. All we learned forever changed how we understood ourselves and, for those of us who were married and moms, our husbands and children. I was embarrassed to admit that an ancient Sufi system based on nine fundamental personality types could bring me such clarity and compassion, but it did. I recognized myself as a Six on the Enneagram: one who was fearful of having no support and guidance; who projected my paranoia onto others; who was profoundly loyal; and who strongly desired security and support. Howard, on the other hand was a Nine: one who avoided conflict at all costs; who was fearful of loss and separation; and who desired inner stability and peace of mind. It helped us time and time again to realize, when we were each slipping into our own compulsion, how to support ourselves and each other as we tried to keep moving forward.

At times our group shared what we had learned from each other. I pasted Chris' words about me into my journal:

Your intellect operates like a lion (a hungry one). You tear through an issue up one side and down the other until you're satisfied that a balanced truth about it has been found. You are tenacious about truth, whether it be an inner or an outer issue for you. I respect that—yet sometime I see you exhausted by it and then I wish I could help you more. Your very quick sense of humor seems to balance the struggle. I've appreciated your Methodist sense of "doing God's work" and hope you've benefited from my Lutheran sense of receiving and living in God's freely given grace.[1]

Chris, the quietest woman I'd ever met, observed well. My roaring intellect, inherited from O.R. and Mom, was so strong that I sometimes felt trapped by its power. I knew little about how to rest in God's grace as I continued to dive into my spiritual practice and work.

Surrounded by people I loved, active within a vibrant church community, and held in a small group of women of faith, my searching lion continued to roar. The more the mystical aspect of Catholicism fed my spirit, the dryer Methodist spirituality felt to me. Since I was raised not to criticize others unless I looked at myself first, every criticism I felt about the church required criticism of myself. Snuggled under the covers in the dark of night, I worried that I'd been too hard on Paul, wasn't doing enough to help Laura with a difficult teacher or hadn't adequately led the adult education committee the night before. From there my thoughts jumped to a long string of disasters that had recently struck our fragile world: Union Carbide ordered to pay the government of India for damages it caused in the deadly 1984 Bhopal chemical leak; the ongoing saga of the savings and loan crisis that cost depositors their life savings, then cost tax payers two hundred billion dollars in a bailout; and the Exxon Valdez tanker that spilled thousands of barrels of oil into Alaska's Prince William Sound.

In the middle of the night, I often felt like I was being swallowed by something terrifying, a lot like the boa constrictor in the song[2] I sang with Paul and Laura. The gruesome idea of being eaten by a snake never bothered us as we belted out the song. From toe to knee, it soon got more graphic as bit-by-bit the snake swallowed us whole.

I learned that sometimes things that started out cute began to eat away at me. If nothing changed the gulping, soon it could be too late. I started out trying hard to be a good girl for Daddy. Then for my teachers. Then for my boyfriends. Then with medical professionals. Bit by bit, my own inner knowing was gobbled up and forgotten. Being a good girl, or a good woman, used to seem virtuous to me, but I was growing to believe that our world suffered from an absence of feminine wisdom. My endless self-criticism didn't leave much room for wisdom or healing.

Sometimes my longing for Mom's comfort left me feeling empty. She wasn't of a cuddly sort of woman, but she had provided a harness to the wild bucking of the world inside my head and all around me. Although I'd often disagreed with or resisted her, I realized Mom had been my dearest role model for being a woman in this world.

After many restless nights during the spring and summer of 1989, a vacation seemed like a perfect way to help lift my spirits. Howard, Paul, Laura and I drove through Montana, Wyoming, Nebraska and western South Dakota. Along the way we stopped for a little culture at a Western museum. Holding hands, three-year-old Laura and I walked around looking at the Texas-sized paintings that filled the room. Cowboys rode across the plains hunting huge herds of bison. On a rocky bluff, Indians sat trading with white settlers. I noticed the color, the technique and the breathtaking landscape.

Puzzled, Laura stopped and asked, "Where are the women?"

Where indeed? I, in my grown-up wisdom, hadn't even noticed their absence. Not interested in feminist talk or gender theory, Laura saw the story held within the pictures—this was a man's world. She missed the women.

What else did she see that I no longer noticed?

On our way home, we stopped to visit an old friend in Boise. As usual, I browsed her bookshelf and found one that sounded interesting—*Women's*

Reality: An Emerging Female System, by Anne Wilson Schaef. In the book, Schaef explored the differences between male and female ways of viewing time, power, morality, communication—so many aspects of life in which I'd long felt out of step.[3] Intellectually, I'd known that our society was set up to value masculine reality and disregard feminine reality, but Schaef's words and Laura's innocent sight broke through my resistance to believing that these realities had an impact on my life.

While I hadn't focused on gender inequities, I had been paying attention to and was disturbed by the economic injustice in our world. In addition, I was beginning to realize that aligning money and faith wasn't talked about in church—other than on Stewardship Sunday when we were asked to make our annual pledge—but I wanted more conversation. In the summer of 1990, I attended my second Ministry of Money workshop near Washington, DC. Once again, I cried as I realized the implications of keeping the global family in mind as we made our own financial decisions. Hearing more stories about their "reverse mission" trips to Haiti, I now believed that one day I'd be brave enough to go too.

One idea highlighted in the workshop was choosing investments that would bring both financial gain and social good. I'd tried to find some socially responsible investments with our Merrill Lynch advisor, but each time he'd discounted the idea of using our values as a guide for making financial decisions. He'd adamantly held that making a profit and following social values were not compatible.

When I shared my frustration with the Ministry of Money presenter, he told me, "You can do this. Do the research yourself and then hold your ground with your advisor. Or find someone new. One day, you may even find that you enjoy it."

Enjoying it sounded ludicrous, but I believed that I could do something about realigning our portfolio. We mustered up the courage to sell our South African diamond stock and gold Krugerrand coins, both given to us years before by Howard's father. Emboldened after the Ministry of Money workshop, I no longer collapsed in the face of my advisor's objections to selling stocks in companies I didn't want and instead bought community investments I preferred like Calvert Foundation notes. Nevertheless, these successes didn't change the fact that we were ready to find a financial advisor who shared our values. Dwain Gump, CFP from First Affirmative Financial Network, was a pioneer in the social investing movement and provided the guidance I needed. Dwain had many exciting suggestions for responsible investments as well as an honest assessment of the difficulty of finding "perfect" companies or funds. Suddenly, investing had become fun.

The stimulus for growth came from all directions—some from investment advisors, some from the mouths of babes and some from the shadows of our past. Memories of what had unfolded during my final semester at Trinity University in 1975 caught up with Howard and me one mid-winter's night in 1990.

In the middle of the night, I bolted awake with a question shouting inside my head:"Why didn't Howard say NO?" I knew it had something to do with what had happened at Trinity. Before I had a chance to say anything, Howard began to share that old college memories haunted him.

Finally, we broke our unspoken vow of silence and talked about what had happened almost fifteen years before. We'd always been clear about the outward details: I had a sexual relationship with Al during the time Howard and I were still dating. The rest was foggy.

The day after our midnight discussion, Howard and I were exhausted, but not done talking. As busy parents, we found whatever moments we could to continue our conversation. The more we talked, the more our old stories didn't feel true.

What really had happened fifteen years ago?

As we poked and prodded our memories and emotions, new clarity began to emerge. I realized that the letter I'd sent to Howard so long ago about my plan to begin a sexual relationship with Al was filled with independent-sounding words. My real message—"I don't know what to do. I'm scared and confused. Help. Come quickly. Do you love me?"—remained unwritten. My midnight wake up call surfaced my hidden desire that Howard would have responded to my letter with a resounding "NO! Don't do it," and immediately come to Trinity so we could talk before I made my decision.

Likewise, Howard admitted that he hadn't written what was true for him.

Unfortunately, we'd believed the words we wrote to each other and were oblivious to the unuttered shouts just below the surface.

As a young woman, I had felt alone and abandoned by the man I loved. But that wasn't a thought I could let in. From the perspective of years, I saw how my fears and confusion had scrambled my ability to think clearly.

I realized that I had walked a similar path dealing with the trauma of Paul's Cesarean birth. At that time, I believed my doctor had fully supported my birthing process. At twenty, I'd believed that things going further than I'd wanted with Al meant that we must love each other and that love for him required me to respond as I did. In both cases, when faced with a situation too traumatic and contradictory for me to understand or digest, I'd shut down emotionally and mentally and made up a story I could live with.

In college, I never stopped to figure out what really happened that night that shook the foundations of how I saw myself and what I wanted in a relationship. Here in Fargo, I was ready to begin to answer that question.

My memories remained cloudy, but I knew that I was pushed farther than I wanted to go that night. Over the years, other women friends had told me similar stories about sexual encounters wherein they had felt responsible because they hadn't said "no" clearly enough or loudly enough, or because no overt force was used, or for a million other reasons. For me, I couldn't reconcile what I knew about myself with what had happened. Instead of sitting with the pain and listening to what I wanted next, I grasped the first solution that occurred to me. It had brought calmness in the moment. But I'd paid a high price during the days and years that followed for that one moment of peace.

In the icy land of North Dakota in 1990, frozen spots in my life were beginning to thaw. As the kids turned eight and five, I was coming to terms with my past memories and present disasters. Whether I liked it or not, life was a wild ride. Like that brave woman on the bucking horse, I was learning to hold on and go where it led.

Ann Mathys, age 34, 1924

Salinas, California

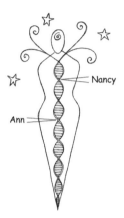

After John and I said "I do," we loaded my wardrobe trunk onto the train and sped across the country. The romance of the world rose to greet us as the miles whizzed by.

Then we arrived in St. Anthony, Idaho. My heart skipped a beat. Maybe several.

St. Anthony. The saint who renounced his wealth and founded monasticism. I wanted to do neither.

The saint known for finding lost things. St. Anthony failed me. Twelve years would pass before I began to find what I lost the minute I arrived in that tiny town in the wilds of eastern Idaho.

Looking outside the small train window when we first jerked to a stop, I gasped. Waiting for us with smiling faces were fiddlers, girls in petticoats and red-checked dresses, and strains of screeching Western music. They wanted us to join in the square dance down the dusty town street. John was glad to see his friends again. I was horrified, but pretended I felt otherwise. Round and round we do-si-doed. My white blouse grew dingy with dust. My frozen smile almost cracked my cheeks. We circled left in front of stores and clover leafed around churches and bars. We promenaded up and down the streets, where concert halls, dance floors, college libraries, and teahouses were nowhere in sight.

Eventually I found friends among the dirt, grime, and western music. I grew to appreciate the beauty of life at the edge of Henry's Fork of the Snake River, with mountains nearby and dunes that reminded me of the ocean's shore. John and I enjoyed the fishing, hiking trails, and sunny picnics on the few Saturdays he was off work.

Luckily, motherly delight reverberated in my bones after our sons Jack then Ed were born. We sang and bopped and bounced together. The itsy, bitsy spider made our fingers pirouette. The rock-a-bye-baby waltz was good before naps. The diaper-changing routine of the little piggies found a place in my heart. The boys and I explored the outdoors. We read book after book after book, turning some of the stories into performances. I remembered what I had written so long ago in my thesis, "Play is the real work of childhood and the love for play in the child would become the love for work in the man." [1]

Nevertheless, with each passing year in the barren West—Idaho, Colorado, then rural California—I grew more parched.

Ann, Jack, John and Ed, circa 1924

14

The Flight Inside

With Paul and Laura both in elementary school, I had more time to focus on my spiritual journey. I was thrilled when Judy Kerr, a friend at church, told me about the upcoming Academy for Spiritual Formation offered by United Methodist's Upper Room Ministries.[1] Participants from around the country would meet together five days a quarter for two years and experience a combination of spiritual education, faith sharing and worship. Reuniting the best of Protestant and Catholic traditions within the context of a lay and clergy community sounded like heaven to me. Vatican II—the 1963 church council that was underway while Mom was explaining Bible stories and ancient church councils to me—had opened the door for this sort of ecumenical program to take place within Roman Catholic retreat centers.

The next two-year Academy was scheduled to begin meeting at Mercy Center, my favorite San Francisco area retreat center. I wanted in.

Attending meant that I was away from family for almost a week every three months. I arranged for Paul and Laura to play at friends' houses after school until Howard got off work. When I told Laura, she smiled. "Goody! We get to eat good food when you are gone."

"Oh really?" I asked. "Like what?"

"Frozen pizza, spaghetti with sauce from a jar, Daddy's potato and egg dish and fish sticks. Daddy cooks real good!"

His menus may have been limited, but evidently he was the more appreciated cook in the family. My children adjusted to my absences without too many glitches. Howard, however, eagerly awaited my return.

For the first session, I left snow banks behind and entered a state filled with winter flowers. We began our quarterly gatherings in the Mercy Center Chapel, sinking into community through worship. Each of our days together included Eucharist, communal prayers, two one-hour guest lectures, silence and gathering of the small group we'd been assigned to that would meet together for the entire two years.

Our first week together started off sweetly, filled with getting to know each other, soaking up the rhythm of the day and wondering what the next two years would hold for us all. I could hardly wait for the second session to begin. When three months had passed, I flew again to California. All of my preparation and travel fatigue slipped away during our opening worship. I was open, eager for what would be given during time together.

The murmuring of discontent began by the second day. I overheard conversations at the break. A small group of people clustered at lunch, and I caught snippets of angry conversation. It broke into our covenant group when George said, "This week's afternoon lectures are insipid and a waste of time. I paid good money to be here, and we deserve more than this."

I was incredulous. Discontented participants rejected the speaker and all of what he had to say because it wasn't what they wanted. He was offering his best. Wasn't that enough? And why were people complaining about what they had agreed to pay for these sessions? Were they really expecting that every lecturer and every session would go exactly as they wanted?

We had a community gathering at the end of the week. This conflict, the elephant in the room as far as I was concerned, was not mentioned. I was too insecure in the larger group to say anything but was disappointed in the silence.

The following week I wrote Don McClannen, Ministry of Money director, to ask if he thought I was crazy to be so upset at the way not-getting-our-money's-worth was a central focus of the criticism.

He replied quickly: "Be grateful that you reacted so strongly and clearly. The dynamic that you observed is entitlement, the belief that when we pay money for something, we get to control what it looks like. Money is a potent force in our psyches and in our spirit."

Don's words settled me. I was slowly but surely becoming more confident and secure with my understanding of the events unfolding around me. It was, however, scary to see what most others didn't see, or at least didn't speak. And I didn't want to say anything if I might be wrong or sound overbearing. Instead, I often burned inside while I tried to understand and figure out what to do.

In the months that followed, I realized that the dynamic I'd encountered within our second Academy session was part of the reason that I had issues with the word "justice." Too often I spoke of justice in the context of getting what I had paid for, or getting service just the way I wanted from a business. This use of justice held elements of truth but was so self-focused. The larger justice or injustice in the fabric of the culture was left unnoticed.

Each quarter we returned to Mercy Center. Conflicts came and went. Lecturers covered a wide spectrum of spiritual formation topics, including mysticism, Biblical studies and spiritual direction. Informally over meals we touched on various ways our daily lives and faith wove together. One evening the conversation turned to dreams. I couldn't remember any dreams from that week, but I told my friends my recurrent childhood dream about the Leaning Tower of Pisa church.[2]

As I described this old dream, I noticed that it symbolized much of my spiritual journey. The red velvet drape hanging in the middle of the church was the divine, and for most of my life I'd had an insatiable longing to touch God. I loved the church too and felt drawn there even during those years when I felt like my Christian beliefs were lacking. Yet I'd often seen the church leaning from its own weight, vital at its core yet unbalanced—like the leaning tower. Part of me had tried to push the church upright, correcting the descent that began so long ago. When I was frustrated, I'd tried to give the church a little shove, hoping to speed up the slow fall of this unbalanced institution and thus free God from its ponderous, tilted walls. The latter didn't happen too often, however, since I'd never been comfortable taking such forceful action toward an institution I loved.

As I looked at the dream with Academy friends, I wondered if my vision of the off-balance institution was accurate or overzealous. But the dream only confirmed that I, like the little girl in my dreams, was willing to reach whatever distance necessary to touch God and cling to him in the middle of daily life as much as in the middle of church.

After I returned home from the Academy session, I continued to work with the dream through collage and drawings. I wanted to figure out what I needed to do now. Suddenly I knew.

I didn't need to shove the church over or push it upright again. It would stand or fall of its own accord. Instead, I needed to focus on my dance with the divine, with God, inside and outside the church.

Whether through dreams, assigned books, lectures or conversations, the Academy gatherings nurtured me. Following each session I wrote about my experiences: what I had learned and what I had begun to understand about myself. I sent them out to my pastors, my old California covenant group friends, my spiritual director, local friends and to my father. As each session became more personal and my writings filled with more details about my spiritual journey, I wondered whether I needed to take Dad off the list. Nevertheless, each quarter I sent letters to everyone, including him.

Dad and I followed up after he'd read my reflections with conversations on the phone. Once Dad understood something differently than I, and we disagreed. He called back the next morning saying, "I just want to make sure that I didn't come across too strong with my opinion. I love our conversations and wouldn't want to do anything to hurt you."

I hadn't been offended. Dad really listened to me even when he didn't understand me or saw things differently. I paid close attention to his ideas. In the tenderness following Mom's death, we'd both taken the risk to speak honestly with each other. The days of don't-tell-Dad had fully passed.

In the winter of 1993, I flew west for the final session of the Academy for Spiritual Formation. I'd already anticipated missing the rhythm of quarterly sojourns across the country. This last week was full of celebrations aimed to inspire us to return home and use what we'd learned in our work.

When I opened the wooden chapel doors for our final worship, the familiar woody smell of the sanctuary greeted me. The stained glass windows glittered like jewels in the late morning light. For two years I'd come to this chapel to be fed by the Eucharist, drenched by prayers, settled by silence and washed in the Word.

After such a full week at the end of a stimulating two years, I believed I had already received all of the grace and gifts I needed.

I was wrong.

Walking up the aisle to my seat, I caught sight of a kneeling prayer bench to the left of the altar. Just beside it lay a pile of different colored cloths: red, purple and yellow.

I gasped. I recognized these cloths. The logo for the Academy for Spiritual Formation depicted a person reaching high to catch a cloth mantle. The cloth in the logo, and on the chapel floor, symbolized the Old Testament's story of the passing on of the mantle of leadership from the prophet Elijah to Elisha.[3] It was time for each of us to receive our mantle of spiritual leadership.

For me, the red cloths also symbolized the sacred drape from my childhood dream.

When they called my name, I walked over, picked up a red cloth and knelt. Loving hands of the leadership team rested on my head and shoulders. My heart warmed as I felt the sensation of electrical currents pulsing throughout my body. I was thrilled to hear the scripture blessing that God was able "to accomplish [in my life] abundantly far more than all [I could] ask or imagine."[4]

When I returned to my seat, my heart remained warm and my body continued to vibrate. I stroked the wood of the pew to ground me back on Earth again.

Dreams and concrete reality
    Wood and cloth
        Words and touch
            Passing of the mantle
                Spirit shot through it all
                    Suddenly anything felt possible.

Where was I being led on this sacred life pilgrimage that promised more than I could ask or imagine? How had God shown up in my life? I remembered a whole string of holy moments including the morning I was baptized and confirmed in my big Texas church, the candle-lit evening when teen-aged strangers prayed for me in tongues of gibberish that lit my heart on fire. Now the holy had showed up again at Mercy Center chapel at high noon where dear friends commissioned me. None of this made logical sense to me. Still, each time the power of the Spirit blew into my life, I felt clearer than before.

After the Academy for Spiritual Formation ended, I searched for ways to integrate the inner growth of those two years with the rest of my life. I so loved the rhythm of the Academy and the stimulation of Ministry of Money workshops, and I wanted to find ways to introduce some of what I learned at my home church.

In the silence of prayer, I listened. In circles of others seeking answers, I explored. I wanted to put myself in the middle of some aspects of diversity that filled our world. Yet I was born into a neighborhood—and had lived in many others just like it—filled with people who, for the most part, looked a whole lot like me: Christian, white, upper middle class, married with kids, at least one of the partners with a professional job and several others with stay-at-home moms like me.

I tentatively pursued conversations with friends about race and class. One afternoon, over coffee after church, a white friend commented about what she had faced during integration. In response, I shared how easily integration had happened in Midland, without protests or overt racism. Mid-sentence, however, I realized that none of my friends had changed after integration. I didn't remember a casual friend, much less a close girlfriend, with dark skin. I was horrified that my pride about my own openness to integration failed to take this critical detail into account.

Unsure how to find diversity in my daily life, I began reading accounts of people whose lives were different than mine. One cold, Fargo morning I picked up a book recommended by the latest *Ministry of Money* newsletter—*Rachel and Her Children*. A world I never knew existed came alive in those pages through the stories of homeless women and their children in New York City.[5] Though our histories and finances, and in many cases our skin color, were drastically different, the homeless women and I were all mothers who loved our children. I monitored my children's activities and checked out their friends' families before playdates; I insisted they wear seat belts in the car. The mothers in *Rachel and Her Children* lived in neighborhoods where their children walked down shelter hallways amidst drug dealing and gunfire.

This chasm between my protected and orderly life and the danger and desperation of these homeless mothers stopped me in my tracks. Life wasn't fair. I couldn't change the lives of these women directly, but hearing the stories of how some people really lived—their struggles and their wisdom—felt like a critical step on the path toward justice for us all.

I didn't want my lifetime of white, upper middle class neighborhoods to mark the edges of my entire life. If nothing changed, the only way I would ever hear a diversity of perspectives was through the pages of a book.

The following week, a newspaper notice announced a six-week volunteer training course for new volunteers at the local homeless shelter. Homeless people made me nervous. I didn't know any of them, but they felt unpredictable and desperate, potentially dangerous. Nevertheless, I mustered the courage to sign up.

For each of the six training sessions, I walked into the shelter with other new volunteers, veteran activists and homeless people. After a few weeks of meeting together, however, "those scary people" became people I'd met—Julie, Sam and Gilbert. My fear shrank.

When the training ended, I volunteered to organize the children's play area. Tentative at first, soon I was willing to take seven-year-old Laura with me. The two of us worked and played together in a place that had once scared me. Few residents, though, remained in the shelter while Laura and I were there. Homeless shelters only allowed residents to stay inside during the day if the temperature plummeted below zero.

The next fall's *Ministry of Money* newsletter recommended a book written by Habitat for Humanity's founder, Millard Fuller—*The Theology of the Hammer*. Soon I wanted to work with low-income people to help build simple, affordable homes. That work seemed part of a solution to improve things and bring about justice, so I decided to leave the shelter and volunteer instead for Habitat for Humanity.

To maximize my partnership with new homeowners, people who were of a different class than I was, I worked on the family selection and nurture committee. I listened with curiosity to the applicants and then to the stories of the home-owners-to-be about growing up in neighborhoods far from mine.

Nevertheless, my well-meaning helpfulness often felt impotent. Though I wanted to live in the middle of our diverse world, my life had given me few tools to work through the issues that inevitably arose. How could I offer suggestions about caring for a home without sounding like a know-it-all? Was my discomfort with things discarded in the front yard a universal value or based on my class? The number of challenges faced by many of the Habitat families at work, home and with money was overwhelming. What did I have to offer that would be helpful?

I questioned my attitudes about my family and neighbors also. Was I too opinionated and controlling? When should I step in with my children, either to help or correct, and when should I let them figure it out for themselves? Which of my opinions were based on my being a white, upper middle class woman, and which were based on my personality or preferences?

Even though things had improved since slavery or the movements of the 1960s, I was beginning to see that consciously or unconsciously racism, classism and sexism were still active in me personally and in society. I wanted to understand these painful historical divisions as well as hold onto the robust threads that tied us all together. The journey inside brought me out into the middle of a wide world with equally big questions.

15

My World Stretches Outward

By the time Howard, Paul, Laura, our basset hound, Porsche, and I moved across the country to a house in Klamath Falls, Oregon, in August 1994, my childhood idea of "neighborhood" was unraveling.

Paul and Laura enrolled in the nearby public elementary school. One of Laura's school girlfriends described her family as "travelers." They lived in a cheap motel at the edge of town and moved on after a few months. Other friends came from some of the wealthiest families in town. Paul and Laura's classmates expanded both my social and economic perspectives.

I'd fallen in love with the beauty of liturgy during the Academy for Spiritual Formation. Howard had been moved by the mystery of Catholic liturgy as a young boy when he went to Mass with his favorite grandfather, Bampa. After the move to Oregon, we were both drawn to the Episcopal church in Klamath Falls where each Sunday our priests, Susan and Peter Champion, presided together at the Eucharist table. Though Methodists began to ordain women as ministers when I was young, the only female clergy in my churches had worked with young people. I'd longed to have a woman as my minister for years, but I found that a man and a woman celebrating Eucharist together was an even more poignant image for me of the fullness of God—feminine as well as masculine.

Approximately ten years before we arrived in town, a bold covenant had formed between three Klamath Falls congregations—Sacred Heart Catholic, Klamath Lutheran and ours, St. Paul's Episcopal. In the early years of ecumenism, these three churches from different Christian traditions decided to gather together throughout the seasons for simple worship and study. As part of the covenant churches, I could be an Episcopalian and still be part of a larger Christian communion.

That was wonderful, but it wasn't enough. My time at the Presentation Prayer Center in Fargo had been an important part of my journey. Kathleen Norris's *Dakota: A Spiritual Geography* inspired me. She wrote about being a Protestant and part of a lay group associated with a Roman Catholic order.[1] For Norris, it involved becoming a Benedictine oblate; for me, it meant becoming a Presentation Associate.

This desire seemed mistimed. I couldn't be physically present for the preparation classes. In addition, Presentation Associates were all Catholics. Despite what felt like insurmountable obstacles, I talked to the Sisters about this possibility.

The door opened. I was lovingly mentored long distance, and I became the first non-Roman Catholic Associate of the Fargo chapter of the order of the Presentation of the Blessed Virgin Mary. The Presentation founder, Nano Nagle, was a contemporary of the founder of the Methodist tradition, John Wesley. Both wanted to take the church out into the streets and homes where people lived.

One of the symbols of the order was the lantern Nano Nagle had used to light the way down the streets of Cork, Ireland, as she ministered to the people. As I prayerfully explored what it meant for me to be an Episcopalian and an Associate, I sketched an image that brought together my childhood dream and Nano's lantern. In my drawing, I was dancing in and out of the church's doors, holding my sacred, red velvet drape in one hand and Nano's lantern in the other. This simple sketch held the essence of my spiritual work – holding tightly to God's presence and light while moving freely between different Christian traditions, within and outside the church walls.

Though I only remained a Presentation Associate for a few years, the process united the Protestant and Catholic aspects of my soul. Since my teenage awakening with the Pentecostal tradition of speaking in tongues, I'd always had a hard time staying put in any one Christian tradition. Between my time as an Associate and at the Academy for Spiritual Formation, the edges of my church membership were stretching wider.

The stronger my draw toward things of the Spirit, the less I was interested in working in a physical therapy clinic. In Klamath Falls I finally made the shift out of my original profession and into a variety of Christian formation and service pursuits—teaching and coordinating church classes and workshops, lay preaching and volunteering at Habitat for Humanity.

In addition to the usual celebrations around Christmas and Easter, our family filled our year with sacred rituals celebrated at home. We anointed the doors with oil on Epiphany, celebrating the wise men's arrival at the side of Jesus. My sister-in-law's childhood stories about her Belgian St. Nicolas Day traditions inspired us to begin December sixth with hot chocolate, Belgian waffles and the gift of a book for Paul and Laura. We gathered with friends on Shrove Tuesday, donning costumes and sharing a lavish meal, to mark the day before the forty-day church season of Lent. In addition, we marked the anniversary of each of our baptisms, the first day of school and other important days in the lives of our children.

The Christian church may have ignored the celebration of Bar/Bat Mitzvah, but we wanted to mark this transition from childhood into adulthood. Always ready to push for things a little early, Paul was ready for his "turning thirteen trek" with Howard the summer before seventh grade and a few months before his birthday. He and Howard returned to Idaho, the state of Paul's birth, and took a strenuous hike into the Sawtooth Mountains. While they were gone, I asked each of the important men in Paul's life to send a letter to him marking this moment. Putting the men's letters into a notebook, we gave them to Paul on his birthday.

Apparently, ritual wasn't enough to ease Paul's predictable junior high angst. Arrogantly confident one moment, Paul wanted my help the next minute. He no longer worried that our refusal to buy him the latest Nike tennis shoes would turn him into a social outcast—he seemed to want to be one with his multi-colored hair, links of chains hooked to his belt loops and ever present skateboard. Paul was unsure whether it was better to get a ride to school from me or to get up earlier and take the bus. He was positive that I was being overly controlling when I checked the lyrics of every cassette tape with a parental warning label. With Paul's first day of junior high school in 1995, Howard and I had officially left the "easy" years of parenting behind.

I struggled to reconcile my desire for safety in my parenting and in the world around us with the realities of life. I remembered someone at the Academy talking about the power of weakness in the upside down Kingdom of God. My heart was beginning to understand the power in vulnerability, but the voices inside my head wanted stronger provisions and guarantees. I hoped that by continuing to expand my neighborhood boundaries, I would find the deeper safety that God offered.

Responding to a request for volunteers on Sunday during worship, I began to return to church mid-week to work in the Food Pantry. While filling out the paperwork to receive his food box one morning, Jay said, "Some people only see that I am homeless, but I am at home in God's world. That's all that matters." His remark rang true. I also met Gail Burkett, a woman whose schizophrenia and profound generosity existed side-by-side. Living in a group home on very limited income, Gail was one of the few tithers at our church.

Gail and I soon became friends. We visited each other's homes and occasionally had meals together. Each week we met to walk through her neighborhood, spending the first few blocks in prayer. Gail always began by saying, "Father, I come to you from the inner chambers of your heart to the inner chambers of my heart." We then named everyone we thought needed to be brought into God's heart. Only then did we talk about our lives, hopes and fears.

Since my first Ministry of Money workshop in 1984, I'd been intrigued by the idea of traveling to Haiti to get a new perspective on the world. This time, when a similar trip was offered, I decided I was ready to go.

Knowing nothing about this small island off the coast of Florida, I did a little research. Columbus had landed on the shores of the island that held Haiti and the Dominican Republic—not America—in 1492 and claimed the land for Spain and Christ. The native Taino Arawak were baptized, then enslaved. Mistreatment and foreign illnesses wiped out the native Haitian population within fifty years. When the Spaniards returned to colonize this tiny island, they imported thirty thousand kidnapped Africans to replace the lost workforce.[2]

The history I learned horrified me. In 1664 France took control of Haiti. French settlers believed that it was economically beneficial to work the slaves to death (usually within five years) and replace them with strong, new slaves. By the mid-1700s, Haiti, a country the size of Maryland, had revenues equal to that earned by all of the thirteen colonies.[3] They exported sugar, cotton, coffee and indigo from huge plantations. Most of the hardwood forests were cut for exportation. Nine-tenths of the population was enslaved.[4]

This colonial brutality ended in 1804 when a slave rebellion made Haiti the first black republic in the Western hemisphere. Colonialism, local and international support of Haitian dictators and unjust "aid" all combined to make Haiti the poorest country in this hemisphere. During all of my years of education, teachers and textbooks never mentioned any of these facts.

By my departure date in June of 1996, I was physically and spiritually prepared to leave my family behind for ten days and join five others in Port au Prince, Haiti. As soon as we stepped onto the tarmac, we were engulfed by intense heat. Dale and Esther, our white American pilgrim-age leaders, and their young, black Haitian friend, Kenson, met us at baggage claim. As soon as we all headed outside toward the rental car, people started asking for money. Two of my traveling companions gave, while I nervously walked away.

We drove down potholed streets filled with traffic. Despite a traffic light, one intersection was completely jammed with cars pointing every direction. Miraculously, we made it through fairly quickly. We passed brightly colored buildings, one after another, with peeling paint and people everywhere. I was startled when a truck loaded with police in full riot gear, including rifles, passed us.

For two mornings I worked alongside my traveling companions and many other volunteers at the Sisters of Charity orphanage, one of their two facilities in Port au Prince that Don McClannen had spoken about twelve years before. Amid rooms overflowing with babies and children cared for by a handful of Sisters and volunteers, a young boy grabbed my hand and wanted me to carry him around. He soon fell asleep in my arms, oblivious to the children playing around him in the bare courtyard out back. Later I snuggled with a little baby, one in a room of forty babies in their cribs.

"Put on a gown, gloves and mask," the sister told us before she walked off.

Some of the volunteers complied; others didn't. I was already holding a child when I got her instructions. I hated the thought of wearing a mask and gloves for my own safety, when they felt like barriers between the children and me. Safety versus hospitality was complicated. Sometimes I wore gloves and a mask, and sweat profusely when they intensified the oppressive heat, and sometimes I didn't.

It wasn't until I woke in the middle of the following night that I realized the mask and gloves might have been to protect the children from my germs. Was it possible that I, like Columbus, was spreading disease? At the orphanage, I'd been completely focused on whether or not I needed to protect myself.

Meeting with Haitian leaders and American expatriates working for justice in Haiti gave me a glimpse of both the effects of US policy on other countries and the wisdom of cultures other than my own. I learned how American charity and national policy were often caught in the mire of assumptions, arrogance and priorities skewed by race and class. European and American actions regarding Haiti, I soon realized, paralleled what my Stanford neighbor Joan had tried to tell me was happening in Nicaragua.

One afternoon we went into Cité Soleil, the slum where Kenson lived. I could smell the open sewers close by. Rubble was pushed to edges of the dirt street lined with shack after shack, each one touching the next one. Some were bare wood, some had tin sides, and some had peeling paint on stucco.

We were warmly welcomed into the three-room home, housing Kenson, his parents, a sister and several grandchildren. They served us each a bottle of Coke, and we had a lovely few hours visiting while Kenson and his cousin translated.

I'd gone to Haiti in June 1996 to learn things I never imagined about this small country just off our shores. I'd come face-to-face with the devastating fact that I was powerless to "just do something" to fix the inequities. I knew I wasn't personally responsible, yet I couldn't shake the fact that the people who had perpetrated many of these inequities had been white Americans, just like me.

And I wanted to stop calling us "Americans," since Haitians and Guatemalans and Bolivians were all Americans too. Noticing a wider world made speaking more complicated.

I returned home filled with big emotions and little idea of my next steps. A friend recommended I read the journal of Etty Hillesum, written in her mid-twenties and published posthumously in 1982, recording the years before she died at Auschwitz. Etty's words quickly became a solace for me. She described how suffering became her doorway to a life lived boldly, even as the powers-that-be increasingly moved toward mass destruction and death. Her words reminded me that we are not, despite our deepest fears, destined to live forever in despair, if we let ourselves fully grieve:

> And finally: ought we not, from time to time, open
> ourselves up to cosmic sadness? ... Give your sorrow all
> the space and shelter in yourself that is its due, for if ev-
> eryone bears his [or her] grief honestly and courageously,
> the sorrow that now fills the world will abate.[5]

How was it possible that giving my sorrow all the space and shelter it needed would help me see the beauty of life? I didn't know. Etty believed that if I was able to give my sorrow "the space its gentle origins demand, then [I might] truly say: life is beautiful and so rich. So beautiful and so rich that it makes [me] want to believe in God."[6]

If Etty could do that in the holocaust, surely I could find a way to do likewise as a witness to twenty-first century injustice and violence.

While I was hip deep in processing history and yearning for a better future, Laura became a woman. If I wanted to be part of changing the world, I realized that I needed to start at home with my daughter.

I wanted Laura's first period to be noted with something more than the introduction of pads and belts I'd undergone when I was her age. I wanted her to know that being a woman was more than continuously keeping her belly pulled in and a smile on her face. I wanted her to learn that 1990s girls could listen to and honor their bodies' unique rhythms and needs.

Laura's period had started while we drove to visit Dad for spring break. Her best friend Courtney was with us, and my cousins, David, Shannon and baby Nathan McCarty, were meeting us in Monterey. Shannon, Courtney, Laura and I carved out one afternoon to step away from the family and honor this milestone in Laura's life. I rounded up some of mother's china, celebration snacks and bubbling apple cider.

All four of us sat on the bed together as Shannon and I talked about our experiences as women. Together all four of us remembered women we admired—those of long ago like Ruth Tipps and Rosa Parks, Mom and Ann Mathys, and others close to our hearts who had died and friends living today. Shannon had brought nail polish for Laura—a bottle of green and a bottle of orange. We playfully painted each other's toenails.

A week later, we were back home again. I went to the Maundy Thursday service in Holy Week's string of worship services between Palm Sunday and Easter. When I took off my socks in preparation to have my feet washed, I realized my toenails were still painted, alternating green and orange. Inadvertently, I'd brought a symbol of the celebration of Laura's first menstrual period into the church.

On Easter morning I wrote a letter to send to important women in Laura's life, asking them to write something to her in honor of this transition. As the letters came in over the following weeks, I slipped them into a memory book for her.

Haiti, however, was never too far from my mind. I kept reading to understand more of the intersection of Haitian and US history. Nevertheless,

Haiti seemed like a million miles away when the phone rang in the middle of Advent. Dale asked, "Could Kenson come stay with your family for Christmas?"

Kenson? Here in the US? For Christmas?

Kenson and his parents had been gracious to me in their home. How could I refuse?

For years Kenson had helped support his family by making good friends of people visiting from the US and raising funds from them for family needs. Among those long-term friends was a well-meaning priest who invited Kenson into his US-based education program for Haitian high school graduates. The priest had made an exception for twenty-four year

Kenson's neighborhood, 1996

old Kenson, who was still in high school but hadn't yet graduated. Kenson was thrilled. He was also underprepared.

Finally in this land of limitless opportunity, Kenson worked hard to make the best of the opportunity. He aspired to get a driver's license and hoped to marry a US citizen so he could legally immigrate here. Kenson wanted to create a better life for himself and still have extra money to send back to his family.

Unfortunately, these activities made it difficult for him to attend school regularly. By the time Christmas rolled around, it looked like Kenson would soon be asked to leave the program and return to Haiti. But first, he wanted to travel to Oregon to visit his friends.

After hearing Dale describe the situation, I replied, "Yes, Kenson can come here for Christmas."

We considered simplifying our Christmas celebration but didn't want to pretend. Instead, we bought Kenson a nerf football, a muffler, warm socks and a few other presents to join our packages under the tree. We gathered small gifts to fill his stocking.

We joined friends for Christmas dinner. Though the food and wine were fabulous, the stark contrast between our home and feast and Kenson's family home and simple meals gave me indigestion.

This "charitable opportunity" for Kenson's education turned out to be very costly for him and his family. As soon as he returned to school, Kenson was told he must leave the program and return to Haiti. Rather than return home in disgrace, he disappeared. Dale wondered if he made his way to the large Haitian-American community in Miami. Months later, he heard that Kenson had moved to the Dominican Republic, the other half of his homeland island. Though close to home, it was not a country hospitable to Haitians.

I never heard from Kenson again.

I'd chosen to put myself in situations that stretched my ability to cope and challenged my desire to control situations or predict what would happen. On my good days, I welcomed being broken open and emptied, yet I struggled to stand steady in brokenness. The wide world was scarier than what I'd imagined during much of my life. Kenson's life was complicated, maybe unraveled, by the good intentions of the priest. Etty Hillesum and millions of others were caught in racial and ethnic genocide. Haitian history was bleak, and the country was impoverished. Yet the wide world also had a rich texture filled with threads of hope. In the middle of despair, Etty was able to see the beauty of life.

In the middle of poverty, we met many Haitians who were building schools and strengthening their communities. These people reminded me despair and distress weren't inevitable. Despite my dis-ease, I was grateful for my growing awareness of the cosmic sadness and beautiful joy that were part of life on this planet.

No journey, I learned, was fully a private matter. I knew that my family stretched with me, sometimes feeling the burdens of my learning and growth. I hoped they would also reap the benefits.

Ruth Tipps, age 79, 1979

Wichita Falls, Texas

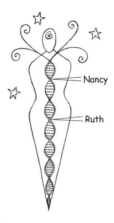

Everyone knew I was a good church-going Christian. Everyone knew I was the woman behind O.R. Tipps. Everyone knew I told stories. But no one knew my favorites—the bold ones that made people stop and think. That was fine with me, but I always hoped that one day people would find out.

Now, at seventy-nine, my memory's begun to fail, and I can't tell stories any more. With my confusion and O.R. coughing all of the time with his emphysema, we haven't been going to church for a long time.

A few days ago O.R. died. I had little idea what to do with him around, but absolutely no idea how to make it on my own. What is going to happen to me? Without him to stand behind, I feel exposed.

Family came from all over for O.R.'s funeral. I didn't recognize some of them, but I pretended.

After we all got back to the house from the cemetery, I saw my grand-daughter Nancy looking through my notebooks in the cabinet beside my reading chair. My heart did a little jig. From across the room, I guided her hand to pick one particular composition book out of the stack—the one filled with stories I'd told and cherished back in 1963. Addled as my brain was, I still remembered their names—"Land of Pilgrim's Pride"[1] about Silvy, a colored girl in an integrated New York school, "The Kitchen Madonna"[2] about two children making sacred icons for their Ukrainian nanny, and "How the Woman Got Her Ring"[3] about how a woman has to hide her intelligence and strength in order to get a husband.

I knew Nancy wouldn't read them for a long time, but that didn't matter. When the time was right, she would be amazed to read the stories I had hand-copied, memorized and told so long before. As I watched her, I smiled. Though she didn't see that we had anything in common, I knew that one day her love of stories would blossom, and she'd feel compelled—like I was—to explore the important stuff of life. Someday my only granddaughter will know me as more than a boring old woman. I can wait. I've had plenty of time to practice patience!

Ruth, 1976

16

It Was True

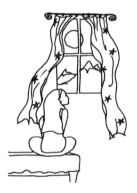

Laura slid into junior high school with greater ease than Paul. She wanted good grades, to do things right and to look beautiful. At that age, I'd played by those rules too and yet still felt bad about myself.

Meanwhile, Paul got a driver's license and enjoyed his new freedom. He also started taking Laura to school. The only trouble was Laura had inherited my belief that ten minutes early was "on time," and Paul followed Howard's lead that "on time" was good enough.

Was life simpler when I was a teen? When I was Laura's age, Martin Luther King, Jr. was assassinated. When I was Paul's age, I'd read about a conspiracy behind the assassination of President Kennedy for my government class. Terrified at the thought, I'd closed that book and pushed the possibility aside.

Thirty-two years after my high school government class, I was horrified to discover that conspiracy theories weren't always hogwash. I longed for the days when earth-shattering news was limited to the fact that there wasn't an Easter Bunny or that women and men had the same number of ribs.

The *Contemplation and Non-Violence* newsletter arrived in my mailbox in January of 2000. The lead article stopped me in my tracks.

The details of King's 1968 murder were never made public because there hadn't been a trial. James Earl Ray confessed. When Ray later claimed that his confession was false, King's family and their attorney, William Pepper, fought to bring all of the evidence to light in a criminal trial. The request was denied. Finally, in 1999, Pepper presented all of the evidence in a civil suit held in a Memphis, Tennessee, court.

On December 8, 1999, the verdict of this civil suit decreed that US governmental agencies were seventy percent responsible for King's murder. The remaining responsibility wasn't shouldered by James Earl Ray but by Lloyd Jowers.[1] Despite that scandalous judgment, few news agencies covered the trial.

Second hand information wasn't enough for me. I located a copy of the trial transcript online and read it myself. It was true. My government had been involved and was largely responsible for the murder of Martin Luther King, Jr.[2]

This news put mothering teenagers into perspective. What kind of world had Paul and Laura been born into?

I had long believed the official discrediting of such outlandish stories, conspiracy theories. But now I wanted to know the truth.

As a child, I thought that King fought solely for civil rights. Many in the 1960s had believed blacks were less human than whites. Many, apparently including the cheering student behind me the day King was murdered, were glad that he died.

In the years since his death, King had been honored as a civil rights leader, with a national holiday and city streets named after him. Ignored, however, were the more controversial aspects of King's community organizing.

As I searched to learn about Dr. King's work, I found a copy of "Beyond Vietnam: A Time to Break Silence," a sermon he preached in Riverside Church exactly one year before he was murdered.

In it King spoke of the hope that was sparked in the US in the early 1960s, when equal rights for everyone seemed possible. Just as programs aimed to eradicate poverty and racial injustice were being implemented, however, the focus—and budget—turned instead toward war. King said, " ... I knew that America would never invest the necessary funds or energies in rehabilitation of its poor so long as adventures like Vietnam continued to draw men and skills and money like some demonic destructive suction tube. So I was increasingly compelled to see the war as an enemy of the poor and to attack it as such."[3]

What good was the freedom of a driver's license, when Paul could only drive around a nation whose long string of wars had diverted our federal money and focus away from building a just nation for him and his generation? What good was Laura trying to play by all the rules if there was something broken with the whole game?

In "Beyond Vietnam" King warned the powers-that-be within the US government that he was calling for civil disobedience in a global, non-violent movement to disrupt inequitable and violent economic and political exploitation here and abroad. Though I had spent most of my life blind to this turn of the civil rights movement, I now believed that King's vision was true and would have sent earthquakes throughout the current system.

I could no longer pretend that I didn't know or that the details were too confusing for my non-expert mind. I couldn't go back to sleep again. I was clear. My life's work must involve transforming the world that Paul and Laura and unborn generations of children would inherit.

17

Letting Go into Death

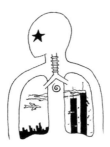

Dr. King and President Kennedy had both focused their work at the intersection of power, money and war.[a] As I prayerfully considered where I wanted to focus my life's work, I kept returning to the intersection of faith and money. I wanted to learn how to unhook my thoughts and behavior from the cultural values that were at odds with the call I heard from Jesus.

In the spring of 2001, I found an advertisement in the *More than Money* magazine about a workshop offered that May just outside Monterey, California. Though I was interested in work intertwining justice with money, my primary motivation for attending was to stay with Dad and have the chance to talk with him each evening. I had so enjoyed our conversations about faith and conscience and looked forward to adding the topic of money to our repertoire.

On the first morning of the workshop, one of the facilitators, Jenny Ladd, introduced herself by saying she'd co-founded an organization called

Class Action. I'd never met anyone who understood the issues that often arose when working across diversity in class. I'd hit a stumbling block around this issue at church. For six months, a friend and I had led a Bible study for people from our church and the gospel mission. In that cross-class group, my fears of sounding entitled because of my relative financial wealth caused me to silence myself. The same dynamic had happened in my work with Habitat for Humanity a few years earlier. I didn't know how to be comfortable when different opinions and encounters, and the feelings that often accompanied them, emerged around class, power and perspective.

When I shared all of this with Jenny, she told me to contact Be Present, an organization that had been working for decades with just those issues. I wrote down the information and planned to call them as soon as I got back to Klamath Falls.

That night, I slipped out of the workshop early so I could return to Dad's home and our conversation. I asked Dad how it had felt for him to manage the family financial inheritance–which came primarily from Mom's family—in the almost fifteen years since she had died.

"I take this responsibility very seriously," Dad admitted. His main focus, he explained, was to keep the money safe and primarily unspent so that it would be intact when my brother and I inherited it after his death.

We didn't have time to explore our feelings and attitudes about money as extensively as I'd hoped, but our conversations were a beginning I felt good about. I was glad Dad was coming to Klamath Falls the following month to celebrate Paul's high school graduation.

Ed and Paul, 1982   *Ed and Paul, 2001*

In June, Dad and I went to the Klamath Union football stadium early to save seats for the ceremony. While we waited for it to start, Dad admitted, "When I first held Paul in my arms eighteen years ago, I didn't think I'd be alive for his graduation." Dad glowed with vitality as he witnessed his first grandchild graduate.

Two months later, the family gathered again to honor Dad's eightieth birthday. Looking through the photos after I returned home, I saw something I'd missed during the party. Dad looked gaunt and much older than he had in June.

In early September, Dad complained of being short of breath. I flew to be with him for an MRI. On the morning of September 11, 2001, the doctor called with the results of the test saying, "Your father has extensive cancer throughout both lungs."

As I hung up the phone, the drone of the television in the living room reported moment-by-moment news, some true and some outlandish guesses, about two planes that had crashed into New York City's Twin Towers.

It was only 9:00 a.m. on the West Coast.

I looked out the window at Monterey Bay. The waves broke and gulls shrieked as they flew overhead. Everything looked normal.

I asked Dad to turn off the television and told him the news. "You don't have pneumonia. The doctor just called to say that you have widespread cancer in both lungs."

"Oh," Dad replied.

In the context of burning buildings and staggering losses, what were we to do with news of a personal tragedy? Dad turned the television back on. I walked out of the room.

After accompanying Dad for a full week of doctors' appointments, I secured a hard-to-get Amtrak ticket to return home. I wasn't going to let cancelled air flights, a national tragedy or Dad's illness keep me away from Paul's move from our home into a University of Oregon dorm in Eugene. This was an important milestone for me. I needed to be there.

While we prepared things for my few days away, Dad talked about his willingness to have chemotherapy. "I'm not afraid to lose my hair," he said, running his fingers through the few hairs remaining on his balding head.

I prayed that he'd manage while I was gone. He wasn't safe driving and was only marginally safe at home alone. I arranged everything I could for him to be on his own, with a little help from neighbors and his brother Jack. I left on Saturday, September fifteenth, planning to return four days later.

Paul, Howard and I arrived at the campus just as the dorms opened. Hundreds of families swamped the elevators, so we took trip after trip up the stairs unloading the van and filling his room. As soon as we were done, we shared lunch before saying our goodbyes. Our six foot, five inch little boy gave us a smile, turned and walked away. He was now a completely free, though financially dependent, man.

Six hundred and thirty miles away, a man who thrived in solitude pondered much in his heart. When I returned on Wednesday, Dad told me in a strong and steady voice, "I don't want any treatment for this cancer. I've led a full life, and I am ready to die. I want you to make an appointment with my attorney so you can know what to do as the executor of my estate."

I was grateful that he'd decided not to pursue treatment but was startled to hear him speak so directly of his death.

As soon as I could be alone, I reached out to my friend Sharon Pavelda, seeking comfort for my grieving heart. She listened to the full range of my emotions, then said, "Just remember, death is safe."

Side-by-side with my sadness, I knew that she was right. Settling into the reality of Dad's illness without fighting it, I became able to accompany him moment by moment.

Dad was an organized man who kept meticulous books recording every penny earned and every penny spent. For as long as I could remember, he had exercised right on schedule and played golf on a regular routine.

Until he began his walk toward death, letting go wasn't Dad's cup of tea. Somewhere in his bones, this man who had never been overtly interested in matters of the spirit knew that these final weeks of his life were a sacred invitation of transformation through release. He let go gracefully, if methodically.

When we met his attorney, Dad released his legal responsibilities. He made sure I understood his bookkeeping, then handed over all financial tasks. He walked independently for another week before he surrendered to a rolling walker.

Over the years, I had spoken of God, and Dad had spoken of conscience. I was thrilled one morning to find that the day's scripture reading seemed to honor Dad's spiritual journey. Over breakfast, I read him Romans 2:15: "They [non-Christians] show that what the law requires is written on their hearts, to which their own conscience also bears witness."

Dad had me write it down for him, then slipped it into his left shirt pocket, close to his heart.

On Wednesday afternoon, Dad made yet another trek down the long hallway to the bathroom with his rolling walker. He stopped at his bed to take off his Pendleton wool shirt because its length got in the way. I offered to shorten the hem. He refused, insisting that there was no need for me to do that.

Later, after returning to his chair, he reflected, "You know, something interesting just happened. You wanted to do something to make things easier for me, and I wanted to do something to make things easier for you."

Thursday, Connie came to clean his house as she had done weekly for the fifteen years since Mom had died. When he told her about his cancer, Connie replied that maybe he would get better.

"No, I am dying," he corrected Connie. "I've had a good, long life and I am ready to die."

On Friday, Dad stopped walking altogether. We sat together in his bed, as his thoughts vacillated between this world and the next.

"I can't think of any brilliant thoughts to say, though it seems like I should," he said. "I am quotable."

All week I'd also felt that I should have been grabbing every opportunity to share profound thoughts about my love of Dad. Instead, we both were learning the richness of shared silence filled with love.

"No one prepares you for dying. Is this the way you thought it would be?" Dad asked me.

He wasn't expecting an answer, but I was fascinated by his question. Mom had died quickly, leaving no time for any of us to live with her dying. In the 1990s my father-in-law had died after a long decline due to congestive heart failure, but we were not present. Five years later, my mother-in-law had died after knee surgery. This was the only time I had walked with a parent on the journey to death. I'd assumed it would be difficult, but these few weeks with Dad had been so gentle and sweet. I wondered what he thought.

Dad interrupted my pondering, saying, "I want to live a natural death." He mumbled something else then chuckled, "I didn't understand that one myself."

I smiled. So many of our conversations over the years had been practical. Here, with death lurking at the door, we felt free to let our thoughts bounce from the absurd to the profound. All thoughts felt welcome that afternoon as we sat propped up on the bed, side-by-side.

"What if butterflies are the good guys?" he wondered.

What did we know of the wonders of life? Of who was good and who was bad? I leaned over and kissed his cheek.

A little later, Dad dozed. I sat at Mom's old desk in the bedroom corner where she spent many hours doing genealogical research. Beside me, Dad's breaths flowed from shallow to deep to silence ... only to start up again. Slowly he slipped into unconsciousness.

Sunday afternoon, Dad was alert for almost an hour. Just long enough to hear the letters Paul and Laura had written him and to speak to my brother and me. His words for me were brief, "I wish you the very best." Tears filled my eyes as my heart overflowed in gratitude for my father.

For years, Mom and Dad had playfully described what they wanted to be in their next lives. Neither believed in reincarnation, but that didn't stop their imagination. Mom always said she wanted to return as a tall, thin blonde. Playfully, she wanted to experiment with life lived in a body so different than her short, round, dark-haired one. Dad joked that he wasn't interested in being a human at all. Instead, he wanted to play and swim in the ocean as an otter. As Dad lay dying, I watched the otters play in the bay and monarch butterflies fly around the bushes just outside the window.

Leaving my brother and the Hospice workers with Dad, I walked along the shore to Juice and Java in the early morning hours of Monday,

October 1, 2001. While waiting for my latte, I noticed a brochure for Reiki treatments by Wendy Cohen. I'd undergone this Japanese treatment before when a practitioner laid her hands over my body and filled me with renewed life force. I had found it more energetically powerful than a massage, and it felt like intercessory prayer. I wanted a Reiki session for Dad to ease his death process and for me as I supported his journey to and following death. As soon as I got back to Dad's home, I called Wendy. She was busy that morning but promised to check back in a few hours.

Wendy called mid-afternoon to say she was coming. By that time Dad was actively dying. "Do you want me to come anyway?" she asked.

I did.

A few minutes later, in walked a stranger dressed in a mini skirt and Harley Davidson jacket, holding a bright red basket filled with little bottles of flower vibrational essences. Wendy silently took her place among the hospice workers, my brother and me as we circled Dad's bed. As soon as Wendy's hands hovered over Dad's feet, my hands touching his face felt his energy soften. His breathing slowed. Two minutes later, his spirit gently slipped out of his body. His final letting go.

It took a week for the family to gather for Dad's funeral. On that day, his casket lay in St. Mary's by the Sea Episcopal Church, a church he'd attended only for funerals and weddings. Draped over his coffin was a cloth of bright red, orange and green—the tablecloth Mom had completed for our Christmas days before she died.

I touched his coffin on my way to the pulpit to preach his funeral sermon. I looked at the family and friends gathered to honor my father, took a deep breath, and began. "In the last journey of his life, Ed Mathys was able to let go. And the more he let go, the more God was able to step in and bathe each day in grace." As I neared the end of my sermon, I said, "Dad died in the living room of his home, where Mom died fifteen years ago. This tired old body he left behind is here in the same church where Mom's funeral was held and is now covered by the same cloth that covered her casket. And our family will again use the tablecloth to cover the family table when we gather to feast together knowing that we are encircled with the spirit of Ed and Sue. ... God, 'give to us now your grace, that as we shrink before the mystery of death, we may see the light of eternity.'[1]"

On September 11, 2001, Dad began his three-week walk toward death. In life, Dad was in charge. But when his crisis hit, he began to let go. He was transformed by the process, and found a new way to live his dying.

On the morning Dad found out he was dying, hijacked planes crashed into buildings that epitomized US economic, military and governmental power. The nation responded with talk of war and patriotic pride rather than grief and introspection. With that choice, the violence continued.

Dad's choice led to life, even in his death.

18

Being Present

I wondered if my grief from Dad's death was still too raw and executor work too demanding to attend an event across the country with an organization I heard about from a stranger. Yet since I longed for help to learn how to "be present" in all areas of my life, I flew to Atlanta for Be Present, Inc.'s National Conference on Power & Class. Kate Lillis, the person who'd helped me with preliminary information and registration, made arrangements for me to arrive on Wednesday, the day before the conference began.

When I checked-in to the retreat center, they told me where to find Kate to get my room key. Peeking into the meeting room, I was embarrassed I had interrupted a candlelit meeting of thirty or so women and girls. A woman I assumed was Kate saw me at the door, welcomed me and invited me to take a seat until their ritual was over.

Startled to be included, I slipped into a chair at the edge of the room and listened as people shared about the impact of Be Present on all aspects of their lives. Gifts were given. More candles lit. At the end, I was asked if I had anything I wanted to say.

I took a long slow breath, and answered, "I am grateful to be warmly invited to witness your holy circle. I am honored to have heard about your journey together. Thank you."

They listened, then completed their ritual. When the lights came on again, a grey haired and pink-cheeked woman came over and introduced herself. Even near midnight, Kate had a sparkle in her blue eyes. As she showed me to my room, Kate explained that the conference leadership, consisting of Be Present staff and the participants in the just-completed eighteen-month institute, had missed their final session and closing ritual due to the travel disruptions immediately after September 11, 2001. I understood, as my life had also taken an unexpected turn.

After a good night's sleep and a day to myself, I returned to the gathering room just before dinner to register. Regina Belle's song about life filled with many colors was playing on the stereo.[1] Large pieces of cloth hung on the walls, intertwined with strings of lights. Almost a hundred chairs were arranged in several curving rows.

Adults and children of all ages and skin colors greeted each other with hugs and squeals of joy. It appeared that I was the only person who didn't know anyone else. Was I also the only one who had never been in a gathering this diverse?

Energetic toddlers sat on laps of people slowed by arthritis. "Flesh-colored" from my childhood crayon box broadened from a single pinkish color to shades from white to brown to black.

Diversity wasn't the only thing that set this conference apart from many others I'd attended. We were given an agenda, but no one stopped anyone whose long sharing didn't fit into the time schedule. Rather than breaks to go to the bathroom or get something to drink, people were encouraged to take care of themselves at any time. Children were invited to speak, and the whole group respectfully waited for their answers.

Several members of the leadership team, including founder Lillie

Allen, shared stories about Be Present's origins. In Atlanta, Georgia, in 1983, Lillie Allen led the groundbreaking Black & Female: What is the Reality? workshop at the first National Conference on Black Women's Health Issues. Five years later, a group of African American women trained by Lillie as self-help group facilitators invited women and girls of all colors to participate in Sisters & Allies, an eighteen-month leadership training project. That project formed the foundation for Be Present, Inc. which was incorporated in February 1992.

Here at my first Be Present conference, the leadership team explained that men and boys would be included in the next eighteen-month institute on the topics of Race, Gender, Power & Class, slated to begin in 2003.

Though I didn't understand the process, I listened closely as people spoke about their own experiences with race, class and power. Something felt new in this approach, and I wanted to grasp it.

I thought everything was going to fall apart on Friday afternoon when Maggie, a white woman, said, "I am very troubled about something that keeps happening at the gym where I work. I don't know what to do. Every few days someone makes a biased comment or tells a racist joke. I hate it. But any comment to counter this sort of thing either gets brushed aside or starts an argument that no one wins. Since I can't figure out what to do, I don't say anything."

I was shocked that Maggie was saying those things around all of these people of color. Even mentioning race opened up the possibility of misunderstanding—weren't we supposed to be color-blind? Maggie's story was even more disturbing because she then admitted that she'd done nothing in the face of racism. Didn't she know how painful her story would be to them? Maggie was beginning to sound like one of those white people who bugged me because they weren't very thoughtful about what they said in mixed race groups.

Everyone turned to look at Maggie. Several people, white and black, moved to her side, gently touching her back in support. Why weren't they mad?

Maggie wasn't standing alone any more.

Lillie walked over to Maggie and said, "Thank you for taking the risk to speak out. What was it like for you to hear those comments at your gym?"

Thank you? Why in the world was Lillie grateful that Maggie spoke of such a thing?

I had been in Maggie's situation before. Sometimes I'd said something as meager as, "That is not how I see it," or "I'm uncomfortable with those comments," but nothing ever changed. I didn't know what to do either. The last time it had happened, I'd felt so dirty. But I'd never admit that here in this diverse group of strangers.

Maggie continued, "I need my job—my three kids depend on it. I'm afraid to make too big a scene and risk losing it." She paused for a moment before saying, "I don't want to just get into an argument where no one changes their mind." She stared at the floor. "I don't want to have anything to do with the three or four people who say those things. I just avoid them."

People were listening. Someone reached out for Maggie's hand, and she gratefully took it.

I avoided people like that too. Why bother? I'd never figured out how to have a conversation with them that had any potential for changing anything.

I was pulled out of my thoughts by the angry voice of a white woman. "How could you be silent? Would you have wanted everyone to be silent if those comments were about you?"

Why was she interrupting Maggie?

No one seemed upset by the outburst. Instead, Lillie turned and asked, "What's coming up for you?"

As I waited for her to respond, I realized that a white woman, not a black woman, had become angry.

This white woman began to talk about justice and integrity and the importance of speaking out rather than remaining silent.

Lillie listened carefully, then asked again, "What is it like for you to hear Maggie speak about what happened in her?"

I answered Lillie in my head. Sometimes it all seemed so hopeless, as if nothing had changed at all since civil rights were won in the 1960s. Some people's beliefs were still racist, and they seemed cast in stone. What could we do?

I got lost in my thoughts, but was startled back into the room when Lillie asked if a black woman in the larger circle would speak about what happened in her when she heard Maggie and the interrupting woman speak.

Why would anyone in her right mind bring up conflict like this so directly?

Tiffany volunteered and stood up. Before she could speak, Lillie started rearranging us. "I'd like all of the white women to stand around Maggie, and all of the women of color to gather around Tiffany."

Tiffany began to speak about racism in the workplace and the effect of silence by white colleagues.

"But how does it feel?" Lillie asked.

Tiffany was silent for a few moments before she began to cry. "It's so unfair that a white woman can have the option of saying something or not—of addressing racism or not. But me, well, being that I have brown skin, my children and grandchildren will have to face racism. I must work to make the world a safer place for them. For me, addressing racism through words or actions isn't an option. Our lives depend on it."

I flashed back to my eighth grade classroom. How many times had I been silent in the face of horrible actions or statements because of fear? Then to my high school government classroom. How many times had my fear, and silence, prevented me from searching out the truth as I'd done with the officially discounted facts about the assassinations of King and Kennedy?

Tiffany continued, "It's complicated for me. My mother is a white woman. My father is a black man. In my body, I experience both realities. And I have brown skin."

As she spoke, I wondered what it would feel like to be inside Tiffany's skin. I had never wondered what it would be like to have both a white and a black parent.

I looked around the room. Some people were talking to one of the leaders, obviously triggered by something that had been said. Many were listening intently. Listening. Really listening. Not exactly sure what was happening, I definitely knew it wasn't about tolerance or politely listening without comment.

The agenda went out the window, and the discussion went on for hours. As soon as we were done, I slipped off to my room for a few minutes alone before dinner. Was it possible to learn this new way to have these conversations, to speak with candor and still keep my heart open? Maggie and Tiffany and others had done it. Yet I couldn't imagine having the courage to speak that honestly, especially in the midst of such diversity.

The next time we gathered, we were divided into groups—white women and women of color. As soon as the instructions were given, a white woman balked. "Why do we need to be apart? Isn't the point to be united? Isn't this the opposite of where we want to be going?"

Several other white women shared their disappointment to be separated from the women of color. The leadership team explained that most of our time was, in fact, together. The race specific groups weren't about being disconnected. These sessions were explicitly designed to give different racial groups time to explore what it felt like to have their skin color in this culture.

Looking at my whiteness had always felt dangerous. The only white people I'd heard talk about their race were white supremacists, and I didn't want anything to do with them. Since I'd usually thought of race in terms of people of color, I had no idea what to say about my whiteness.

Throughout the conference many people had openly acknowledged racial differences without dividing participants into either the "oppressed" or the "oppressors." When the leadership team reread the vision statement Sunday morning, some of it began to make some sense. Maggie and Tiffany had definitely "risked being different," and both seemed committed to "self-knowledge." Speaking out in the circle, they replaced "silence with information" and "powerlessness with a sense of personal responsibility."[a]

I was full to overflowing by the time we gathered to bring the conference to a close. Kate Lillis offered to be available on the phone if I had questions about using the Be Present Empowerment Model®. Kate had been in this work for over twenty years, and I knew I'd be calling her.

A few hours later, on the flight back home, I reflected on all that had happened in my four days with Be Present. The conference broke many of the rules inherent in a good conference—set agenda, well prepared presentations given from notes and regular breaks. I wasn't sure what

Be Present conference participants

had happened. I couldn't remember the three-step empowerment model they'd taught. I often didn't understand what was going on.

When participants had spoken honestly about things usually considered taboo, others met them with respect and support. People listened or spoke out loud when they were too triggered to hear the other person. I'd witnessed something that I knew I needed and wanted in my life. Though I had no idea how I'd fit one more thing into my schedule, I knew I'd be back to the next eighteen-month training.

As I tried to sleep cramped in the airplane seat, my thoughts returned to Dad. We had found a way to be present with each other in the fifteen years after Mom died. Both of us had been able to step outside our old patterns as father and daughter and hear each other afresh. I'd learned how to listen to Dad even when his frustration flared and had been able to remember how much I loved and respected the man I'd grown to know. I hoped that Be Present could help me learn to do that with other people and organizations.

Margaret Tipps, age 35, 1807

Tipps Dogwood Plantation, North Carolina

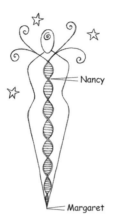

As the year ends, I been looking back. This past year has been the hardest one of my life. It's been a long string of hard years, to be sure. Married at fifteen, then my Jacob headed off to war. 'Twas mighty afraid he'd never return. But he did, strong and ready to carve a place for us in this wide-open North Carolina territory.

A few years after the war, we began our family and moved out to Kentucky, then back home near Salisbury again. Finally, with five youngins we settled in Burke County and planted our roots deep. When Jacob and I first stepped onto this land, I imagined our plantation with slaves to do the hard labor. I was ready to get started right away.

That seems like lifetimes ago. My baby, our fourteenth, is four now. Seven of 'em still lives at home, the rest close-by. They are a big help when we need them, but meals, cleaning and gardening are still on my shoulders. Just yesterday I baked five loaves of bread, washed three tubs of laundry on the old scrub board out back, hung it out on the line, then folded some and ironed the rest. All that along with the usual three meals for nine of us. I've become a worn out old Hausfrau.

I do love this land with the hazy, smoky mountains out a'ways. I try to spend a few moments each day just looking around, noticing the beauty. And appreciating how far we've come. I'm mighty grateful and all, but it was beginning to look like our plantation dream had vanished into thin air. Instead, we'd worked ourselves to the bone.

Sometimes I feared this was our lot in life forever.

Finally we saved enough to buy two slaves. God is so faithful. We agreed that Jacob should buy two men first, to work in the fields. Made sense at the time, but I've grown to regret it. Jacob's load is lightening while mine remains unchanged. The men are a help around the fields but they are worthless to me around the house.

I sometimes feel resentful. How long, O Lord? How long?

Grace, age 19, 1807

Grey's Plantation, North Carolina

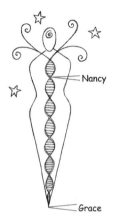

De good Lawd
is crazy as a coot
His ways
ain't muh ways

How else can I make
heads or tails
of long hours and de whip
knowin' what I knows

When I was a babe
jes' learnin' muh words
I talked to angels
dreamed with de Lawd

Round dat next summer
four nights a goin'
woke with a start
bustin' with a dream

Blue mountains
Spirit smoke
where heaven meets earth
down de road a long piece

Der I was workin'
in a fancy house of white folks
muh feets chained
muh heart free
plantin' grace

Dat dream was
so crazy
I knew den
musta been de Lawd's plan

Never forgits
muh dream
Jes told granny
she sees too
tired eyes
shiny grace eyes

Nothin'
not lashin's in de fields
not screamin' in de kitchen
can binds muh spirit

19

Rolling in the Dough

Mom had said that the Tipps family followed the "three generations from riches to rags" pattern like many other early "American" settlers. Margaret and Jacob Tipps were wealthy, but their grandson David and his wife Elizabeth struggled to make ends meet. During O.R.'s childhood, his family had little money on their farm, but his purchase of a ranch in natural gas country had brought wealth to my parents.

For most of my adult life, I knew I would inherit money. I didn't know exactly how much, but I knew. I wanted to be prepared.

Through my participation in Ministry of Money, I'd learned many facts about financial wealth. Tax cuts for wealthy folks, which had shot up in the early 1980s, had widened the gap between people of wealth and the rest of the people living in the United States. By 1976 the richest one percent owned twenty-three percent of all wealth. Thirty years later the same group owned forty percent of the nation's wealth.[1]

I'd also learned the importance of aligning my spiritual values with my money. This involved how much we donated—a minimum of ten percent of our income—but equally applied to how we earned our money, invested our savings and shopped. I'd learned that my financial decisions impacted the earth, the global family and generations yet to come.

Dad's death initiated the yearlong preparation for Howard and me to receive my family's financial legacy. Inheriting money proved to be demanding and complicated. Did we keep the same investments as Dad? How much did we keep invested for our future use? Did we continue donating the ten percent of our income, or give a larger percentage?

Some days it seemed like our lives were consumed with money conversations.

Just as we had announced our plans to join the Peace Corps to prevent us from slipping back into the American Dream during our twenties, I wanted to do something bold to mark our commitment to live justly with this inheritance. As the money began to flow into our bank accounts, Howard and I debated for months about how to do that. We settled on giving away twenty-five percent of the money off the top as it came to us.

In addition, we reconnected with Jenny Ladd for coaching about the rest of our financial decisions. Jenny knew the pitfalls and challenges of inheriting wealth and asked excellent questions to help Howard and me find our path forward.

"Do you want to support many different organizations or to deeply support a few?" Jenny asked. We decided to whittle down our list to four or so organizations dear to our hearts and focus our giving there.

When I began to attack my investment and donation to-do list with urgency, Jenny recommended, "Let it go for now; let things unfold slowly. And what do you do for fun?"

That was a harder question for me to answer. Although the leader of my 1990 Ministry of Money workshop was correct that working with our investment plans had become enjoyable, I didn't think it qualified as "fun." It was hard for me to step aside from trying to work with our money in just ways and still enjoy other parts of life, even though I knew that workaholism was a pervasive value in the very system I so wanted to change.

Jenny knew that we needed ongoing support of others wrestling with these issues. She suggested we contact Harvest Time, a ministry that worked with Christians of wealth. I knew Harvest Time's founder, Don McClannen, from Ministry of Money. In addition, my friend Sharon Pavelda was already involved in their first retreat circle, the Beloved Community. Since Harvest Time held the truth about the inequities of the world alongside listening for God's leading, I contacted Don immediately. Howard, on the other hand, wasn't sure Harvest Time was for him.

I struggled to find the big picture that could guide the rest of our decision-making. Jenny suggested that we take a stab at outlining our values by writing a letter to Paul and Laura explaining our thoughts about the legacy we wanted to leave them.

As we drafted the letter, clarity emerged. We wrote stories of their great-grandfathers and grandparents, through whom the money had flowed. After sharing about O.R. Tipps and John Mathys's remarkable business acumen, we reminded Paul and Laura that their financial success was only partially a result of all of their hard work, vision and saving decisions. The laws of our nation had long supported opportunities for white men—from education, to health care and housing—while too often thwarting those same possibilities for women and people of color.

"Without those opportunities," we wrote, "doors would not have opened so quickly for my grandfathers to become successful and prosperous. That doesn't negate their success, but it does put it into an important context."

Howard and I wanted to invest in creating a world that would support our children and future grandchildren. Given what we knew about the effects of financial disparity, we felt that leaving all of our money to Paul and Laura would do little to provide them with true security and happiness.

We explained in the letter:

> We consider our extended family to be the global family. Ultimately what is best for all people is best for our little family of four. The world will be a safer place for us all, the earth will be more vibrant, and the community between people will be healthier when there is more financial equity between all peoples. There are

enough money and commodities globally to provide for all on the earth, but it has gotten dammed up in the hands of wealthy individuals (like us) and corporations. In our own small way, we want to allow much of our portion of the world's wealth to keep flowing.

With Jenny's guidance, we found ways to keep our rolling-in-the-dough lives in line with our core values. We hoped that joy and our money would one day flow freely, with abundance for all.

Elizabeth Tipps, age 47, 1865

Near Short Creek, North Carolina

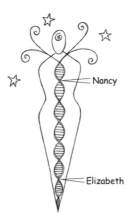

Ever'thing we touched turned to dust.

Ma always said to marry into a family with good bloodlines. Like we was cows or somethin'. Thing is, I thought I did. David's pa died 'fore he was two. It was tough on his mama. But his granddaddy lived high on the hog back at his plantation. We never saw the place, but David grew up feastin' on them stories. David was a man of mighty big dreams, and we jus' knew we'd git the family riches back.

When we talked 'bout marriage, we was already thinkin' 'bout David and his brothers buyin' land next to his mama's place. They wanted all that territory on Short Creek 'tween Marble Hill and Elk River in Franklin County, Tennessee. Sounded mighty good to me.

In them early years, we worked hard and planned big. We decided to save money for our place by movin' right in with David's mama, Barbara, and her girl, Rebecca. That was tough, but we knew it would jus' be for a short while.

We was dead wrong.

Trouble is, we got the hard work in aces but the good life never showed up. Even when we bought our own land, we couldn't afford to build a house.

Worked our backs to the breakin' point. And the babies! I was pregnant, birthin' or had a little one in my arms for what seemed like forever—fourteen in all. Each year the burden got heavier and my spirit sagged lower.

The first threatenin' letters from the bank came in 1861. On the days them letters come, I hollered at them children somethin' awful. Then the letters stopped for a time when the war started.

Damn Yankees. Thomas and Wilson both marched off to war. They looked sharp in them uniforms. Strange to be so proud and so terrified at the same time. The followin' year, a'fore my last baby was borned, we got word that Thomas died of exposure at Camp Chase, a Union prison camp in Ohio. Right then and there somethin' broke inside me. I jus' kept explodin' like a pot of boilin' grits.

20

Playing with Dynamite

Geptember 11, 2001, had marked the beginning of Dad's transformative walk into death and my country's march into a war on terrorism.[1] As fall turned to winter, I journeyed from Klamath Falls to Monterey monthly to fulfill my duties as executor of Dad's estate. Between visits to bankers, brokers and Dad's attorney's office, I missed my father. Luckily the sadness was softened by gratitude. In contrast, I hardened with frustration at my nation's frenzy toward war. I was grateful that Be Present had shown me an alternate way to navigate some of the big topics that emerged within my nation and myself. But I was still caught in reactive anger, and I was eager to learn more.

During the weeks between trips, I relished the changing of seasons in my high desert home. By late April 2002 the snow had finally melted, and the Klamath Falls flowers were in full bloom. Delighting in the first warm and sunny morning, I decided to walk the mile and a half to church for

Sunday morning worship. Down at the bottom of our hill, I was greeted by red tulips and the explosion of pink and white blossoms on the cherry and plum trees. The air was crisp and clear, and a gentle breeze made the new leaves sway on the trees. Along the way, backyard dogs barked hello. Passing a sign listing the Old Testament's Ten Commandments planted in someone's yard, I noticed purple blossoms in flowerbeds and red, white and blue flags carefully taped in windows.

Every Sunday for eight years our family had driven these roads from home to church. Laura and Howard didn't come as often any more, but St. Paul's Episcopal Church continued to be a place where I was fed by weekly worship and work at the food pantry. Different church friends popped into my mind as I walked. Did Bob finally get a job interview after months of looking? How was Medea's husband doing after his surgery last week? I wanted to be sure to recommend the book I was reading to Piper; she would love it. Were Ramona's legs doing better as the blood clots healed? Nature's beauty and thoughts of friends and family filled me with gratitude and love.

I was just a few minutes late, so I slipped into the back row pew. Glancing up at the altar, I gasped.

Just to the left of the lectern was an American flag moved forward from the back of the sanctuary. I could see nothing but the flag of a nation at war, and it was blocking my view of the Christian symbols around the altar. I knelt on the kneeler and struggled to breathe. I considered going outside for fresh air to regain my composure. I missed the first few songs and prayers. I didn't hear the sermon.

It is only a flag, I reminded myself, my country's flag, and I loved much about my country. For a few weeks after September eleventh, the flags that popped up all over town seemed to be symbols of love and unity in our pain. Quickly however, as our government moved toward retaliation and war, they seemed to mark support and agreement with this response. Here, in the sanctuary, the flag's new proximity to the cross indicated, to me at least, that the church believed that Jesus supported US political actions. Where were the Christians who kept asking, "What would Jesus do?"

I was profoundly sad. For months, the church had mirrored our nation's move toward retaliation and patriotism. I'd been waiting for someone to speak about how we, as Christians, should let our faith—not the culture— guide our lives. I wanted Jesus, not my nation, to guide my way. Where were the prophets willing to counter this "righteous" march into war?

This wasn't the first time Christianity had baptized a government's actions. With Constantine's conversion in the fourth century, the church had gone from the margins of society where it had been during the time of Jesus into the center of governmental power. Over the years, the church had also supported crushing indigenous people, slavery and the holocaust. I was furious and brokenhearted that the church had absorbed the state's values yet again.

In the weeks that followed, I had to do something with the emotions that raged in my body. I wrote purging sermons I would never preach and wailing letters I would never mail. I cried out to friends. Within my church I did speak, gently yet clearly, to everyone from the Bishop to the altar guild. The Bishop volunteered to instruct the church leaders to return the flag to the back of the sanctuary, but I wanted a congregation-wide conversation instead of a top-down solution. Be Present had shown me how supported conversations could bring transformation and healing. Instead, the board decided on a compromise: the flag would move to the front of the sanctuary only for national holidays. Days, I promised myself, that I would worship elsewhere.

I did have an official place where I could speak out: the pulpit. I preached monthly as one of the parish's lay preachers, but I had no intention of mentioning the flag during a sermon. I wanted conversation, not merely a place to speak only my side. Also, I found the discipline of sticking to the assigned scripture of the church lectionary to be a fruitful guide for the sermon topic and had usually been amazed at its timeliness.

I was scheduled to preach in June 2002, but I was grateful to be out of town for a few weeks first. I needed distance to get back my perspective before writing a sermon. Howard and I had rescheduled our twenty-fifth wedding anniversary celebration, postponed eight months by Dad's illness and death. We began our vacation staying at my parents' house for one final time before it was transferred to my brother as part of his inheritance. Our trip was to end by meeting members of Harvest Time's Beloved Community. In advance of this meeting, Don had sent me written reflections from several of the group members.

Every morning Howard and I woke in my parents' home filled with almost twenty years of memories. I brewed a cup of tea, sat in the living room and watched the light come up over Monterey Bay. Later Howard and I headed down a block to the ocean's edge and walked along the path through a carpet of purple flowers clinging to the rocky coastline. I'd meandered along this part of the coast hundreds of times, from vacations as a child to my adult visits with my parents, listening to the sea gulls cry and watching the otters play. Remembering my ancestral ties to Monterey Bay, I realized that this little piece of earth was where I felt most at home.

Driving up to the San Francisco Bay area, we passed the exit to El Retiro San Inigo where I'd attended my first Ministry of Money workshop twenty-two years ago. That workshop was still sending transformative ripples, waves and tsunamis into our lives.

We veered off the highway and drove through our old stomping ground at Stanford, stirring up memories of intellectual stimulation alongside snippets from Paul and Laura's preschool days. The light playing on the red tiles and stone of the central plaza of the campus was as breathtaking as always. From the university, we headed into the hustle and bustle of downtown San Francisco where we'd spent our honeymoon. While walking the streets and savoring delicious meals, we remembered all that had filled our twenty-five years of marriage.

After three days in the city, we headed south to a retreat center in Cupertino. As Howard drove, I read aloud the Beloved Community reflections Don had shared. I was intrigued by one account that described the transition from planned gatherings arranged by a leadership team to communal leadership grounded in prayerful listening. One of the members, Sharon Gerred, wrote,

> We are definitely moving from the first stage of
> community Scott Peck describes as pseudo community

and rapidly cruising into the second, chaos. Somehow, I think miraculously, I remember Peck saying that the way out of chaos and into community is never through organization—it's in surrendering and emptying one's self of all expectations, preconceived ideas, etc. The agenda had served its purpose, but now the "winds of the Spirit" were definitely carrying us in an unplanned direction. As [one who loves clear structure] I listened attentively and anxiously to comments, then I mentally said a prayer of surrender.[2]

I didn't know exactly what following the "winds of the Spirit" looked like, but it sounded exciting to me. Another Sharon—Sharon Pavelda, my friend whose reminder that "death is safe" as my father began his journey of dying—was now also going to be my companion on this journey of working openly with our wealth in community. I was eager to be with Sharon and Don and to meet five others in the Beloved Community.

By the time we arrived, Howard decided he could no longer refuse to do this work. I was surprised that he'd made this decision. Here on the brink of our second quarter century together, we were stepping into a new partnership.

The Beloved Community had just finished its weekend together, but most had stayed behind for twenty-four hours to meet Howard and me and to give us a taste of the community that gathered twice a year. Sharon Pavelda and pregnant Rose Feerick greeted us and showed us to our room. As soon as we were settled, everyone began to gather. I held onto Howard's hand, nervous that he might change his mind and try to slip away.

We heard the CD playing before we made it to the room. Inside, Sharon Pavelda was already dancing to the music, Rose was adjusting something on an altar and Don and the rest were visiting quietly. Don and Sharon introduced the people we hadn't yet met: Bryan Sirchio, Judy Bork and Sharon Gerred. We were informed that two others had to leave before we arrived.

As soon as introductions were made, Sharon Pavelda invited us all to dance—quite a challenge for Howard. I kept an eye on him, afraid that dancing with strangers might be too much, but he seemed to be holding his own.

When the song ended, we sat down in a circle together. Sharon Pavelda asked us all to introduce ourselves using our "purple names," playful names indicating what we were feeling in the moment. I was "Twittery," that wild combination of excited and nervous at the same time. Howard named himself "Terrified." He knew we were about to set off on an unknown path.

Later Howard told the group, "There was a sign in our hotel room last night that read, 'In case of fire, do not open the door.' Sitting here in this circle, I realized that I am now ready to open the burning door leading to the hot topic of wealth with this community."

I'd never heard Howard talk that way. I was thrilled to be in this with him.

In the twenty-four hours we shared together, little nuggets of wisdom that had become important to the Beloved Community worked their way into our conversations.

"Money, shit, that's just the tip of the iceberg" pointed to the community's experience that when they talked about money, all sorts of stuff came pouring out. Money, they had discovered, had connections to relationships, feelings of security and issues of self worth.

"We will love you in the mess" reflected their experience that talking about money brought up big issues, and each person had at some point felt like a mess. While in most social situations, falling apart resulted in embarrassment or trying to hide the melt down, this community not only honored those times of emotional breakdown but also promised to love each other through them. Harvest Time's Beloved Community sought to hold the paradox of a world brimming with both pervasive injustice and the extravagant love offered to each of us by God. I felt at home immediately.

In this circle, I could also talk freely about my issues with my church's patriotic fervor symbolized in dueling symbols displayed near the altar: the flag and the cross. In the circle, those feelings weren't considered scandalous, unpatriotic or unrelated to faith. Conversations kept returning to the ways our national values usurped prophetic gospel values, from the days of Jesus up through ours.

I remembered Annie Dillard's image that too many people come into God's presence as if they were "children playing on the floor with their chemistry sets, mixing up a batch of TNT to kill a Sunday morning," or women dressed up to the nines as if for a tea party.[3] They forgot that living a life filled with God was a wild ride. Dillard believed, as I did, that "we should all be wearing crash helmets. Ushers should issue life preservers and signal flares; they should lash us to our pews."[4] The transformative power of God was nothing to be trifled with.

The Beloved Community knew that trust in the wild ride of faith, not an agenda, was needed for this journey. While peace was certainly part of the spiritual journey, God's call could also be explosive with demands that we address oppression within ourselves and in the world around us. Knowing how much it helped to have friends at our side when life seemed to require crash helmets, Howard and I were both excited to return to this circle when it gathered again in six months.

We arrived back in Klamath Falls just a few weeks before I was scheduled to preach. In preparation, I read the passages assigned by the lectionary for that Sunday and gasped when I saw the Old Testament reading: Jeremiah 20:7-13. In these verses Jeremiah wailed,

> O Lord, you have enticed me, and I was enticed; you have overpowered me, and you have prevailed. ... For whenever I speak, I must cry out, I must shout, "Violence and destruction!" ... If I say, "I will not mention you, or speak any more in your name," then within me there is something like a burning fire shut up in my bones; I am weary with holding it in, and I cannot.[5]

God exploded in Jeremiah's life and propelled him to speak hard words to people he loved. Face to face with this scripture, I felt I had to follow Jeremiah's guidance. I knew many in the congregation would not hear my words as the good news I believed they were.

I wrote. I prayed. I met with friends to excise unnecessary, inflammatory lines from my sermon. I called in all the prayer support I could muster.

That Sunday, I woke feeling clear and ready. I arrived at church early so I could pray in the sanctuary before the service began.

When it was time, I walked to the pulpit. I took a breath to settle my few remaining jitters and began to preach. Feeling Jeremiah's presence at my back, I spoke to the people I loved,

> Right now, American Christians are on a danger-ous path by letting nationalism and patriotism take the front seat and letting our nation, rather than our faith, set the questions we are willing to ask and the answers we are willing to explore. ... I know that the flag stands for so much more than our refusal to see things from any perspective other than our own. But right now, Christians have an important alternative to live in the world. ... As Christians, our family includes the global family, not just our immediate families. As Christians, homeland security must be worldwide homeland security. ... [T]he choice is to say yes to this Gospel way or walk away. And the time for response is *now!* God's people and God's earth are being destroyed while we sit back unquestioning.[6]

Four people heard my words as a holy challenge: a visitor from California, Howard and two friends who had come to support me. Most of the rest were silent.

"Those were hard words this morning," Piper said as we picked up cups of weak coffee after the service. Deacon Dewey, with a flag pin on his lapel, affirmed the clarity of my words. Otherwise, little was said about the sermon as we chatted and munched on chocolate chip cookies. Despite all of my fearful anticipation of delivering my sermon, no sparks flew. I returned home exhausted.

A call came a few days later. "Nancy, the worship committee had a special meeting yesterday, and we would like to talk to you sometime this week."

Since I was leaving town again the following day, three of us, all friends, gathered in the church basement within the hour.

Medea spoke first: "The worship committee feels that it's divisive when you preach on a controversial topic when we don't have a priest. Please stop preaching like you did last Sunday until the new priest has been appointed."

I cried but was very clear when I responded, "No. I can't promise to preach, or not preach, anything. I preach what is laid on my spirit in response to the day's scripture. I am given no guarantee that what I write from my heart is, in fact, true. But I must speak it anyway. Anything else would be disobedience to God." I stopped to regain my composure, wanting to make sure I was understood. "If you want to stop me preaching here, you need to pursue the process to have me officially removed from lay preaching."

As we prepared to leave, Piper asked, "May we show your sermon to the Diocesan office? We contacted the regional office yesterday to find out about what content was appropriate for sermons."

At a less emotional moment, I would have laughed at the thought of church rules laying out what subjects could, and could not, be spoken from the pulpit. "Certainly, share it with whomever you'd like," I replied.

A few weeks later our church board reaffirmed my license to preach, and the topic was officially dropped.

I didn't want it dropped. I desperately wanted to have a conversation within our congregation about the intersection of patriotism and Christianity. I longed for a process where we could respectfully hear one another across our differences and learn from the wisdom and experience of others. I'd seen that happen at Be Present trainings and knew that it was possible to bridge the gaps that divided us.

For me, this conversation had global ramifications. We worshiped a God who called us to be neighbors with everyone, even our enemies. This call was to a life filled with the dynamite power of love, not a toy chemistry set. I wanted to scream out to my congregation of friends that we needed to find a way to speak and listen to each other. If reconciliation was impossible here, I feared our world was doomed.

I shared with the church board my hope that we could find a process to help us hear each other and move beyond our impasse. After several weeks, Medea told me that everyone was fine now and that they didn't think the topic was important enough for such a meeting.

She smiled, as if the topic were settled.

I cried.

No matter what everyone else thought, things were not fine for me. Though part of me longed to leave and find another church, I'd never been one to jump ship when things got tough. My loyalty to this community compelled me to stay and work things out. I loved these people. I keenly disagreed with them. How could we be a community?

The stark contrast between church and the Beloved Community was hard to bear. I wanted to stay within both.

Elizabeth Blackwell's words echoed in my heart. "I have an intense longing to scream, and everyone here speaks in a whisper."[7]

Ruth Tipps, age 85, 1985

Monterey, California

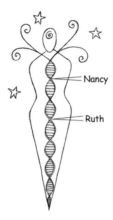

I found my voice one Sunday morning at the Restful Valley Nursing Home.

Each week a different preacher set up church in the corner of the dining hall. This week's preacher was droning on and on and on about Matthew 13:47-50. He took that great story and started shouting about how God's going to separate the evil people from the righteous people and throw the bad ones into the fires of hell.

I tried to stand up to speak, but my legs were too wobbly, so I just shouted out: "I am sick and tired of all of you preachers babbling such nonsense. You pick at the carcass of the scripture, but the meat and skin is missing. You are taking that wonderful Jesus parable and messing with it. Jesus and me are both storytellers and we are mad as hell."

The nurses interrupted me with their urgent order, "Shhhhhhhhh. Hush Ruth." When I didn't hush up nice and quiet, they quickly wheeled me out of the room.

I wasn't finished, so I continued straightening him out in my mind.

"You must be one of those folks who sees but does not perceive and hears but does not listen or understand. Jesus knew that even preachers' hearts could grow dull. Read the rest of Matthew 13, why don't you?"

I guess that last sentence must have made it to my lips as the nurses jumped all over me trying to get me to shut up again. I was unstoppable.

I continued (in my head or out loud, I have no idea which), "All that finger pointing as though the evil ones were someone else and we alone are the righteous ones is damn arrogant and stupid."

A few holes in my thinking finally freed up my mouth to say what I'd held back all those years. I finished my first and last sermon by saying, "Amen. So be it. The word of the Lord, and all of that. Thank you, Jesus."

They told me not to come to church again. Oh well, I don't guess the Good Lord will be too upset with me about that, given that they kicked me out for speaking the gospel truth. Doesn't matter much anyway. Jesus will come fetch me soon enough.

Ruth, circa 1920

21

Wailing and Gnashing of Teeth

My patriotic act in honor of Independence Day 2002 was to write a million dollar check to Uncle Sam to pay Dad's estate tax. Howard and I had participated for years in Responsible Wealth's Tax Fairness Pledge. We were disturbed by the ever-increasing tax cuts for high income Americans and wanted to give back what we'd saved to organizations working for economic justice. We had also fought to keep the estate tax in place even though Dad's estate was in the two percent of US citizens who would have to pay it. That big check seemed like a small price to pay for roads, schools, water, libraries, museums and national parks. I was glad to do it.

Howard and I were grateful for our friends from the Beloved Community who were willing to talk about such things, since few church friends understood why that kind of economic justice was critical to our faith. One new friend from the community, Judy Bork, came to visit us in December, and I was excited to strengthen our friendship while we explored the beautiful southern Oregon countryside.

Howard's photo captured it all. Crater Lake, brilliant blue and almost one thousand feet below the crater's rim, glistened in the background. In the foreground, two middle-aged women stood close, grinning like we didn't have a care in the world. In that moment, I had no idea that soon a wail would erupt from deep within my belly.

Judy and Nancy, 2002

Klamath County covered a lot of territory in south central Oregon just east of the Cascade Range. It stretched from Crater Lake captured in our photograph—all that remained of Mt. Mazama after she blew her top almost seven thousand years ago—to Klamath Lake a few blocks from my home, to the potato farms and ranches near the California border twenty-five miles to the south. This was semi-arid country, very different from rainy Oregon on the west side of the Cascades.

Klamath Falls was the county's largest city, with forty-five thousand living in the area. As we drove back through town, I pointed out the sights to Judy. After the stunning beauty of the surrounding area, the twelve-foot metal bucket in front of the City Government Building in the middle of downtown stood out like a sore thumb. This bucket, I explained, symbolized a four-month protest against the government's decision to cut off irrigation water and thus protect the endangered suckerfish in Klamath Lake during the drought of 2001. A US flag affixed to the top of the huge bucket snapped in the breeze. I shook my head at the irony that a flag which had been flown upside down during the water protest had suddenly taken a prominent place, upright and proud, after the attacks of September 11, 2001 ended the demonstration and initiated a season of patriotism.

Howard, Judy and I returned home at dusk to the smell of chili in the crock-pot and, soon, the sweet scent of oak burning in our wood stove. Relaxing in the warmth of our home, we visited late into the night.

Just before bed, we talked briefly about the following morning's church service. Judy, a white woman, worshiped in a predominantly black church. Her Sunday mornings were full of praise, swaying bodies and Bible teaching. I preferred the ancient prayers of liturgy from the Episcopal *Book of Common Prayer*, weekly partaking of the bread and wine and a variety of preachers in the pulpit. Though I wished it wasn't so, my congregation was almost exclusively white.

I was excited for Judy to come to church with me. I wanted her to meet our friends and be part of the Sunday liturgy we loved. Mary Jane and Paul, co-workers with me in the church's food pantry, warmly greeted us at the door as we arrived. Emily hurried over and pulled me close; she loved to hug. I nodded at Eleanor, sitting in her usual spot, near the front left. The sun streamed through the stained glass window, lighting the dark wood of the pews.

Susan and Peter, our priests, had left in the fall, leaving worship leadership to lay leaders like myself. But this Sunday I was released from preaching or reading the scripture so I could sit with Judy. In the middle of the four weeks of Advent, the liturgy slowly moved toward Christmas—a refreshing contrast to the shopping malls playing "Jingle Bells" the day after Halloween.

A large Advent wreath hung from the ceiling. Four candles were nestled around the evergreen circle, three blue and one pink. Starting the first week of Advent with the lighting of one candle, symbolizing hope, each Sunday a different person from the congregation relit the candles from the past weeks and lit a new one—honoring hope, joy, peace and love.

That morning Bob lit the candle of peace and read a short meditation. During a week that our nation moved closer to war, I was grateful that an alternative was lifted in prayer here in the church—peace.

Later, in the Prayers of the People, we prayed for those enlisted in our Armed Forces.

My prayers went out to the soldiers, not only for physical safety, but also for protection of their spirits from the inevitable horrors of the war. But I was startled that no prayers were offered for the people, civilians as well as soldiers, whom we might soon be bombing in Iraq and who were already under fire in Afghanistan.

Then we prayed a prayer for Peace from the *Book of Common Prayer*, which asked that "our dominion may increase until the earth is filled with the knowledge of your love."

The words were beautiful, but they ignored the contradiction between God's unconditional love and human control. In history around the world, when the "God of our nation" was invoked to support "our" side during wartime, blind patriotism fueled by religious fervor had too often led to violent and dangerous conflicts.

The realities of that particular moment in history as well as hope for peace were missing from the prayer. Nationally, there was escalating talk of our bombing Iraq for suspected weapons-of-mass-destruction and for their alleged role in the September eleventh Al-Qaeda attack. No one in my congregation mentioned the lack of national introspection about our nation's actions before and after the 2001 tragedy. No one reflected on how our Christian faith could help us find our footing of faith during this fearful and angry time.

And no one had helped me find a way to transmute my rage and grief at our government into my own compassionate stance for peace. For the last year my church and nation had acted as if Jesus fully supported the US going to war.

Something inside me crumbled as I sat on the familiar wooden pews, painfully aware that I was at home with strangers. I gasped for air throughout the rest of the service.

Finally we sang the closing hymn. Embarrassing even myself, the only word I could sing, which I cried out loudly, was "wailing."

I couldn't leave the pew when the service was over. I hadn't heard Jesus in the liturgy. I was furious that our President was leading our nation into war, and I felt no hint of forgiveness toward him. The day's liturgy of peace felt lost alongside the prayers for war. I reacted like a caged animal trapped inside my skin, unsure how to release the wails that crashed around inside me.

Once I was able to join them in the fellowship hall, everyone else seemed fine. They all sipped coffee, ate cookies and visited as if nothing was awry.

Where was Jesus when I needed him? Was it possible that my pain was a sign of God's presence? If so, this was an excruciating love.

After we left church, as Howard, Judy and I drove around town, I poured out my grief and anger.

Judy was baffled by the enormity of my reaction and feelings. She believed that the war on terrorism was a just response to the horror of September eleventh. From previous conversations, I knew that we held different political and theological views. Yet Judy listened to me without getting defensive.

"What's happening for you?" she asked, using one of the Be Present tools I'd shared with her.

My emotions calmed as I shared the fullness of my grief with the two of them. Howard had heard my feelings before and agreed with me. Judy listened respectfully even though we disagreed.

After I finished, I asked Judy, "What has it been like for you this morning?" I was able to hear her thoughts without spiraling downward again. In Atlanta the year before, I couldn't imagine how merely taking the time to speak of my emotions could let them move through and out of my body and make it possible for me to listen to Judy's very different perspective, but I had just done it myself.

I had been a mess that morning. Yet in our car driving home, Judy, Howard and I experienced true community, each speaking what was true for us and listening to each other. My grief remained, but I felt loved.

Elizabeth Tipps, age 52, 1870

Near Short Creek, North Carolina

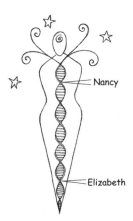

Right after the war ended, Sheriff sold our land out from under us, all 'cept our forty-two-and-a-half-acre homestead. In one dark day, all our land was gone. Ever'thing went to pay our bills. The shame felt like a millstone 'round my neck.

I woulda died boilin' mad and draggin' the rest of 'em down with me, but the Lord stepped in. Snatched my heart and turned it 'round right.

I didn't never like them wild tent meetin's they had right over there at the edge of town. Methodist evangelists comin' in and out of town makin' a whole lot of racket. Folks talked 'bout salvation, but nothin' ever seemed to change.

My friend Liza tricked me into goin'. I shoulda known she was up to somethin', 'specially wearin' her favorite blue dress with her hair braided real purty 'round her head. But gittin' away from the farm sounded real good. I was tickled to go anywhere she wanted to take me.

I figured it out when we hit the edge of Marble Falls and saw the big revival tent. Truth was, I coulda slipped off once I realized what was happenin'. But somethin' held me steady inside while Liza was holdin' my hand.

Walkin' down that aisle towards our chairs, suddenly I knew, clear as day—if I took another step, wouldn't be no turnin' back. Amazin' thing was, I kept on walkin'.

Somethin' happened to me that night, plum in the middle of strange singin', wild prayers and a sermon I forgot. God reached out and called me home. Grace it was, amazin' grace. Love reached out to a self-pityin', furious old woman like me.

The deep thaw begun that very night. Under the moonless sky filled with twinklin' stars, my heart broke open like the ice on Tennessee mountain rivers come spring. Only heard that sound once, but I'll never forgit it. A short crack that shot back and forth across that ice and sounded like a giant chick bustin' out of its shell.

My frozen heart did the same thing that night. Tears was runnin'. Tears of gratitude. Tears of confession. All at once. Cleansed me clear down to the bone.

I may have been brand new on the inside, but folks around me couldn't see that. Livin' my faith out day by day, in the middle of the family I'd been so mad at all them years, was somethin' else entirely.

22

Whites Only in a World of Many Colors

At Be Present's National Conference in 2002, one of my small groups had explored whiteness, asking each other what it was like to live in this world with our white skin. For most of my life, I hadn't thought that race was a factor unless someone—almost always a person who didn't have white skin—brought it up. However, I was beginning to understand how not paying attention to how whiteness influenced life meant that I was de facto accepting the belief that the white experience and perspective were the norm.

After Paul began classes for his ethnic studies major at the University of Oregon, the two of us had lively conversations about race and class. One semester he loaned me one of his favorite textbooks—*The Possessive Investment in Whiteness*. The title itself was provocative. It was one thing to have white skin, but another thing to be unconscious about our selfish clinging to the perks and values that our culture had invested in white skin color. Lipsitz, the white author of the book, wrote about the unearned, and rarely acknowledged, benefits gained by white skin in everything from housing, to education, to inherited wealth. [1]

Lipsitz made it clear that fighting racism and racial privilege was the responsibility of everyone. The more I read, the more eager I became to begin my quarterly sojourns to Atlanta for the six weekend sessions of the upcoming eighteen-month Be Present Institute.

I was excited when January 2003 rolled around, and I was once again at the Atlanta airport about to begin the first session. I waved when I spotted Kate waiting for me at the curb. I'd enjoyed visiting with her over the phone during the past year and looked forward to deepening our friendship.

On the way to Kate and Lillie's home where I would stay the night before the institute began, I talked about the damage racism had caused in the culture around me. Kate listened before she said anything.

"Don't do this work of addressing racism, or any of the 'isms,' for others, as a way to help. Instead, do it for yourself," she advised.

Of course I wanted to do this work for others. Even though Lipsitz had said much the same thing, I'd spent much of my life wanting to help others, and racism felt like an important wrong to set right.

As Kate and I continued to talk, I began to understand. Addressing racism with a goal to help others kept the issue at arm's length—"their" problem that I was qualified to help by virtue of my white skin color. Acting as if I was unaffected by a racist culture was a lie. Racism, I was learning, affected us all.

Thursday afternoon, a group of us drove to the conference center for our weekend together. Struck by the diversity of skin color, class, family history, gender, faith tradition and age, the shyness that I always felt before any group gathering had intensified. I knew that I would be changed by our work together, and despite how I seemed to pursue it, change scared me.

This time men and boys were also in the circle, and I was interested to see the new dynamic. Men spoke. Sometimes women reacted to a man's tone of voice or phrase that reminded them of their past experiences with controlling men. Women spoke. Old gender dynamics sometimes emerged, but other times conscious listening occurred. Assumptions, cultural biases and events that had traditionally separated us one from the other became the opening that began to bring us together.

Friday afternoon, Lillie Allen explained how this work began when she was a young woman, elaborating on the origin stories she'd shared at my first Be Present gathering. Lillie had set out to discover if there was another truth about people than what she'd personally experienced. Could white men be different than the violent white men of her childhood? Could she be freed from returning to her old memories every time she was face to face with a person or situation that looked like, or felt similar to, something from her past? Lillie discovered that each moment was a fresh one and didn't have to be hooked to past occurrences, assumptions or beliefs. "The present moment is the best place for change to occur," Lillie said.

Lillie had begun her organizational work within the black Women's Health Project, simply by asking groups of black women and girls, "What is the reality for you to be black and a woman in this culture?" Initially, the women had no words—only wails. In time, they found words to speak about their experiences. Remembering wasn't a way to get stuck in the past but to begin the movement toward knowing themselves outside of the distress of their oppression.

I was mesmerized by Lillie's story. She may have shared part of it at my first conference, but I heard it in a new way. I was grateful for the women in her story who had laid the foundation for this organization by wrestling with the reality of their lives as black women. I wanted to be able to see the reality of my own life as a white woman.

When Lillie finished speaking, Margherita Vacchiano, Be Present's Associate Director, stood before us. Tall and slim, Margherita had long, black curly hair and was impeccably dressed from earrings to boots. Longing for a practice to embody the theory she had learned in her graduate women's studies program, Margherita told us that she got involved with Be Present in the early 1990s. The Be Present Empowerment Model, first used by Lillie in her own life and then adopted as the heart of the organization, had given Margherita the tools she needed not just to understand gender justice in analysis but also to bring her actions in line with her values.

We talked about this model during my first training, but I'd only understood part of it. This time I paid careful attention, hoping it would begin to sink in even more.

Margherita identified the first step of the model: "Know yourself outside the distress of oppression."[2]

I'd spent all of my adult life trying to know myself, so that part of the step was clear. In addition, I was very familiar with my tendency to get triggered and slip into distress when I was confused or felt misunderstood. Regardless, I had no idea how I got caught in the distress of "oppression." I was aware of the oppression of sexism, but other than that, I was structurally in the oppressor, or power, position. My thoughts were spinning, but I continued to listen.

The second step, Margherita explained, guided us to, "Listen to others in a conscious and present state." My friends had often commented that I was a good listener. Even so, while appearing attentive, sometimes I got caught in my thoughts—judgments, opinions, problem solving, relating what I was hearing to my own life—and my hearing of the other person went out the window. I had much to learn about really listening.

The third, and final step, Margherita explained was to, "Build effective relationships and sustain true alliances." Relationships and alliances had always been a central part of my life. But at the cross-class Bible study, at St. Paul's church, and in a few groups I'd dearly loved over the years, too often things fell apart when members strongly disagreed. I wanted something different. I hoped these steps would guide my learning.

After the session, we gathered around the tables for lunch. I sat next to Alease Bess, a woman I'd felt drawn to the first time she introduced herself. Her hair was close cropped, her skin a pecan tan. Her short stature, softly rounded curves and no-nonsense manner reminded me of Mom.

In groups, I could usually tell when someone was angry or confused or happy or sad, but Alease stumped me. Watching her across the meeting room during the morning session, I'd noticed that she usually maintained the same expression: not a frown, not a smile, just even in her lips and eyes. During our introduction the first day, we'd both been vocal about the centrality of our faith. Alease called herself an apostle and openly talked about things God told her. I called myself a seeker who had had a multitude of roles in the church—teacher, education coordinator and licensed lay preacher. I'd often felt guided by God and willingly followed divine nudges, but I had never felt comfortable claiming that God told me to do something. Over our meal, we began to get to know each other.

Saturday afternoon we divided into two groups, women and men. We were to practice using the model while talking about our lives.

Cynthia Renfro was the first to speak. I listened intently as she shared about living in Portland, Oregon, and Southern California neighborhoods with few other black families. Cynthia's dark skin was suddenly considered a problem when she and her friends entered junior high school. Invitations to sleep-overs and birthday parties ended. Friends pulled away. Old friends occasionally made racial remarks.

Most of the African American women nodded knowingly. Since all of my friends growing up were white, I had no idea that this sort of abrupt severing was common with cross-race friendships during the transition into the teen years. My heart was heavy with the sadness of it all.

Cynthia told us about an incident that had occurred in 1965, before she was born, when her mother Pat moved from the West Coast to Dallas, Texas. Days after the move, Pat thought the WHITES ONLY sign propped in the laundromat window referred to her white laundry. A few hours later, home again with clean laundry, Pat realized the sign referred to skin, not clothes.

I gasped.

Texas? 1965?

I'd never seen any WHITES ONLY signs. Had I missed them? Couldn't blacks eat at my favorite restaurant? Shop in the same stores I frequented? If the signs were there and I never noticed them, what else hadn't I noticed growing up as a young white girl in West Texas? Tears flowed. I had a hard time listening to the rest of the women's group sharing.

The first session of the institute ended the following day, and that evening I flew home. I started talking to friends and family to find answers to the questions that Cynthia's story had brought up in me.

Most didn't remember window signs. A few older women recalled separate water fountains and bathrooms at the bus station until the mid 1960s. Wanting to know more, I returned to my whitewashed childhood memories with new eyes.

In my search to find out about segregation in Wichita Falls during the first six years of my life, I discovered that the West Texas "colored" schools used our old and discarded schoolbooks. I'd never seen any of those schools and only crossed the tracks to that side of Wichita Falls or Abilene or Midland once or twice with my mother to take our maid back home. I had never questioned why all the maids I knew as a child were black. I certainly hadn't known that every time I'd been issued a brand new textbook, a black student across town got my old marked up and outdated one.

Officially the Midland Independent School District unanimously voted to desegregate the schools in August 1956. However, the first move in that direction was in 1968 due to a federal court order. My research also uncovered the fact that lawsuits aimed to enforce full desegregation in Midland continued into the 1980s and 1990s.

When Midland's schools began integrating my freshman year, it had never occurred to me to ask any questions. What had happened to the rest of the teachers from Carver High School, the closed black high school? What about their school traditions? Thirty-three years later, I pieced together the answer. Most of the teachers lost their jobs. The school's traditions screeched to a halt. By contrast, Midland High School's traditions continued year after year, little changed by integration.

I also remembered Beatrice, the women who cleaned our house in Abilene and whose photo I had snapped with my new camera. In my neighborhood, maids were always referred to by their first name only. Southern girls like me in the 1960s always addressed adult women outside our family with the title Mrs. or Miss, followed by their last name. My calling her "Beatrice" had marked her as an adult not worthy of respect. That was not my intent, of course, but the impact was the same.

In the mid-1960s the Midland Community Theatre had hung a

"Everybody's Different" by Sue

piece of Mom's art in their lobby, a large appliqué stitchery covered with bright-eyed children's faces. The fabric used for each child was a different piece of cloth—black, white or a black and white pattern. Some members threatened to withdraw their annual subscriptions unless the wall hanging was removed. The theatre refused, and Mom's art stayed put. After I heard Cynthia's story, I remembered my teen-aged pride at this liberal decision by the theatre. Forty years later, I realized that I'd never looked beyond this incident to see how race had played out in the theatre as a whole. I never paid any attention to the fact that the kids in my children's theatre group, the adults in the plays, and the audiences were overwhelmingly, if not exclusively, white. I hadn't wondered how skin color was used to determine who was included, and excluded, from Midland's "community" theatre.

Combing through my memories, I recalled Mom telling me of an incident that had happened when she attended a conference in Colorado in the mid-1940s. After the morning session, she and a group of colleagues walked into a restaurant for lunch. They were refused service because one of the women was black. She'd told me the story when I was in high school, and I'd been proud that she'd known discrimination was wrong. Pondering it again now, I realized that Mom's shock at that awkward moment wasn't because she was unused to segregation—that was all she'd known in Wichita Falls and at the University of Texas in Austin. Perhaps that day was the first time Mom had ever walked into a restaurant with a black woman and thus the first time she witnessed a colleague experiencing the rejection of segregation. It had stung her. But I had no idea what she said or did in or after that moment.

Something was shifting in me as I traveled between Oregon and Georgia that year. Gathering with others in these rooms of many colors, I was seeing the world I wanted to live in, but I still had a lot to learn.

23

Called to Leave

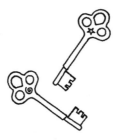

Despite the controversy with my Jeremiah sermon the previous June, I continued to preach at my church once a month until late January 2003 when the new priest arrived. He announced that he wanted to preach every week, and I heard the doors to my leadership in this congregation creaking closed. Though my preaching was no longer welcomed at home, the Friends (Quaker) meetinghouse often invited me to their pulpit for Sunday morning worship.

At the same time, a good friend offered to let me use her office for researching and writing sermons. Whether or not I would be actively preaching, I loved exploring my thoughts and spiritual journey through words and was thrilled to have a beautiful, one-room office where I could create undisturbed for a few half days a week.

That spring, through prayer and reflection alone and with friends, I developed clarity about my next steps with my church. I would still return to that parish to be with the people I loved and participate in the liturgy of worship that so fed me. Yet, after years of preaching, helping with Christian education and fully participating in the life of the church, I knew that my time of being active in that congregation was over. Though I wished I could share what I had learned from Be Present and the Beloved Community, the new priest wasn't any more interested in these topics than the congregation had been.

Sunday March 2, 2003, dawned bright and sunny. Laura and I chatted as we pulled into the church parking lot. We hopped out of the car, slammed the doors and turned around to walk to the church. Glancing up, I gasped. A big US flag was hanging just outside the church doors. It waved gently in the breeze. I froze.

"I don't know if I can do this," I sputtered to Laura.

Her eyes widened. She hadn't been paying any attention to my problems at church, but she believed I had a tendency to "freak out" about crazy things.

"Mom, don't make such a big deal out of everything," she said.

I took a long slow breath, and continued walking.

Entering through the back door, we walked into the fellowship hall where people gathered before worship. Laura hurried away as the deacon and several friends hugged me, welcoming me back after several weeks away.

"How are you?" Dewey asked.

Before I could think, I answered, "It looks like I have come to say good-bye." As soon as those words came out of my mouth, I knew it was true. I had to leave this church. Now.

I found Laura, kissed her on the cheek and told her I was going. Grateful I didn't make a scene, she nodded and said she would find a ride home. With tears on my face and pain in my heart, I hugged a few more friends on the way out. I said goodbye, walked out of the front door and drove away.

Passing the Friends church on the way home, I felt the urge to pull into their parking lot. My friend Faith Marsalli was the pastor, and I'd long been warmly welcomed there.

I slipped into the back pew and cried through the whole service. I closed my eyes and let the music wash over me. Faith's sermon soothed my spirit. Just before closing, Faith asked if anyone had prayers to share. I stood with shaking knees.

"I stand here knowing that I've just been called out of my beloved church this morning. I hate to leave a community of people I love and a liturgy that touches my soul. But I felt the call of God to walk away, and I did. I am grateful to each of you here this morning. Your presence has gently held me. Thank you."

At home that afternoon, I realized the impact of leaving on that particular Sunday. The following week was Ash Wednesday, the beginning of the season of Lent. Since my first trip to Haiti, the Ash Wednesday liturgy had a special place in my heart. It is the only time when the Episcopal community asked for forgiveness for our cultural sins:

> We confess to you, Lord ...
> Our self-indulgent appetites and ways,
> and our exploitation of other people ...
> Our intemperate love of worldly goods and comforts. ...
>
> Accept our repentance, Lord,
> for the wrongs we have done: for our blindness to human
> need and suffering,
> and our indifference to injustice and cruelty ...
> prejudice and contempt toward those who differ from us,
> For our waste and pollution of your creation,
> and our lack of concern for those who come after us. ... [1]

These words of confession spoke the things I so longed to address in my life and in the world. Often Christians focused on personal sin but ignored institutional and organizational sin that we all participated in together. Now without a church community, my Lent had started early and I felt alone.

In the middle of the next week, I returned to St. Paul's to drop off my key. The building was vacant and silent. When I reached for my keys, I discovered that two of them looked identical—the one for St. Paul's and the other one for my friend's office. I laughed knowing that a different door, the one to the cozy space where I wrote each week, had already opened for me.

I entered the empty building that had been my church home for nine years. Recollections of sweetness and community jumbled with present sadness. Wandering through Sunday School classrooms, the small chapel where we'd held mid-week Eucharist and the parlor where I'd held the cross-class Bible study, I was flooded with memories.

Passing through the Food Pantry, I stepped into the tiny, basement library. I'd rarely gone there looking for a book among its meager shelves, but years before I'd volunteered to clean the small room. While dusting the bookshelves, I'd found a photocopied chapter from a book written by Abraham Heschel and titled, "What Manner of Man is the Prophet?"[2]

I'd smiled when I first read those words. It was easier to laugh than scream at how often I'd had to expand the definitions of "man" or "men" to include women. Curious, I'd read a few lines, then paragraphs. Time seemed to slow down as I read words that felt strangely familiar.

Despite the task at hand on that long ago cleaning day, I couldn't stop reading.

This day, on my way to slip the church key under the office door, I once again pulled the pages off the library shelf and began to read the words that felt so familiar. Heschel explained that the injustice that felt minor to most people was a crisis to the prophet.[3]

I had just left this church about such a paltry thing as a flag moved to prominent places in the church. Most felt it wasn't an issue. For me, it was a catastrophe.

Mesmerized again, I kept reading. Heschel detailed the sleeplessness of prophets, plagued at night by loud divine messages.[4]

I put the pages back on the shelf. Who in the world was I to feel that my own experience was reflected in Abraham Heschel's descriptions of the Biblical prophets? I made mistakes all of the time and tended to make assumptions that sometimes proved wrong. But I couldn't deny the situations, overwhelming in their intensity, when I felt "something like a burning fire shut up in my bones."[5] During those moments, I was too weary to hold it in. During those terrifying times, I'd had to speak what I saw. Jeremiah and the prophets felt like my brothers and sisters on this journey of faith.

I offered a prayer of gratitude for Abraham Heschel's words. Be

Present was teaching me to stand steady in the fullness of my experience, including my prophetic sight. At our last gathering I'd heard Alease Bess say that God spoke to her. I was fascinated that I observed none of the dogmatic righteousness I'd long associated with that sort of claim to spiritual authority. Studying the Biblical prophets as their words inspired my sermons, I'd learned how prophets were people with a combination of clarity, authority and personal shortcomings.

Though I knew I had clarity in some instances, I also had a tendency to erupt when my feelings were hurt, when I thought someone believed something untrue about me or when the conversation didn't make sense to me. My flaws seemed much bigger to me than my spiritual sight. This had made it hard to believe my Fargo spiritual director's observation that in some situations, my feelings and understandings were prophetic. In that dark, poorly-stocked church library, I'd discovered what manner of woman was a prophet. Me.

Softly closing the door, I went into the sanctuary and knelt in prayer. The foundation of my church world had cracked beneath me. I had preached hard, unwelcome words. I'd walked away from my congregation. Here in this beautiful church, I had violated one of my cherished values—staying and working through differences. When God had called last Sunday morning, I knew I had to take the next step into the wildly diverse world I'd glimpsed in Be Present circles and in Haiti. New foundations were needed for the journey ahead. My white Euro-American worldview and principles, so affirmed in this church, needed reevaluating.

As so much around me seemed to be falling apart, I continued to reach out to touch God. Similar to my childhood dream, I kept reaching until I grasped the edge of the velvet drape at the center of my Leaning Tower of Pisa Church. Things might rip. I might have to leave. I might fall, again and again. Holding tightly to God, however, I trusted that my life and the world around me was filled with grace.

I wasn't sure exactly where I was heading, but the details didn't really matter. I was dancing with God and Life. What more could I want?

24

Front Page News

Leaving St. Paul's church might not have made the news, but it was the lead story of my life during the spring of 2003, and one that left me with questions.

I looked to books for answers and came upon Gandhi's autobiography, *Experiments with Truth*. I loved the image of my life filled with experimentation in which failure was as important as success. From that vantage point, my last couple of years at St. Paul's had been an extended experiment in community and listening to God's guidance. I wasn't positive that I hadn't been caught in distress. But I'd walked through that time as faithfully as I knew how.

Howard and I also experimented with financial transparency in the Beloved Community's bi-annual gatherings. We shared the details of our investments and bank account balances. Most of us were proud of some of our investing and spending choices and embarrassed by others, but we discovered new possibilities when we explored our feelings and numbers together.

Following Harvest Time's encouragement, the Beloved Community retreat circle wanted to experiment with a small portion of our portfolios as commonwealth rather than private wealth. Wondering how we could let our money flow freely into a "common pot" and then out into the world, we gathered around our altar, lit a candle and sat together in the silence, listening.

All of us agreed that we would each determine how much to donate to our common pot. Then we would decide together where to gift the money. We would all have equal say in the decision even though the amounts contributed would vary greatly.

Howard and I talked about how much we would donate to the common pot in the evenings, on the plane home, and over the next few weeks. Not wanting this experiment to be just another financial decision, Howard and I prayerfully listened and soon arrived at the amount we were to give.

It wasn't quite as easy, though, for us to see eye-to-eye on our personal donations.

Why, Howard wondered, had he agreed to give away twenty-five percent of our financial inheritance? In response to his anxiety, Howard set out to develop a plan to calculate how much money we would give away over the ten-year period from 2002-2012. He determined that a bold giving goal was the sum of the Christian tithe (giving away ten percent of income annually) added to the Islam zakat (giving away two and a half percent of assets each year). To calculate what that meant for us in the upcoming nine years, he subtracted the twenty-five percent that we had already given away in 2002.

When he explained his plan to me, I thought his calculations were nonsense and his bottom line stingy. I struggled to listen to his logic. Likewise, Howard had a hard time hearing me, afraid I wanted to give away even more.

For the next three days, we returned to this conversation. Nothing shifted.

The Beloved Community had taught us that an impasse such as this one was the perfect time to stop conversations and start listening instead. Howard and I agreed to take the following week to prayerfully see where we each felt led, hoping we'd find a way forward that felt good to both of us.

A week later, I suggested we take a giving sabbatical, a period of time where we could have conversations without any need to make a decision. Howard was excited by that idea and suggested we do this for six months. We honored the few remaining donation commitments for 2003 and began our experiment.

While on our giving sabbatical, I pondered the roots of my own thinking. Released from having to make any decisions, I was finally able to hear an inner voice that had been there all along, taunting me about being a wealthy woman in an unjust world. For me, the decision to give away twenty-five percent was based on prayerful discernment, and my intent with the gift was solid, but somewhere in the background I was also trying to appease my guilt.

In addition, I caught sight that my desire to give money had also been influenced by my sense of responsibility to the organizations I feared had become dependent on the large gifts we'd just given. As I brought my money guilt and fears out of the shadows, I began to understand my feelings and reactions more clearly.

Howard had felt the impact of my unnoticed feelings. Something in him knew that I was unconsciously driven to give away more, and he countered with his formula to limit our donations. Our Sabbatical gave us time to reflect and let our distress surface and dissipate, allowing our wisdom to become clearer.

In a recent Be Present training, Lillie had emphasized the importance of coming to terms with who we were. She'd pointed out that as a wealthy white woman, even if I gave away all of my money, I still would have access to privilege with my white skin, education and family connections. Instead, I needed to know what was true about myself and consciously use my resources—money and otherwise—in ways that were aligned with my values.

Likewise, I found guidance in Harvest Time's acceptance of money related paradoxes. On one hand, we were called to respond to the cries of an unjust world—as in the admonition of Jesus to a man who wanted to inherit eternal life. Jesus told this man to sell all that he had, give to the poor and follow him. On the other hand, God's economy was based on an extravagant outpouring of love, highlighted by the loving affirmation of Jesus to the woman who anointed his feet with costly nard (that could also have been sold and the money given to the poor.) Despite the greedy and addictive ways money was used in our culture, Harvest Time understood that working with money could be a doorway to spiritual transformation.

Since I'd loved the process of giving away the twenty-five percent, I struggled to imagine slowing down our giving when that money was gone. Our six-month giving sabbatical gave me the time to look inward and to share my thinking openly and honestly. Howard's mathematical scheme was born of his own fear, but it allowed us to find a new way to meet in the middle of our opposing money concerns.

It turned out our Sabbatical made way for other decisions as well. One afternoon, Howard said, "I think we should buy a condo in Portland."

I was silent for a few minutes. We'd never wanted to have a second home. Nevertheless, my response was clear. I nodded and smiled. "Yes, I think you're right."

Howard was stunned. He presumed I would disagree.

We knew we wanted to move to a larger town, a more progressive town like Portland, after Laura left for college. Howard was also eager to leave academia and open his own engineering business.

We contacted Mary Mather-Slac, a Portland real estate agent, who asked us to write down our home manifesto: a statement of all the things we hoped to find in our condo. I loved starting this process with a vision of what we wanted rather than looking at random two-bedroom condos. Lately, rather than starting cold or limiting ourselves to what only seemed practical, Howard and I had been trying to begin with our "high dream" or intention for everything from what we'd like to do over the weekend to our new condo. Our list unfolded quickly—human scaled (not a high rise), near public transportation, with a library, bookstore, pub, restaurants and a park within walking distance.

Within the month we owned one of the twenty Rosegate Condominiums in the Hollywood neighborhood, a vibrant part of the city.

At the same time Howard and I were being interviewed by Portland's newspaper, *The Oregonian*. Through our long-time support of United for a Fair Economy's Responsible Wealth, we were asked to be one of five families with varying income levels from "lower" to "high" to highlight how the recent Bush tax cuts benefitted people of different classes. Believing this information was important to share broadly, we agreed.

Saying "yes" became a comedy of one exposure after another.

First, the family who had greater wealth than we did dropped out. Suddenly, we were labeled the "high income family."

We imagined the article would include a few general figures about our financial portfolio. We were naïve. They printed details of our income, capital gains taxes paid and deductions.

In the end, even a detailed financial profile wasn't enough. They sent a photographer to take our picture. Howard struggled with each new request, wondering about the sanity of his initial assent. Personally, I was grateful that none of our extended family lived in Oregon; I was ready to go public about our unconventional financial lives to strangers and local friends, but not our family.

The Oregonian reporter wasn't sure when the article would appear.

One warm August morning while visiting our Portland condo, Howard walked to Wholesome Blends for a cup of coffee. On the way, he glanced at the bright yellow newspaper machine at the corner. On the front page, smiling back at him was us. He bought a copy and hurried home.

We were still strangers in Portland. Would our new neighbors recognize us? How would old friends in Klamath Falls react when they saw the newspaper?

We read the article for the first time. That year the Bush tax cuts saved us thirteen-hundred dollars in income taxes. [1] That figure was lower than normal because of the tax benefits of closing my father's estate and our large initial donation. Despite President George W. Bush's assumptions, Howard and I did not strengthen the economy by spending our tax savings. We had enough extra money to do that before the tax cut.

Laura was waiting for us at the dining room table when we returned home to Klamath Falls.

Her interrogation began. "We're wealthy? And you're going to give most of it away? What about my college?"

Laura hadn't been interested in these conversations before she read about our finances at her best friend's home. Now that we were front-page news, she wanted more information.

Paul was in college. Even his parents appearing in the newspaper didn't prompt him to call home.

I was shy in public during the first week after the article appeared. Most people said nothing. A few friends mentioned the article. Some admired our values; others thought we should save more for our children. Some warned us that we would be inundated with requests for donations. A pastor in Portland called to see if we had heard about Ministry of Money, since he'd seen the kindred spirit in our story and their work. Only one person called to ask for money. After recovering from my initial embarrassment, I was eager to talk about money with friends and strangers and hear their perspectives.

By the time our story was old news, our giving sabbatical ended. We didn't emerge from this time with a formula. Instead, we'd begun to trust each other enough to have donation conversations that weren't stuck in the polarity of strongly held opinions. We found middle ground where our different perspectives brought richness to our decision making process.

Even though I had been exploring the intersection of money and faith for decades, I preferred opening up this topic in workshops or classrooms to having it be front page news. Nevertheless, publicly sharing our financial situation helped me remember the relationship between my private wealth and the global family. When I wasn't trying so hard to either protect my self-image as a wealthy person or fight my fears that my money automatically brought me in conflict with middle and lower income people, I began to taste freedom.

Sue Mathys, age 50, 1976

Houston, Texas

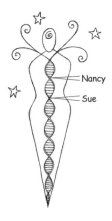

Wednesday, June 2, 1976

Dear Troops,[a]

I want to report that I passed my 50th without too much trauma. Ed took me out to dinner the night before—because Nancy would never forgive him if he didn't. We went to the Mason Jar—a local restaurant that Nancy discovered on her first trip to Houston. The evening was almost spoiled just prior to leaving home. Nancy's high school friend Jack had lived with us for a few weeks, and had moved out the day before to get settled in his new apartment. Fully dressed except for shoes and hose, I decided to wash my bare feet one last time before joining the world of the proper for my big birthday dinner. As is my habit of long standing, I stepped into the bathtub and turned on the faucet to anoint my feet. It was then I discovered that Jack had committed the GREAT NO NO—not turning off the shower faucet when getting out of the tub. So I stepped out dripping from my head to my tail. That meant completely re-dressing. Fortunately with my simple, short haircut I didn't ruin a $7.00 hair-do! But Jack's name is mud around here right now. At least I had another clean dress.

My favorite exchange of the day, however, happened when O.R. called and asked, "How does it feel to be old now that you are 50?"

"A whole lot better than it would feel for my daughter to turn 50!" was my quick reply.

He had no quip in return. O.R.'s silence was golden ... and extremely rare. That moment was my favorite birthday present.

A note from Aunt Betsy, a card from Mother and a call from Martha rounded out my birthday greetings from the rest of the troops. So all is well.

See some of you soon.

Love,

Sue

Sue, 1976

25

Two Texas Tarts Take Over the White House

Change was in the wind in the spring of 2004. Laura was graduating in June, and we planned to move to Portland in August. Our Klamath Falls real estate agent called one day in April to ask if we'd be willing to show our house that afternoon—two months before we'd wanted to put it on the market—to a potential buyer who was in town for the day. After looking around for ten minutes, he bought the house with the agreement to let us rent from him until August.

We had lots of preparation work to do, but first, I was about to turn fifty.

Some people fear saggy chins, droopy breasts and achy knees as their half-century birthday nears. Not me. I wanted to celebrate turning fifty in a way that combined sacred ritual, play and freedom. I was searching for the portal between the foundation I'd laid in my first forty-nine years and the beginning of my wilder second half-century. Coming out in the

Oregonian article gave me a taste of speaking my economic vision boldly. Painful as it had been to leave my church, I was also gaining skills at following my inner guidance.

Lauri Leaverton and I had celebrated our twelfth, thirteenth, fourteenth and fifteenth birthdays together back in Midland, Texas. Skinny, awkward and sure everyone else was prettier, we had invited a gaggle of teen-aged girls to come to her home on January eighteenth and mine on May twelfth to celebrate. We contorted ourselves into awkward positions playing Twister and gambled with poker chips in Tripoli. We sang "Happy Birthday," ate cake and opened presents.

Back in the late 1960s, Lauri and I had listened to our favorite 45s spinning on the record player or rocked with my transistor radio. We sang "Born to be Wild"[1] and "The Impossible Dream"[2] even though we lived as if we were born to be tame and were unable to imagine dreaming anything that wasn't practical. At fifty, we were finally ready to live some wild dreams and celebrate this milestone birthday together.

I checked bed and breakfasts not too far from our condo in Portland, halfway between Lauri's Yakima, Washington, home and Klamath Falls. The White House was top of the list. Were Lauri and I, whose friendship started when we were both shy West Texas girls in the hometown of President George W. Bush, ready to step out and take over the White House?

Damn straight we were ready. Things needed a little shaking up by a different kind of Texan.

Lauri and I issued an invitation to a few female family members and friends announcing that two Texas Tarts had taken over the White House and would be mighty grateful to have folks join us on April 23, 2004, to celebrate our birthdays.

Unbeknownst to her, Allie Mae Tipps Weatherwax picked up the full tab for the weekend gala. She'd died exactly a year before our celebration and had generously bequeathed some money to me, one of her great-nieces. Allie Mae was a back-yard vegetable farmer, family historian and home economics teacher whose life of frugality turned to hoarding in her later years.

Despite a lifetime of behavior to the contrary, I believed that Allie Mae's heavenly spirit would be thrilled to have her money underwrite a party. Though I'd never thought much about healing through the generations before, it made sense to me as I thought about

Allie Mae, 1991

Allie Mae. I knew that family traits and conduct, endearing as well as annoying habits, moved from one generation to the next. Intuitively, it made sense that if any one of us shifted an entrenched family behavior, it could shift the influence of that trait in future generations. Dad and I had been able to shift what I presumed was a generational admonition not to talk to fathers about hard stuff, and I hoped our grandchildren-to-be wouldn't be caught there as we had been. Likewise, since money had flowed into my family, I wanted it to open up a channel for outrageous hospitality and hilarious stewardship, as Ministry of Money had suggested. Celebrating on Allie Mae's money felt like a way to honor her, the Tipps family, my mother who gave me life, Lauri and me, our daughters, Laura and Katrina, and our friends. I wanted to see if play and extravagance, two things not particularly valued in my family, could stir things up in me and mend the legacy of ancestors like Allie Mae.

Wondering what had been written about generational healing, I discovered the work of Barbara McClintock. Allie Mae and Dr. McClintock were contemporaries and both loved vegetable plants. Dr. McClintock had won the 1983 Nobel Prize for her discovery that stress to a corn plant caused genes to change their position on the chromosomes. She proved that genes, the genetic building blocks passed through the generations, were mutable and could be changed. If this change could happen due to stress, I presumed it could also happen due to a positive stimulus. It appeared to me that generational healing through changes in our DNA was scientifically possible. Lauri and I set out to see if an extravagant gift flowing from Allie Mae to me to our celebration could bring about healing for us and our families.

For our women friends and family, the party was luxurious and free. The only requirements were spelled out in the invitations: do what you want to do at any moment; take care of no one except yourself; and have fun. I was just beginning to learn that such freedom could pave the way to deeper connections and joy.

After months of dreaming, the day finally arrived. The White House had let us choose the flags for the gala, so Lauri and I decided to flank the big-starred Texas state flag with the Stars and Stripes of the US flag on one side and the multicolored, World Peace flag on the other. All three flapped their greeting to us from their perch over the front door.

Sun filled the White House on this occasion of celebration and joy. All fifteen of us hugged each other in the huge foyer before the owners gave us directions to our rooms, most located up the grand staircase to the second floor.

Within the hour, the women began to gather in the parlor. They sat on the antique couches and chairs and browsed through the photographs we'd set out around the room. The few who had known my mother and had met Allie Mae poured over their photographs. People giggled at childhood pictures of Lauri and me. Jill and Karen took turns playing the grand piano in the corner of the room.

Wine and chocolates were offered as Lauri and I gathered the women together to officially begin our celebration. Here in elegance that I imagined rivaled the other White House, we honored Allie Mae and my mother, Sue, through stories of their lives. Lauri's mother, Carolyn Leaverton, was a friend of Mom's and had her own stories to share. Lauri and I told of our first meeting when I knocked on their door one August morning in 1968 and said that my brother had noticed that some girls around my age lived there. The rest, as they say, was history.

Over dinner, we continued to share stories about growing up, friendships and each other. We all, from maiden to crone, roared in laughter as we told stories of our first periods—including our mothers' guidance about that biological initiation into womanhood. As the hour grew late, some went to bed for a luxurious night's sleep while others played games and talked into the night.

After a breakfast feast, we each did what we wanted to—walks, visits, massages, shopping, naps. Despite a lifetime of taking care of my daughter, Laura, I found it uncharacteristically easy for me to trust that she could fend for herself. I wanted to follow my desires throughout the day.

In the waning afternoon sun, we put on our party clothes and gathered in the garden surrounded by flowers and trees. We sipped elegant cocktails and nibbled on exquisite hors d'oeuvres. Lauri was dressed in a stylish 1970s-era tie-dyed dress, and I wore my low-cut, long black dress—the only party outfit I owned.

Lauri, 2004   *Nancy, 2004*

Sharon Pavelda herself wasn't coming to this part of the party. In the ten years of our friendship, Sharon had often disappeared from the scene and returned transformed into one of her performance art characters.

After we were settled around the patio table with fancy drinks in hand, in walked the Rev. Dr. Toolie Rogers, dressed to the hilt with an auburn wig, sexy shirt, big jewelry and a bold attitude. She introduced herself and offered a blessing to our gathering: "Welcome to this table, all who have journeyed here unknown. Sit, eat, drink, laugh, for at this table we are one. This is for you, no strings attached. Here your heart can rest and know you are at home. Your name is Love."

A gift with no strings attached. A bold, sexy minister welcoming us all. A table offered for laughter and rest. Apparently, turning fifty was a blast.

The Rev. Dr. Toolie brought gifts, too. She offered Lauri and me a bottle of Old Vine Zinfandel to underscore the fact that although we were middle-aged, we certainly weren't dried on the vine! In addition, she presented the two of us with necklaces of huge "pearls," in honor of our ovaries. My mother had married in pearls. I had pearl earrings. I'd never before thought of pearls, exquisite gifts of the oyster—or plastic look-alikes—as symbols for a woman's creative energy, yet it rang true.

Lauri and I had been friends for almost forty years, but our ovaries had never been on the same cycle. As teenagers Lauri was jealous that my period started years before hers. By the time we met at the White House, I was four years into menopause, and Lauri's ovaries were still going strong. Though our bodies' ovaries were out of sync with one another, we both now sported identical pearl/ovary necklaces.

After a delicious dinner, we descended into the basement ballroom for more festivities planned by Lauri's sister, Karen. She divided us into three groups and instructed each team to choose one member to model a soon-to-be-created newspaper ensemble. Karen had photographs of fifteen-year-old Lauri and me, sporting clothes crafted from the daily newspaper. I looked jaunty wearing a high-necked mini-dress, complete with hat and go-go boots that Lauri and another friend had created.

When we were all done, we had a short fashion show. One team modeled a pleated-skirt outfit reminiscent of the 1920s flapper style. A more risqué team had outfitted their model in pasties and hip-hugger pants with a photo of George Bush in front of her own "bush." I wore my team's two-piece—i.e. with my belly showing—outfit with a newspaper "grass" skirt. We rolled in laughter at our creations that left much less to the imagination than those of our teens.

Once we were all in our cloth clothes again, Karen played a few Herman's Hermits songs on the piano. With gusto, Lauri and I sang along. We hiked up our skirts and danced the samba with teenager Lora leading us on. At one point Jill picked up a vase-of-tulips "microphone" and belted out her life-long favorite, an imitation of Petula Clark singing "Downtown."[3]

Life slowed down and was savored. Gratitude flowed. I never imagined that I would get to share women's freedom and joy with Laura, now eighteen and still in the senior-in-high-school-swirl of complicated relationships. Our worlds usually felt far apart, but there at the White House we enjoyed partying together.

Lauri's and my fiftieth birthday celebration had become a ritual marking the beginning of a new phase in my life, a freer life than I'd ever imagined possible. Allie Mae's posthumous generosity set the foundation for our whole celebration. As the women parted company on Sunday, my heart beat stronger, full of confidence and joy. I was ready for my second half century to begin.

John Mathys, age 50, 1942

Minneapolis, Minnesota

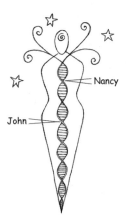

I turned fifty today but I'm in no mood for celebrating. The Nazis took over Belgium two years ago. It is the end of February, and there is still no word from my family. Jews are being herded out of the country into camps and losing their homes and businesses daily. Here in America, we are still reeling from the December seventh bombing of Pearl Harbor. It is just a matter of time before Jack and Ed enlist. Rumors have it that Japanese Americans all along the West Coast, including those from Salinas, our old hometown, will soon be herded off into camps and lose their homes and businesses, too.

In the midst of all of that, who would want to have a birthday party?

I am grateful that my work with Northrup King's home garden seed division is so critical to the war effort. I've helped develop a strong seed stock, essential to thriving Victory Gardens across the nation.[1]

I marvel at the string of fecund fields and quality seeds that have led me to this point. Opa and Oma's garden before I understood anything about soil or vegetables. Seed warehouses in St. Anthony, Idaho, and Greeley, Colorado. Fertile Salinas Valley with rows of lettuce and other crops. And now state-of-the-art garden seeds in Minneapolis.

Here at fifty, I am grateful that I've been able to spend my entire career with my hands, or at least my mind, in the fertile soil. In peacetime and wartime, the fruit of my work feeds people. Remembering that is my birthday gift to myself this year.

John, on a happier day, 1942

26

Following the Trail

We were both fifty. Howard had left his job at the university and was about to open New Paradigm Engineering in Portland. He had bold visions of rounding out the practice of civil engineering to include the effects of building or remodeling a home on such things as the local economy and ecosystems, social equity and health, and abundance for all. I had finally dropped my physical therapy license and wondered what was next.

Laura was next. In mid-September she had packed and was ready to head to the University of Oregon. We carried box after box of Laura's worldly goods up the stairs with other nervous parents and eager freshmen. "Leave (Get out)" blared from a CD player in a room we walked past.[1] Was that what Laura was thinking?

While I teared up at the poignancy of my youngest stepping into her own life, I was almost as excited as Laura. Howard and I had spent months planning our first empty-nester adventure. Soon after dropping Laura off, we flew east for a month-long vacation. We wanted to relax, see fall colors and mosey our way around the Northeastern United States doing whatever we wanted to do each day. I'd tasted that sort of spontaneity at my White House party, and Howard and I wanted to experiment with our first itinerary-less vacation.

After visiting with Beloved Community friends in Philadelphia, we got a late start heading into the Pocono Mountains. We were tired of night driving when a billboard directed us to Jim Thorpe, a small town wedged between steep foothills. Magnificent old wooden buildings, twinkling little lights and a huge grey stone Episcopal church lined the two downtown streets. We rented a room at the historic Inn at Jim Thorpe and dropped quickly to sleep in a comfortable antique bed.

After eleven hours of rest, we headed out to explore the area. Sun filtered through the yellow and orange leaves as they floated to the ground, some landing on huge piles of discarded coal tailings. Billboards picturing clean, smiling miners advertised mine and museum tours. These larger than life miners looked very different from the exhausted, sooty men I'd seen in photographs. Tourist signs and brochures told how the local Lehigh Coal and Navigation Company's mining had fueled the American Industrial Revolution, tamed the river and developed creative ways to get the coal to market. Soon Jim Thorpe had become home to over fifty wealthy residents—millionaires by today's standards.[2]

Each new piece of information brought up more questions than answers. Why was it that none of these historical accounts mentioned the disparity between the millionaire mine owners and the miners who, despite their smiling faces on billboards, had lived in poverty across town? Why was a mining town named after Jim Thorpe, a Native American man? Unexpectedly, our brief visit to this town began a journey that felt more like solving a mystery than vacationing.

A quick Internet search showed that Jim Thorpe had no direct connection with this area. He was part of the Sac and Fox tribe, born on the Oklahoma reservation in 1888. As a youth he attended Carlisle Indian Industrial School near Harrisburg, Pennsylvania, seventy-three miles away.

A tourist brochure spoke of parallel paths between the town and the

man. Both had wildly successful heydays. The town, originally called
Mauch Chunk, "mountain of the sleeping bear," was established beside a
mountain with a belly full of coal that brought prosperity to mine owners.
Likewise, the athletic genius of Jim Thorpe became quickly apparent at
Carlisle Indian School. Thorpe then competed in the 1912 Olympics in
Stockholm where he won gold medals in the decathlon and pentathlon.
Sweden's King Gustav V called Jim Thorpe "the greatest athlete in the
world."[3]

Then, the story continues, both the town and the man hit hard times.
When the coal market declined, Mauch Chunk's economy plummeted as
well. As for Jim Thorpe, a few years after the Olympics, he was stripped
of his medals when it was shown that he earned two dollars a game playing baseball during his summers off from Carlisle and thus had been a
"professional athlete." Thorpe continued to play in professional sports but
died penniless. His fame had dimmed, and his home state of Oklahoma
had no interest in building a monument in honor of his record-breaking
athletic abilities.

The year I was born, the residents of Mauch Chunk had built a monument honoring Jim Thorpe, the man, in exchange for the use of his name.
The town leaders hoped that the new name of Jim Thorpe, Pennsylvania,
in honor of one of the nation's greatest athletes, would help revitalize the
area. Despite this "honor," most of the sites that popped up in my "Jim
Thorpe" Internet search referenced the town and not the man.

Sitting at my computer, I kept reminding myself that this was supposed to be a vacation. Finally I stopped trying to figure it all out and
picked up my latest novel for some light reading. In the middle of *The
No. 1 Ladies' Detective Agency*, I met Obed Ramotswe, a man who had
just learned he would soon die of lung disease caused by his years in the
African mines. He spoke about working deep in the mines that threatened
his life by day and haunted his dreams at night. Obed remembered a song
the miners sang about how "the mines eat men."[4] Meanwhile, the white
mine owners stayed safe above ground and grew rich.

Truth had been spoken amid fiction as the worlds of African and
American miners intersected. My reading had taken me right back to my

questions. I laid my novel aside. Life was unfair. People suffered. It was hard to enjoy my vacation.

On our third and final full day in town, I picked up my *More than Money* magazine to take a break from history and read about current issues. I was drawn to a short article outlining several studies that found that one-quarter of the children in contemporary Harlem had asthma. Common triggers for asthma, it explained, were air particulates and ozone that were emitted predominantly by the thousand coal-burning power plants in the Ohio valley. Power plants ordered to clean up emissions ten years ago, still spewed pollutants illegally.[5] I'd never thought about coal before this trip. Now here I was surrounded by coal and its collateral damage—coal brought a fortune to a few and illness to many, both miners of long ago and today's children in Harlem. The coal legacy had continued, it appeared, with the costs and benefits divided along economic and racial lines.

In the end, my curiosity was stronger than my desire for relaxation on this vacation. Luckily, after twenty-eight years of marriage, Howard was used to this sort of thing. And at that point, he was hooked too.

I wanted to know more about Carlisle Indian Industrial School and why a young boy from an Oklahoma reservation ended up going to school in Pennsylvania. I spent the afternoon reading online facts and articles, following one link to the next. Jim Thorpe's tribe, the Sac and Fox Nation, long lived on the land that became Wisconsin, which meant that Ann Cahoon and John Mathys had grown up on land that once belonged to Thorpe's tribe.

In several waves of displacement, white-skinned settlers forced Thorpe's ancestors farther and farther south. In the end, the entire tribe was exiled to an Oklahoma reservation.

Meanwhile, Calvary officer Richard Henry Pratt, inspired by Hampton Institute, a school for Negroes, was getting excited about the idea of similar residential schools to "civilize" the American Indians. He explained his vision for these schools to the 1883 Baptist Ministerial Convention: "In Indian civilization I am a Baptist, because I believe in immersing the Indians in our civilization [in the same way Baptists use full immersion under the baptismal waters] and when we get them under, holding them there until they are thoroughly soaked."[6] Pratt convinced the US government and wealthy white financial supporters to underwrite the cost of these schools. He planned to take "Indian children from the reservations, remove them to a school far away from tribal influences, and transform them."[7] Carlisle Industrial Indian School in central Pennsylvania was the first of many off-reservation government boarding schools for Native Americans. In 1904, Jim Thorpe left his reservation far behind to attend that school.

My eyes hurt after two hours at the computer, and my heart chilled at the facts I was learning. Was this sort of behavior by men in power inevitable? How had a Christian nation worshiped the idea of Manifest Destiny and thus felt entitled to take land that had belonged to Native American tribes for thousands of years? Where was the critical analysis of this behavior in our tourist or historical records?

All of my questions had become unsettling souvenirs from this part of our vacation.

As Howard and I drove away from Jim Thorpe, I slipped into a slower rhythm and focused on the scenery outside our car window. Questions still popped up, but I nudged my ponderings onto the back burner so I could stop trying to figure out that convoluted historical saga and instead enjoy my vacation moseying through Vermont, New Hampshire and Maine.

We followed the trail of our moods and curiosity, stopping when we wanted, driving in circles some days and covering miles on others. I turned my attention to the red and gold of the maple trees, cool breezes and the Red Sox coming from behind to defeat the Yankees in the 2004 American League Championship.

Never too far behind, however, was my overwhelming desire to understand how topics of race, class and power affected both my life and the evolving history of my nation.

27

A Diverse Portfolio

W hat Howard and I learned about money and power in Jim Thorpe, Pennsylvania, strengthened our desire to establish congruency in all aspects of our financial life. Our first step was to open an account with Albina Community Bank, a locally owned and operated neighborhood bank. Alongside opening our checking account and deciding how much to give away, we wanted to invest our savings in bold ways that supported justice and honored our planet. I was on the hunt for financial practices and pursuits that carried the scent of God.

Taking responsibility for our investments after my Ministry of Money workshop in the early 1990s had been a huge step for me. Yet classic, socially responsible investing wasn't enough for us anymore. Too many of the mutual funds in our portfolio still included stocks in companies that could best be described as "greenish." We wanted to have our money support businesses and work that improved our world, not those that merely did less damage.

The month after our return from Jim Thorpe, we were delighted to find Upstream 21. Before making a financial decision, this corporation looked at how doing business would impact two areas: the natural environment through sustainable use of natural resources and waste disposal capacity, and the human environment through employees, customers and suppliers and local community. This was an investment anchored within a business paradigm and principles we believed in.

The "parent" of Upstream 21, called Portfolio 21, was located in Portland. The company, and its mutual fund of the same name, focused on "environmental sustainability as a fundamental human challenge and a tremendous business opportunity." Though few investments were completely "clean," the Portfolio 21 global equity mutual fund invested in companies "designing ecologically superior products, using renewable energy, and developing efficient production methods."[1] Howard and I were excited to have such far-sighted financial advisors in our home town.

Working with Portfolio 21 got me thinking about investment in a broader way. The vast majority of our donations were earmarked for Be Present, Inc. and Harvest Time, whose work supported the transformation that Howard and I longed for in ourselves and the world around us. I invested time, insight and money into these two organizations; they invested time (and thus money) in me, sharing insights and teaching me skills to continue aligning my values with my actions. The flow of resources went both ways.

Philanthropy, a word associated with making donations, was defined as a love of humanity. Yet my experience with both Be Present and Harvest Time's Beloved Community had shown me that this act of love was sometimes very complicated. Too often a skewed sense of power and a desire for control flowed with the cash and thus impacted the expression of love. For me, money and power collided in my over sense of responsibility for an organization's financial situation; while appearing generous, I was influenced by an unconscious belief that I had the power and, thus, the obligation to be a "savior" of an organization. Part of me understood that money in my bank account also meant that I had more social power, and I was uncomfortable with that. Another part of me knew that I did have a spiritual responsibility to invest in the people and organizations I had been called to support.

Now that I saw my "savior" thoughts clearly, they didn't just disappear. I chose to continue to dig for their roots because I'd learned that otherwise they would show up sideways, continuing to influence me to behave in ways contrary to my values.

The Beloved Community explored the implications of Jesus's statement that a camel could slip through the eye of a needle easier than a rich person could enter the Kingdom of God. I understood that Jesus was highlighting the true difficulty of having financial wealth in a culture—two thousand years ago or today—where money easily intertwined with status, power, privilege and greed. Instead of excluding the rich from God's Kingdom, Jesus offered reassurance that anything was possible with God. Rooted in the belief that our relationship with money was a spiritual issue, the Beloved Community became a critical place for Howard and me to bring our portfolios in line with heart and spirit. I needed a strong community or two to hold me as I opened up these challenging issues. And sometimes I needed to support others.

Be Present's Capacity Building Campaign Team (CBCT) was a part of the organization's Vision Based Social Change Fundraising Committee. The CBCT was composed of women who defined themselves as wealthy. Be Present wanted to give wealthy people an opportunity to work with issues of power and class in a supportive community of practice, while simultaneously raising the money to staff the organization. That way the financial capacity of the organization and capacity for inner and outer congruency of the CBCT members could be increased together.

When asked to join the CBCT, I was conflicted. I didn't like fundraising, yet I wanted organizations doing amazing work in the world to have an abundant money flow to support staff and programs. Lillie, Be Present's founder, had told me that far too often the human spirit gets taken out of the equation when money is involved, and I wanted to practice raising funds while remaining fully in my spirit. I also wanted to understand more about my own dynamics with fundraising—both giving and asking for money—outside my own personal distress and skewed cultural values and behaviors around class and power. I knew that sustainable partnerships within the CBCT and with individual and foundation donors would give me that experience. This work was an investment in the growth of my own capacity—spiritual and otherwise—as much as in our communal work.

For most of my life, I'd understood portfolio to mean a collection of investments and investments as limited to finances. I was beginning to see that "portfolio" meant so much more. I cherished my mother's art portfolio, filled with thirty-two years of her silk-screen and woodcut prints and photographs of her stitchery. Her talent and love of creativity that she so freely shared throughout her lifetime had begun to blossom within me.

Over the years, countless people and organizations had invested their time and talents in me. But a bigger question remained: How would I live if I remembered I was an investment in God's portfolio? For me, that was the key context as I decided how to invest my time, money and love.

I wanted my own portfolio not just to be page after page of numbers, but to reflect the value of people, time, talent, service, spirit, compassion and wisdom. Only then could I have a portfolio diverse enough to equip me for the journey ahead.

28

Womanly Arts

While preparing for our White House birthday takeover, Lauri and I had strolled through a shop called Healing Waters & Sacred Spaces. Although she lived out of town, Lauri had signed up to receive their weekly emails. A year later she forwarded one to me. I scanned through it quickly. My eyes caught sight of a description of four different rituals offered by "Earthmother" and massage therapist Candice Covington.

Earthmother?

Rituals?

I'd never thought of anyone as a mother of the Earth before. I wasn't sure what she did, yet I was clear that I wanted the ritual Candice had titled "Mountain Top." Somewhere in my bones, I knew this session would support me as I continued my exploration of portfolios and the ways money and power got tangled up.

When I arrived at Healing Waters & Sacred Spaces for my appointment, I followed Candice—a petite woman with big hair—up a flight of stairs into a cozy, candle-filled room. Spicy scents filled the air. We walked past the massage table in the center of the room to sit at a small cloth-covered table nestled into a corner.

Candice, 2005

Candice poured tea for both of us before handing me a deck of cards, instructing me to shuffle, then choose three cards and place them face down on the table.

Cards? Were these fortune-telling cards? Not understanding what cards had to do with my ritual, I nevertheless did as she instructed.

When I finished, she handed me a second deck and asked me to repeat the action.

Though I was unsure of what was going on, I felt as at home as I'd felt in the room of many colors at my first Be Present training. All was strange; all felt exciting with sacred opportunity. I sensed that a gift was about to be given.

When instructed to do so, I turned the cards over—first the Faeries' Oracle cards,[1] and then the ones from the Medicine Cards deck.[2] At peace in Candice's presence, I listened attentively as she interpreted each card's meaning for me. I was shocked that they spoke so eloquently of the ways I'd been writing my way toward understanding all that had been churned up during my time in Jim Thorpe.

Candice pointed out that the "writer" oracle card sat in the middle of my reading, indicating that I had an inclination for writing or some other creative medium as a way to explore areas that interested me.[3] Another card spoke to the importance of my looking for messages and patterns in nature and the little details of life.[4]

At the end of the reading, Candice said, "This is an amazing journey you are about to embark upon—your writing and spiritual journey join together like wine and fill the chalice of life to overflowing.[5] You, like the skunk card you pulled, are a woman with a strong scent of power—some will be frightened of you.[6] You will learn how to live with joy and hope on a daily basis as you grow to trust yourself and the divine, and grow in your belief in miracles."

Although much of what Candice said confirmed things I already knew, other things she shared gave me a fresh perspective. The cards indicated that writing might be a means for me to come to terms with myself: what I did and didn't notice growing up; the different ways I'd used power; and how I'd reacted to people and events around me. Candice made my work feel part of a sacred heroine's journey, one part of a larger pattern of change in the world. Contemplating an increase in joy and hope felt like a wonderful balance to my times of sadness and despair about all I was learning. Even being at the appointment with Candice felt like a miracle unfolding.

Next, Candice intuitively selected several essential oils—cajuput, rose, peppermint, clary sage and opoponax—to add to the massage oil. "This blend will support your pure heart with Mother Mary energy, clarify your Solomon-like wisdom, and strengthen aspects of the wounded healer, like Chiron or Christ, in you. In addition, this blend has a splash of deep, crone-goddess energy."

I was startled to hear this Earthmother speak of energy using Biblical examples, especially since Candice knew nothing of my faith path.

Before I prepared to get on the massage table, Candice asked me, "What is your intent for this session?"

My intent! How should I know? "I trust you to know what to do," I said.

Candice assured me that she would indeed follow her guidance, then gently asked again, "What is your intent for this session?"

I struggled to listen inwardly for a moment, just in case I might hear something I hadn't realized was there. I took a long slow breath and said, "I want to release the things that are blocking my sight, keeping me from seeing this work that God is calling me to do." I was amazed to hear myself speak exactly what I needed from this session.

"Wonderful," Candice replied.

At one level it was just another massage, and I'd had many over the years. But everything in those strange cards confirmed the work I so longed to do, and the scents in the oils seemed to open my senses and clear my thoughts. Each massage stroke kneaded this clarity into my muscles. Candice's ritual knitted my body, creativity, mind and spirit together in a new way.

I left my first session with Candice knowing that I would be back soon.

When I returned a few weeks later, I asked Candice how she'd started in this work.

Her eyes gleamed as she told me about mixing essential oils as a young girl. The secrets of plants, and their oils, had always fascinated her. She talked about plants with the same intimacy I'd found in the writings of George Washington Carver, who talked to the peanut and listened to its response. I wondered if Grandpa or my great aunts Allie Mae and Kate talked to the plants in their gardens.

While Candice and Carver had listened to plants, my work as a physical therapist had taught me to listen to the human body. I now remembered that when working with my patients, I often felt like my body wanted to offer me support or guidance in a particular way. Several times my mind had no idea what to do next during a treatment session, but I found my body leading or reaching to support my patients' movements and gently nudging them to take the next step forward, be it catching their balance in sitting, rolling or walking. Here in this exquisitely scented room, I was ready to receive healing touch and guidance, whether it came from a rational place or not.

By the summer of 2005, I'd also begun to work with Rosemary Beam, Candice's friend and colleague at Healing Waters & Sacred Spaces. Rosemary's purple-walled room had shelves and shelves of crystals and a velvety purple cover over the massage table topped with half a dozen soft pillows. Rosemary's treatment included Reiki—the same hands-on offering of energy that Wendy had used with Dad on his deathbed—and crystals.

Crystals?

My body's energy shifted under Rosemary's firm hands and beneath the crystals she placed on my body. After her session, Rosemary told me that she had spent most of the time trying to loosen and release emotions stuck throughout my body like food baked on a pan. Her choice felt right, as I'd had a hard time releasing my sadness about the vast, inhumane treatment of native peoples my research had uncovered.

Rosemary told me that I could release these pent up emotions in much the same way she had done during my session. I merely needed to imagine opening a door behind my heart and letting all of these feelings pour out into the Earth. When I felt complete, she instructed, I could energetically close the door.

Both Candice and Rosemary worked from a point of view that was wise and grounded in the feminine qualities of deep listening, creativity and nurturing touch. It felt like a much-needed balance to the more

Rosemary, 2005

traditional institutions in my life like school, church or medicine. The work of these two women was different than any I'd experienced, yet it felt as if I had come home to a long forgotten part of myself.

I began to gather my own collection of essential oils. Each morning I would choose one with which to anoint myself. Initially, it had seemed as if I was picking a random bottle of oil, yet often the energetic properties of the one I'd chosen were exactly what I needed for the day.

Navigating life with intellect and logic and those left-brained skills had served me well but left me hungering for the feminine. With Candice and Rosemary, I'd been invited to honor my gentle intuitions and intentions, receive guidance from cards and absorb support from plant oils and crystals.

I was eager to learn more. My trust in this woman's way felt tenuous, threatened by my inner cultural bias for concrete facts and scientific proof. I knew I needed to step away from institutions steeped in the status quo and give myself time and space to nurture the balance I was seeking.

With great trepidation, I took a sabbatical from Western medicine. After Paul's birth, I realized that I had a tendency to lose my ability to think and follow inner guidance in the face of the expert authority—the doctor. That had not changed.

Just before moving away from Klamath Falls, I'd declined to follow my doctor's advice. My annual pap smear showed irregular cells, as it had off and on for most of my adult life. Instead of waiting a few months and retesting, which had always resulted in a normal pap smear, she recommended I have a cone biopsy performed. Horrified that such an invasive procedure would be performed without retesting, I refused. My next pap smear was normal. At the same office visit, the doctor recommended that I have a bone density test. Knowing that I wasn't interested in taking hormones for the normal changes of menopause, she warned me that if my scan showed that my bones weren't as dense as they had been when I was twenty, the report would recommend hormones to improve my "condition." I refused to have the test.

I increasingly believed that the US medical institution as a whole was seriously ill. Doctors ordered more and more expensive tests for those who could afford to get them, while fewer and fewer people had access to even basic care. Those two facts collided in my body in ways that made me sick.

In addition, the influence of pharmaceutical companies in medical education and practice had resulted in the skyrocketing use of drugs for "healing." Cancer treatment facilities grew larger while little was done to stop the carcinogenic chemicals and products in everything from baby bottles to lipstick or to address the unhealthy manipulation and degradation of our food supply. I felt crazy participating in an institution that was part of such a system.

Still, the biggest problem was within me. I came to my senses after making a fool of myself in a dentist's office. I went in to see a new dentist, clear that I didn't want to have a full set of dental x-rays. I didn't mind x-rays when needed to check out a specific issue or occasionally for whole mouth checkups, but I'd had them fairly recently and didn't want to have them taken at that appointment. Nevertheless, within the first ten minutes, I'd agreed to x-rays of my full mouth. Two of the pictures were blurry, so I was asked to come back to have them re-taken. My irritation was growing, but I obeyed. One of those retakes needed to be taken again, and I exploded. I don't remember what I said, but I know that every patient and staff in the office heard my tirade. My anger touched everyone, but it was primarily directed at myself. I had violated what I felt was best for my own health and was furious at my inability to say "no."

I no longer trusted myself to listen inwardly in a medical office.

Simultaneously, I realized that I was in the midst of experimenting with alternative ways of healing, ones more centered in the womanly arts I was learning from Candice and Rosemary. With their support and my use of essential oils, I felt things shifting throughout my body, mind and spirit. I hoped one day I would be able both to honor my own knowing and to receive the wisdom of Western medicine, but for a while I needed to abstain from doctoring.

My inner voices roared their objections: *You can't be healthy without having regular tests.*

I knew I was seeking wellness, but the fearful warnings kept returning: *Doctors, not you, know how to keep you healthy.*

Concurrently, I took a sabbatical from attending church. I needed to step fully into the feminine aspects of spirituality that had been shoved to the side for two thousand years of patriarchy within the Christian church.

My inner church elders pronounced their judgment: *Going to church regularly is the only way you can stay close to God.*

Candice and Rosemary encouraged me to talk about my powerful encounters with Jesus. But the voices yelled out: *Don't be ridiculous, Nancy. You are drifting away from your faith.*

At my fiftieth birthday party, I'd made a commitment to begin to live life following my belly's inner guidance and not fearful voices that chattered in my head. I was grateful I'd now been given two excellent Earthmother guides for staying true to this commitment.

I was learning that divine guidance could come from anywhere. A magazine advertisement about protecting my assets for my heirs had sparked my understanding that all children needed to benefit from how I used my money. A few sentences in the photocopied chapter I just "happened" to find in the church library helped me understand the prophetic experience. Even my cat reminded me to slow down and luxuriate in warm afternoon sun. If guidance came from something as mundane as a magazine advertisement, then it could certainly come from the fruits of the earth—oils and crystals—and from Earthmothers who embodied feminine wisdom.

A simple email from Healing Waters & Sacred Spaces forwarded by Lauri held an invitation. Even without understanding what was being offered, I'd responded. A gift was given. The first step of a new adventure, I was learning, was as simple as that.

Elizabeth Tipps, age 52, 1870

Near Short Creek, North Carolina

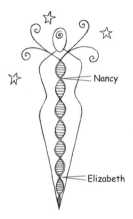

When I got home from the revival meetin', my heart was 'bout to burst but I still couldn't say nothin'. After I got to bed that night, I lay in the moonlight and dreamed.

> I was in a beautiful and lush garden. A big woman was bent over weeding. When she straightened up, her black skin glistened in the sun. She looked me clear in the eyes with a love that filled me up. Grabbing my hand, she started to show me 'round the garden. She lifted a purple flower for me to see the little yellow stripes down each petal. She pulled me over to the bright red tomatoes and caressed their smooth skin. She pointed out the big yellow blossoms beside the dark green squash.
> Motioning me to smell the red rose, she laughed when I squealed with joy. Row by row we went, noticing the colors, the textures—the bounty of the garden.
> She stopped and looked at me for a few minutes. Then she turned and motioned for me to follow. We walked through the huge garden to the very back. Just on the other side of a gnarly old peach tree at the

garden's edge was the strangest sight I ever did see.
There stood a row of people, their feet planted in the
soil. Young and old, tall and short, with every color of
skin and hair and eyes that you could imagine. She
stopped by each one and stroked one woman's hair,
another man's cheek—introducing me to this strange
yet beautiful row.

I was awed at the beauty and the variety of these
human "plants." Her eyes twinkled with delight. She
reached 'round and gently touched my heart, then
kissed me on my forehead.

I woke up feelin' strange. My heart warm like I walked outa' cold rain
pourin' down and into sunshine. Since then, life looks brighter to me! In
my dream, the whole world was a garden, full and ripe. There was a bunch
of different things jus' growin' and bustin' out all over. Never told nobody
'bout that dream 'cause they wouldn't understand it no ways. They wouldn't
understan' how I see coloreds different now.

Now, when I pray, the Lord I'm a talkin' to looks jus' like that woman in
the garden—black as night with smilin' eyes.

29

The Trail Leads Back Home

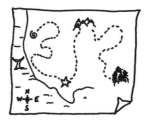

Months after our empty nest vacation to the Northeast, I was still hooked. I couldn't stop trying to understand the dynamics of race, class and power that I'd glimpsed in Jim Thorpe, Pennsylvania.

I wanted to write my way to understanding, then bridge some of these gaps between the world and me. Twice a week I took my computer and notes and headed to the downtown Portland library's Sterling Room for Writers. Passing clusters of homeless folks congregating in front of the library, and greeting those who caught my eye, I walked up the wide steps through the doors into the majestic old building. The massive marble staircase opened into the lobby much like antebellum plantations or Jim Thorpe mansions. Step by step, my creative juices flowed as history I'd once thought boring began to come alive.

I scoured the stacks, researching US history around the time of the coal boom in Mauch Chunk, the life of Jim Thorpe and general information on the issues of racism and classism. With a head full of facts, I'd return to the writers' room to sort them into some semblance of a story. This was a pattern I repeated many times throughout the day.

I was intrigued by the connections that surfaced between Jim Thorpe and my family. Mom wrote about the "Indian hostilities" that kept Lorenz Tipps, our family's original immigrant from Germany, waiting in Pennsylvania for twenty-two years before he proceeded to North Carolina. What had happened during those decades to the Native Americans in the Carolinas?

In the mid-seventeenth century, British settlers had moved into the land that was to become Virginia and the Carolinas with a bold dream of becoming wealthy farmers. They soon discovered that their best cash "crop" wasn't fruit of the earth. It was Native American slaves. Numbers vary, but it was estimated that between thirty-thousand to fifty-thousand Indian slaves were shipped out of Charleston, South Carolina, to the West Indies or New England.[1] The Native American slave trade continued for a century.

How could it be that I, the civilized and educated one, knew nothing of Native American slavery? The trail of facts I'd never known stretched out far in front of me.

Through continued battles, small pox epidemics, enslavement, destruction of some of the coastal tribes and treaties made and broken, the borders of the Cherokee's land shrank and their population decreased. The native people fought back. By the middle of the eighteenth century, the rebellions were squelched, and the Native American population diminished, thus reducing "Indian hostilities." Only then did Lorenz eagerly join the Southern migration to the land of his dreams. As he and his family built their farm, however, new conflicts began to brew between the settlers and the native people.

I stopped reading. I had a bad taste in my mouth and felt queasy. Several reference books, pulled from the library shelves, lay open on the library desk. I doubted the story would lighten after my ancestors arrived in North Carolina.

What was happening in the colonies as Lorenz's son Jacob grew to adulthood? What was the rest of the story about Jacob Tipps's Revolutionary War commander, General Rutherford? Though part of me wanted to run away as quickly as I could, my curiosity propelled me to continue my search.

A few years after tea was thrown overboard in Boston, the first corporate land speculation was under way in North Carolina. Daniel Boone's description of the amazing frontier in and around the Carolinas captivated the imagination of North Carolina's Judge Richard Henderson. Inspired by Boone, Henderson formed a private company, the Transylvania Land Company, and set out to gain control of twenty million acres of Cherokee land.

In the end, the land purchase was shaved down to two hundred thousand acres of Cherokee land, as the English colonial government in Virginia and North Carolina refused to concede the whole land sale.

I knew that corporations had a powerful influence in the US starting a hundred years later, but I had no idea that a company had paved the way for an even bigger land theft than what had been done by the colonial governments. Even without post-civil war legislation giving a corporation the same civil rights as a human person, the Transylvania Land Company was still influential enough to play a crucial role in buying land for a pittance. Again, I'd learned nothing about this in school.

Cherokee retaliation to this land purchase was swift. Under the leadership of Tsíyu-gûnsíní (Dragging Canoe), white settlers squatting on Transylvania Land Company acreage were killed. The Cherokee action toward the unauthorized settlers on Cherokee land was legal under the royal treaty still in place at that time.

Legal or not, the white settlers' retaliation under the leadership of General Griffin Rutherford was fierce. Rutherford was brigadier general of the North Carolina Militia, the backcountry component of the Revolutionary Military Force. He was given a regiment of two thousand men to carry out a counter attack. Lorenz's sons, including my ancestor Jacob Tipps, were among these soldiers. Their orders were direct: Destroy the Cherokee Nation. Together with militias of surrounding states, the North Carolina militia burned and killed its way through Cherokee territory. Thirty-six Cherokee towns were burned to the ground. Cherokee who didn't go into hiding were killed or imprisoned.

My family's side "won." By 1838 the Cherokee were forced off their remaining land and held in temporary concentration camps before being marched to Oklahoma along a trail of tears and death.

There it was, stark and horrifying. Generations of my ancestors had lived in the South where slavery, first of native peoples then of Africans, was considered acceptable. Living on land stolen from Native Americans. How could they?

I headed out to walk under the huge trees surrounding the library. The facts I'd just learned were worse than I'd imagined. Not just random white people had committed these atrocities; they were my family.

On that warm afternoon in mid-June 2005, I slipped into Tango Coffee Bar and tried to calm down with a mug of jasmine tea. I was frustrated with the land theft by my nation and family ancestors. Before I took the last sip, though, I realized that my ancestors and other early white-skinned settlers weren't the only ones who claimed Native American land for their homelands.

I did, too. Twelve times.

Every neighborhood of my life had once been Native American land. Because the land had been bought and sold many times between its theft and my living there, it had been easy for me to forget that I too lived on land claimed in the name of Manifest Destiny.

I returned to the library to find out which tribes had called "my" neighborhoods home long before I got there:

> Wichita—Wichita Falls, TX
> Comanche—Abilene, TX
> Comanche—Midland, TX
> Tonkawas—San Antonio, TX
> Atakapans—Galveston, TX
> Wichita—Fort Worth, TX
> Wichita—Arlington, TX
> Western Shoshone—Boise, ID
> Costanoan—Stanford/Palo Alto, CA
> Dakota—Fargo, ND

Klamath—Klamath Falls, OR
Chinook—Portland, OR

In addition to these twelve places, I was also connected to twelve thousand acres of land in the northeast corner of the Texas panhandle. This "neighborhood" was once home to huge herds of buffalo and Plains Apache then Comanche tribes. In 1876, after the buffalo were slaughtered and tribes exiled by white settlers, Roberts County, Texas, was established.

In the late 1930s my grandfather O.R. and a partner invested in an oil financing exploration. The deal failed, but O.R. convinced his creditor to give him a second loan for a guaranteed-to-succeed second oil well exploration.

This second deal was wildly successful. O.R. paid off his debts for both loans and had an additional forty-five thousand dollars profit. He didn't want to take the cash "due to the tax situation,"[2] so he and his partner made another offer to their creditors. They exchanged their "equities in these oil payments for a ranch out in Dickens County and the cattle thereon."[3] The creditors, O.R., and his partner all earned money in the transaction, and taxes were minimized. A few years later, in 1943, that ranch was traded for another ranch in Roberts County. O.R. and his business partner ran cattle on this land under the name of the "Indian Creek Cattle Company."

Natural gas and a little oil were discovered in Roberts County in 1945. In the 1970s, oil and gas prices jumped. As a result, more wells were drilled on the ranch. New wealth began to flow into our family just before O.R. Tipps died in 1979. Seven years later, in a legal arrangement that would have boggled the minds of this land's original human inhabitants, my family sold the surface rights to their land but kept the rights to the minerals beneath the land's surface.

I loved my grandfather. I admired his vision, his determination and his intelligence. Likewise, the owners of Pennsylvania's Lehigh Mining and Navigation Company and North Carolina's Transylvania Land Company had vision and were willing to take economic risks to set up their companies. Many of the things I had enjoyed throughout my life were financially possible due in part to O.R.'s work and business acumen. Unfortunately, success stories for men like O.R. rarely mentioned the cost to other groups of people and the earth.

I struggled with the paradox of admiring my ancestors and cringing at some of the consequences of their actions. I felt like I was living in multiple worlds at the same time. Creative writing and research were magical. One idea led to another. Hours flew by before I noticed. My emotions bounced from pleasure at finding an unexpected connection between history and my family's experiences to despair at the behavior of white settlers. I couldn't stop.

Jumping forward a generation, I also wanted to understand more of what African American slaves on small US plantations like those of Jacob Tipps had gone through. I read several books of slave narratives. From there, I began to read about the post-Civil War period. I discovered that life for free slaves only improved for a few years before the Jim Crow brutality began. After reading for a few days, I was again agitated and troubled.

Yearning for a change of focus, I picked up the handful of papers I'd written, trying to put together all I was learning. Settling in Costello's Travel Cafe with an extra-foamy latte, I lined up my pens—red for editing, yellow for highlighting passages that needed more depth and purple for new ideas that came as I reread the pages.

Out of the blue, a flash of nausea swept over me. I stopped momentarily and then continued reading. Before I'd read another sentence, though, I remembered Candice and Rosemary's advice, "When your body speaks, she has something important to tell you. Listen."

What was going on? Where was my nausea coming from? Was it related to what I was reading and writing?

My thoughts were too jumbled to figure anything out through words. Instead, I grabbed my journal and began to draw. A side view of my body emerged on the page. Red and yellow lines swirled together in my belly. This churning burst out of my solar plexus, down my legs, and filled the bottom of the page. Swirling, pouring, splashing continued to emerge long after my mind thought I should have been finished. When done, I stopped and studied my drawing. It looked like blood and pus flowed out of my belly.

Was something physically wrong with me that I needed to pay attention to?

I didn't think so. The wave of nausea had disappeared.

I reached for my manuscript and looked over the pages I'd just pushed to the side. A quick glance reminded me that I'd been perusing a long litany of sickening aspects of the human condition: greed, violence and arrogance. Slavery, families divided forever, brutality. Disregard for nature. Children taken from their parents and reservation and sent to far away schools where they were forbidden to learn about their native culture or speak their language.

What if these things had happened to <u>my</u> children?

The churning in the pit of my stomach returned.

Pus and blood. Shame and anger. Nausea.

I'd grown up with a strong work ethic and knew how to push aside my body's messages and continue working. This time, though, I was ready to stop and hear what she had to say. In the middle of the coffee shop, the impact of all that I had read finally became too much for my body and spirit to bear. I couldn't hold it in any longer.

The weight of it all felt like a boulder in my belly. My writing energy was gone.

Breathe in and out, I reminded myself. Slowly my muscles relaxed, and my mind's swirling slowed. Finally, I remembered.

Rosemary had taught me a meditation to release the psychic gunk that kept building up inside me. As I had been working with these difficult topics, a mishmash of judgment, sadness, anger and grief was again sticking to me, like food burnt on a pan.

Wanting to be outside to do Rosemary's meditation, I gathered up my pens and papers and walked to a nearby park. Lying on the grass, I relaxed and took a few more deep breaths.

I imagined mopping every nook and corner inside my body, scrubbing grief stains and scouring sticky shame. I kept gathering and mopping from my toes and fingers, then legs and arms, belly and shoulders, always moving in the direction of my chest. From there I imagined wringing the "dirty mop water" out of my body just behind my heart, allowing it to flow harmlessly into the land and into the heart of Jesus.

When I'd tried mentally to make sense of it all or shove what I'd learned back into the shadows, nothing had changed. Nonetheless, this simple meditation, an act of ritual and imagination, opened the way for me to walk right into the middle of big emotions and big topics, feel what emerged and glimpse a way to hold what I'd learned a little more softly so I could keep moving in the direction of healing.

A week after my emotions burst into my writing session at the cafe, I flew into Atlanta for the next session of my eighteen-month Be Present training. Each time I arrived in Atlanta, Kate Lillis picked me up. On the drive across town, we'd catch up on our families and lives, continue to build our relatively new friendship and get to know each other. Just as we pulled up into her driveway, Kate turned and asked me, "Where did you grow up?"

"Texas," I snorted with disgust. The harsh tone of my voice surprised me, but I was too excited to be in Atlanta with Kate to give it any more thought. Until later.

Alone, snuggled under the covers in Kate and Lillie's guest room, my body was tired, but my mind was wide-awake. I'd loved growing up in Texas, but my world expanded after I moved away at twenty-three. Year by year, I'd broadened my understanding of life. Simultaneously, I grew more self-conscious about my narrow childhood perspective, packaged in Texas-sized confidence.

Almost thirty years after I'd moved away from the land of my birth, under the covers in Kate's home, I was horrified to realize I'd spent many of those years trying to cut out the Texan parts of me. Around midnight, I also recognized a larger pattern: I'd long been trying to extricate other parts of myself as well.

When I finally noticed that we had more money than many, I was embarrassed by my family's upper-middle class and, later, upper class status. For a time, I wanted to give my family money away, not wanting to be wealthy in a world where so many had so little. Simultaneously, I wanted to keep all of the options that money gave me.

Likewise, I had recently realized how white my world had always been. As I heard story after story of experiences and perspectives of people with darker shades of skin, I wanted to rip off my white skin and the white-colored glasses that had kept me unaware of signs of racism during childhood and into my adult years.

The glow from the streetlight gave the room an eerie light as I considered other parts of myself that had faced the knife. It wasn't easy for me to admit being a Christian, either. Jesus didn't embarrass me, but far too many Christians did. Too often the radical heart of the faith was usurped by traditional US cultural values.

As a strong girl turned woman, I thought I'd avoided sexism. In the dark of night I realized that I'd been largely unaware of the ways I'd absorbed patriarchal beliefs throughout my life. I'd grown to respect my use of reason and logic—the skills honored in my family—and ignored my subtler intuition, gut and heart. I'd slipped unaware into the patriarchal way of valuing only one part of me. In addition, I was disgusted that it took over thirty years for me to discover how slowly liberation had come to my home state—married Texan women didn't even have full legal rights until the late 1960s.

I felt full of holes, like a hunk of Swiss cheese. So much of who I was brought me shame. Projecting that onto Texas and onto the United States of America at the height of her world power, I tried to increase the distance between myself and the culturally affirmed values I no longer accepted.

Were these holes I'd cut out of myself destined to remain empty forever?

Nestled in bed, cozy in Kate and Lillie's home, I was weary of apologizing, to myself mainly, for who I was. Trying to distance myself from my native state, my family money and everything in between had exhausted me.

In the following days during the training sessions, I participated in the conversation but always circled back to Texas in my mind. I talked with others about their feelings about the places they grew up. Within an hour of landing back in Portland, Howard and I were in our favorite neighborhood pub talking about Texas.

In the next week I began to put some of the pieces together. North

Carolina, with a history of stolen land and slavery as well as magnificent white oaks and black walnut trees, was a vital link in my family's "American" story. I had lived on the plains of West Texas and North Dakota, nestled against Idaho's foothills, on Stanford's campus in California, and in the high desert and then fertile valley of Oregon—all beautiful in their own right and all taken from a wide variety of native tribes and peoples of Mexico. On our trip through New England, Howard and I stayed in luxurious accommodations surrounded by trees in full fall colors in a town built to serve a few wealthy white men but named after a legendary (yet penniless) Native American man. This nation was filled with a blend of beauty and injustice—in Jim Thorpe, Pennsylvania, in North Carolina, and in my own life.

Be Present had taught me the importance of making room for everyone's experience. In the Beloved Community we were learning how to welcome all parts of ourselves, not just the parts that made us proud. I knew I was tired of being stuck and full of holes. I trusted that if I kept writing, I'd find a way to thrive and find wholeness right in the middle of the mess and the miracle of my life.

30

Money Made Howard Stupid

One fall morning in 2005, Howard headed to his office to continue his civil engineering work on several small home remodels. That evening he stepped through the front door, dropped his backpack onto the chair and announced, "Money makes you stupid."

This was no broad, societal judgment. The more money we had in our portfolio, the more he worried that we wouldn't have enough and the less confidence he had in his own professional ability to earn a living wage if an economic collapse wiped out our accounts.

Howard was fascinated by the way his fears looked for holes in his wisdom and fought hard to win control of his mind. His fearful voices fought like a loud, chaotic gang, determined to win. His wise voices were quieter, more resonant and fewer in number.

Late into the night, drinking a pint of beer, eating dinner, washing dishes and relaxing on the couch, we tried to understand the two different voices that had battled in Howard's head. And the ones that fought in mine.

Howard named the "supposed-to's" he'd heard that encouraged his menacing mind gang. For instance, online retirement planning formulas estimated that we'd need several million dollars in savings to ensure a comfortable retirement. This "fact" only confirmed Howard's fears that we'd given away too much money and consequently wouldn't have enough to live comfortably in our golden years.

After considering old age shortfalls, he moved to disasters. The news was full of catastrophes that had devastated other families. Would we have enough to pay for an accident or multiple accidents that just might happen to us? Had we kept enough to weather an economic crash? Would we have enough to financially support Paul and Laura if a catastrophe hit in their lives?

If I focused on these sorts of possibilities for too long, my fears and insecurities erupted too. Part of the reason I'd hated Howard talking about his anxiety was that I didn't want mine to start screaming.

In the face of wealth, Howard felt as if his own ability had shrunk. Suddenly money, and only money, held the key to our lifetime security. More often than before we became wealthy, half of Howard's mind believed that our money portfolio was the only investment that counted. He kept careful financial spreadsheets, hoping that one day the numbers would be high enough that his fears would retreat.

As the son of an accountant, Howard took financial responsibilities very seriously. Sitting on our living room couch as the sky darkened, Howard wondered which of his concerns were valid and which ones were caught in the compulsive money fears that gripped our nation.

I reminded him of our experience at "Levi's table" during a recent Beloved Community gathering, and we both laughed. One of the tools used in Harvest Time was to playfully listen to the parts of ourselves we had labeled sinners and thus excluded from the conversation about wisdom and money. We were following in the footsteps of Jesus who had eaten dinner with Levi, also called Matthew, and his tax-collector friends, despite the fact that the Pharisees and scribes thought Jesus had no business dining with such people. Howard's most recently identified sinner had been "Excel," who pontificated on the value of organizing life according to a carefully crafted worksheet.

"Spreadsheets don't lie as long as they are programmed correctly," Excel had said. "If everyone organized their lives within these columns and rows and kept them full of big numbers, all of our problems would disappear."

Excel was wrong. High numbers hadn't made all of Howard's problems, or at least anticipated problems, disappear. But the laughter helped us sleep that night.

A full week followed for both of us, so we put our conversation onto the back burner.

The next weekend Howard and I headed to nearby Laurelhurst Park. We walked round and round under Douglas-firs, giant sequoias, ginkgos and dawn redwoods. Beneath towering trees, it was easier to hear the softer voices that spoke wisdom in the presence of fearful stupidity.

We recalled that Sunday twenty-five years ago when we had agreed to heed the warning I'd heard from my spirit to step outside the American Dream. Though we hadn't yet understood what we were stepping away from or into, we'd begun a journey of waking up to the difference between our spiritual longings and the status quo. Under the trees, we realized we were still on that journey.

We also remembered how moved we'd been by that first Ministry of Money workshop, when it became clearer how our faith could influence the way we worked with our money. Over the decades, Howard and I had spent hours dreaming about the world we wanted to invest our money and life's energy into and how profoundly our vision contrasted with the current state of affairs.

The calmer, wiser voices we'd nurtured were clear that our security wasn't based on the amount of money in our private financial portfolio. Instead, it was based in our faith, in the strength of our community—i.e. the commonwealth—and in the abundance of life itself. Even if the bottom fell out of the economic system and the numbers on our spreadsheets dropped precipitously, these wise voices reassured Howard and me that we would face the crisis with our community of friends and together be divinely guided. Some of our friends already knew how to thrive on far less money than we could imagine, and we trusted that our collective best thinking and experience would help us figure out what to do.

We knew many marriages struggled when the two partners had different values and ways of working with money. For us, exploring these differences through the lenses of love and justice usually brought us closer together. Yet, during those periods when Howard opened the doorway to his money fears, we struggled. It was a dance we'd perfected and both disliked. He wanted to hold onto more money, and I reacted by building a wall within my heart to protect myself from his downward spiral.

This time, though, something different happened. Howard and I both had seen clearly the two different voices, in his head and mine, at the same time.

In the weeks that followed Howard's pronouncement, we tried to understand the bigger picture of what had happened. Some of the menacing gang of voices had come directly from the events of our lives, but most of them felt rooted in something much stronger and more pervasive—and related to the American Dream. We also wondered how the stupid, fearful thinking had increased in Howard's mind rather than decreased, as we had expected, after we had more money in our financial portfolios.

Some of Howard's extra angst appeared to be a direct confrontation of our bolder actions outside the culture's "best practices." While we had been clear about our donations and investing decisions, culture's voice remained inside Howard's head and screamed warnings that we'd given away too much. The values and beliefs of our culture hadn't disappeared.

In the midst of our questioning, I flew to Washington, DC, to visit Beloved Community friend Sharon Gerred and her husband Bill. Howard was busy with work and couldn't join me. Despite a tiring and delay-filled trip across the country, the three of us gathered around their kitchen table for a midnight dinner and a glass of wine. Our excitement rose as we touched on all that we hoped to cover during our visit together, including understanding what had happened to Howard as two different voices battled in his mind. We wanted to explore fears and faith, justice and reconciliation. Big topics at midnight.

Sharon, Bill and I knew that the battle wasn't Howard's alone. The three of us also longed to trust God's mysterious love and desired to live from a place of abundance, but our own fears of scarcity were loud. We shared about struggles with our over-commitment and busyness, and how we sought, instead, a rhythm of life that included regular Sabbath rest. Together we explored our choices by trying to reconcile our desire to be grounded in the welfare of the global community and the earth with the times we acted as if our wants were the only important ones. One topic bounced to the next.

Surrounded by a culture obsessed with saving for a future presumed to be filled with danger and never ending needs, we sought out ways to align with Jesus's teachings on living simply, while remembering that all people were our neighbors. We knew that we were addicted to the very values in our culture that we disliked, and we yearned to be free.

The next morning Sharon handed me Anne Wilson Schaef's book *When Society Becomes an Addict.* Sharon agreed with Schaef that the biggest addiction problem in our country wasn't individual addicts but the fact that society itself was an addict in serious denial that anything was amiss.[1]

I remembered years before I had been intrigued by Schaef's perspective in *Women's Reality: An Emerging Female System in a White Male Society.* Reading her book in the early 1990s was the first time it had occurred to me how profoundly my understanding of reality was clouded by patriarchy, what I now understood as an entrenched part of cultural addiction. Despite my thirty-something mind knowing that women were equal to men, I had struggled most of my life with self-esteem issues, particularly around the "ugly" parts of body, my "unfeminine" fiery personality and my compulsive sense of responsibility that required me to take care of others without taking into account the cost to myself. I had internalized the culture's sexist beliefs even though my conscious mind felt liberated.

I shared with Sharon how I had dutifully learned, and internalized, many of the cultural values I now struggled to release, such as, "Good girls are nice and quiet." I toned myself down as a three-year-old and still struggled to free my wilder and more creative side since I turned fifty. Given that my niceness was also valued in Christian culture, it had been even harder for me to follow divine guidance when I felt nudged to say hard, i.e. not nice, things.

"Do what the teacher says," I was taught in school. I wanted to be extra good in school, so I learned how to write within the lines, ignore my need to pee until recess and follow all of the rules so I would get good grades. In retrospect, I found that what I'd learned best in school was to follow rules and schedules and be obedient to the expert.

My teacher also taught us that hiding under our desks would keep us safe from a nuclear disaster. That neither children nor parents questioned this practice illuminated the depth of our mindless belief in what we were told, even when the instructions were ludicrous.

My schooling about the Native Americans had been presented through an art project focusing on Indian artifacts and architecture followed by a vague mention that the Indians left their lands. The heroes, I learned, were the white settlers who had to fight against Indian hostilities and savagery. Few adults in 2005 believed such a simplistic story, but tourist signs and brochures and too many museums still whitewashed the massacres and exile of the original inhabitants of this land. History, then and now, was taught from a white man's perspective.

As a thirteen-year-old school girl, I was given training about what it meant to be a woman—including the warning that I could avoid the disaster of a middle-age bulge if I practiced model posture at all times. I laughed with Sharon that my attempts at good posture hadn't prevented my middle-age bulge, after all.

I learned the fine art of acting like nothing was going on inside me. Not wanting to appear too emotional or be too vulnerable, I'd pretended I was fine. Never meaning to lie or be deceitful to another person, I'd thought I was being polite. That had happened in my high school Sunday School class when an earthquake shook the foundation of my faith, but I continued in the discussion as if nothing was going on. That sort of culturally expected behavior overlooked the power of vulnerability.

As Sharon and I explored addictive thinking, I shared with her

"America is not a Flag" by Sue

what I'd learned about Edward Bernays. He was unapologetic about his motives. Furthermore, his work represented the ways that manipulative power, twisting of truth, and financial gain with no consideration of the impact of these actions were at the heart of far too much US behavior. Bernays, I explained, not only developed a scheme to make our nation believe that Árbenz, Guatemala's democratically elected president, was a communist dangerously close to our shores, but also launched a campaign to convince women that smoking cigarettes was a step toward their freedom. Bernays called his campaigns "engineering consent," the art of manipulation wherein the public or individuals were kept unaware that manipulation was taking place. In *Propaganda,* he wrote, "The conscious and intelligent manipulation of the organized habits and opinions of the masses is an important element in democratic society."[2]

Bernays's campaigns made the American Tobacco Company rich and allowed the US government to violently influence world affairs, but he didn't seem to consider the benefit or cost to the exploited. Nevertheless,

Bernays was heralded as the father of public relations, and his approach was woven into the fabric of our institutions and society.

Sharon, Bill and I walked through the arboretum, visited the Church of the Savior's Potter's House bookstore and shared meals together. Our conversations continued wherever we were and remained unfinished when they dropped me off at the airport to fly home.

Shortly after I landed back in Portland, Howard and I sat at the neighborhood pub for dinner. I shared highlights from my conversations with Sharon and Bill, admitting that I'd returned with more questions than answers.

Receiving my family's money legacy had evoked Howard's and my fears and our desire to do it all right. We had inner battles and external disagreements about what parts of our thinking were full of wisdom and which parts were stupid and addictive. Simultaneously, we'd found rich connections among our dreams, our global neighbors, organizations dear to our hearts, friends and our marriage. Money may have made us sometimes think in stupid ways, but it had still proved to be a "doorway to spiritual transformation."[3]

Ann Mathys, age 67, 1957

Minneapolis, Minnesota

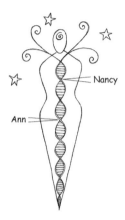

I felt like my life began anew in October 1929. John sold his seed business in Salinas, pocketed the profits, and we headed across the country for his new position—Vice President of the Home and Garden Division of Northrup King. John, our sons, Jack and Ed, and I arrived in our new home—vibrant Minneapolis—a city that sang with class and culture. I had finally returned to civilization.

With Gloria, our live-in help, doing the housework and helping to care for the boys, I was able to step into the niches of society for which I had been groomed all of my life. I Foxtrotted in the halls of the League of Women Voters, Women's Club, Republican Club, local Kappa Kappa Gamma Sorority Club, and Bridge Club (the latter included a private box overlooking the Minneapolis Millers ball park). I was thrilled to be involved with other women monitoring congressional legislation, educating voters, and lobbying my senators and representatives. In the evenings, while sipping our bourbon-on-the-rocks, John and I filled many hours with political discussion. I felt like I was in college again!

After the boys grew up, I traveled with John on almost every business trip, here and abroad. In 1956 we were part of a private agricultural mission inspecting crops of field corn produced from early hybrid seeds Northrup King had sold to Russia, Rumania, and Hungary. Little did we know our trip would end in a hair-raising escape from Budapest.

Things had been peaceful when we arrived. Later that night, however, on our way back to the motel after the opera, we passed army tanks filled with soldiers in complete battle dress. We woke the next morning to sounds of machine gun fire just across the bridge.

We were dismayed to discover that the anarchy of revolution made the American Embassy impotent. We were on our own in the middle of the Hungarian Revolution! Luckily the Europeans at the motel began to plan for our escape. A few days later we left in a convoy of fifteen cars, each waving a white flag of truce as well as an American and a Dutch flag. The one hundred and fifty mile trip took seven hours because we had to stop at checkpoint after checkpoint.[1]

A few weeks later, we learned that the revolution failed and thousands of Hungarians were killed by the Soviet crackdown. Never again will I take my freedom for granted.

Ann, circa 1950

31

Did My People
Survive Slavery?

My musical repertoire expanded through both Rose Feerick in Harvest Time, who loved to share songs that spoke to her, and the music that flowed in and out of the Be Present training sessions. Sweet Honey in the Rock's songs rang through both organizations as their lyrics embodied both spirit and action.

I loved to sing Sweet Honey's "I Remember, I Believe"[1] at the top of my lungs whenever it played on the stereo. As I tried to come to terms with my slave-owner ancestors, I attempted to imagine how these women's black-skinned ancestors had survived the brutality of slavery.

One afternoon as I sang along, my perspective flipped. I, Nancy Ann Mathys Thurston, didn't know how <u>my</u> people survived slavery.

Who was I to think that my ancestors—white-skinned, privileged people—had survived anything worth mentioning? My people were the ones who were free, who could come and go as they pleased, the ones who enslaved others.

The question wouldn't go away. Did my people survive slavery?

How was it possible for my ancestors to love their own children, enslave others' children in their fields, and not suffer deep spiritual damage?

What happened to the moral fiber of men who fought for our country's freedom and then held human beings captive?

Even when slavery was abolished, Jim Crow[a] laws were unjust and brutal. What was the psychological cost of my family participating in those laws, even if—as I hoped—they weren't personally violent or hateful?

What about me as a young person? How was I able to sing about God holding the whole world in his hands and often forget that the whole world included people who weren't all white like me?

Had I survived racism?

Maybe we didn't survive slavery. We'd sowed seeds of indifference, hatred, blindness, hardness of heart and violence. My family planted healthy seeds too, of course, but these destructive seeds were the ones most often overlooked in historical accounts. Believing that it was moral to own another human being, something white society seemed reconciled to, must have wounded my family's bodies, minds and spirits. I was afraid their long-ago actions had planted seeds that were now bearing the fruit of greed and domination across the world.

In my research on race in the US, I'd read about the Southern Christian Leadership Conference, formed by black church leaders in 1957. As my fears ran through my head, I remembered that their motto was "To save the soul of America."[2] They knew that racism threatened the soul of my nation and, I feared, my soul as well.

I wanted to understand. Sitting with my ancestral family's compliance with cultural immorality and my own blind acceptance of "modern" cultural mores filled me with shame. My Tipps family was Christian, and we had all promised at our baptisms to resist evil, injustice and oppression in whatever form they presented themselves. Nevertheless, my ancestors went along with the church's "baptism" of slavery, injustice and oppression.

Would I have behaved any differently than my ancestors had I lived long ago?

I wanted to know more about the years my ancestors lived in North Carolina, hoping I'd find some answers there. The only person I knew who lived in North Carolina was Alease Bess, my friend from a Be Present training. I wondered if her ancestors had been slaves in that state. Though we'd only visited once in the year since our training ended, I hoped she might have some information or a perspective that would help.

I brewed a cup of tea, sat down in the rare Portland, Oregon, winter sun that streamed through my front window and dialed her phone number. Alease answered from her log cabin nestled in Durham's pine trees.

After a quick catch up about our lives, I dove right into the middle of my story. I told Alease that Jacob Tipps, my great grandfather's great-great-grandfather, destroyed thirty-six Cherokee villages during the Revolutionary War and owned thirteen black human beings on his plantation in North Carolina. I told her I was haunted by dreams of Grace, the only slave mentioned by name in a family will.

Alease's family had indeed lived in North Carolina for generations. Her grandfather's grandfather was a slave. In addition, she told me, she was part Cherokee and Lumbee. She didn't know any of the details about her ancestors during the time of slavery.

"Do you think it's possible that our families might have lived on the same plantation?" I asked.

Both of us were quiet. I felt my heart beat faster.

My family lived in North Carolina for two generations, while Alease's family stayed there after they were freed. Despite the obstacles of post-slavery legalized racism, Alease's grandparents owned a thriving neighborhood store at the edge of their farm just outside Chapel Hill. The store was a gathering place for the surrounding African American community. This changed abruptly when the city of Chapel Hill took steps to build federally mandated public housing. Rather than construct this housing within the predominantly white Chapel Hill, the city government extended its boundary to include her grandfather's land. They immediately forced him to sell his farm, claiming it under the laws of "eminent domain." The city hired a local black preacher to convince their neighbors to accept the city's below-market offer to buy their homes, promising them an apartment in the soon-to-be-built public housing. Some of the neighbors were giving up small homes with wood heat and outhouses. For Alease's family, though, this deal required giving up their two-story home with central heat and bathrooms, a thriving private business and a productive farm in exchange for a public housing apartment.

Chapel Hill fulfilled its federal obligation while Alease's grandfather lost his livelihood, his land and his zest for life. The wealth and security of her family land did not flow through the generations as it had in mine.

While I silently pondered the differences between our families' experiences, I listened to Alease talk about Community Wholeness Venture, a ministry she'd founded. They created and taught "tools, strategies, and processes for very busy people to experience intimate, right relationship with God, with themselves, and with others in order to manifest the fullness of their purpose on planet earth."[3] Community Wholeness Venture did all of this through community plays, consulting and a mentorship program. To deepen people's intimate connection with God and to guide the way for healing, Community Wholeness Venture practiced a transformative form of prayer-filled foot washing.

The wider work of the ministry, Alease explained, was addressing issues of injustice and inequality, building bridges across differences, and creating sustainable communities through helping people to identify and develop their spiritual gifts, leadership competencies and collaborative organizing strategies.

The biggest obstacle, however, had been securing funding for the heart of Community Wholeness Venture—their mentorship program. Rather than working with a large number of people, as funders often required, this aspect of the ministry focused on mentoring a small number of people to become spiritual leaders through healing of body, mind and spirit, building financial skills, nurturing self-esteem and supporting the development of each person's unique spiritual gifts and leadership. The current participants were black women working their way off welfare. Alease said, "We can't change the world if we can't change ourselves."

I suddenly realized that each of the women in Community Wholeness Venture's mentorship program had her own ancestral story impacted and scarred by legal and illegal racism.

I felt God's hand at work bringing Alease and me together in ways I never imagined when I dialed the phone. I knew beyond the shadow of a doubt that my family—past, present and future—had mystically reunited with Alease, her family and the women she served.

Was the increased income that had just begun to flow into our bank account supposed to flow through us into the work of Community Wholeness Venture? I was too nervous to speak my jumbled thoughts aloud to Alease. Not yet. I needed to pray about it first, ponder some more and talk to Howard.

When the call ended, I shut my eyes and soaked in the sun's warmth. My heart pounded.

I knew that something that had long been ripped apart was being woven together during our call. This conviction didn't stop my mind racing to list all the reasons bringing money into my relationship with Alease was crazy. How could our income have anything to do with a larger plan for an organization like Community Wholeness Venture? Was l caught in another crazy scheme to feel better about my past by trying to buy my way into peace? How in the world could money given today have any relationship to something that took place generations ago?

A few hours later I spoke about the afternoon's events to Howard, expecting his usual cautiousness. Instead, he listened, then nodded. It seemed like a strange idea, yet it made sense to him too. Together both of us felt guided to step further into relationship with Alease and Community Wholeness Venture. We waited a few days to see if any other concerns emerged.

Those three days hovered in the thin place where daily life was just a breath away from the larger, divine movement in the world.

At the end of that time, Howard and I remained settled with our decision. I called Alease back and said, "We believe that we are to give to Community Wholeness Venture as an act of restitution."

Alease rejected my framing of the conversation in terms of restitution, an act of paying for deeds done in the past. "I am not interested in a partnership that begins with you trying to pay for what somebody else did a long time ago. When you act out of guilt, it diminishes our work together. Back then it was like somebody was over and somebody was under. If you are operating out of guilt, all that does is flip it around. Do you understand what I am saying?"

I did.

Alease explained that it was better for us to start to build a brave new world instead of trying to fix the old broken one. She spoke of the chasm that inequity, hatred and oppression had cut through our world and touched all life. Her words flowed into Ezekiel's, "The people of the land have practiced extortion and committed robbery; they have oppressed the poor and needy, and have extorted from the alien without redress. And I sought for anyone among them who would repair the wall and stand in the breach [gap] before me on behalf of the land."[4]

"Do you want to stand in the gap with me?" Alease asked.

Gulp.

"Yes," I said.

Standing in the gap together underscored the fact that our connection was about much more than money. Yet, I was still afraid about the money.

"But what happens if our income drops?" I asked her. "How will we know when it is time for us to change the amount of money we give each month? If we feel our donation needs to decrease sometime in the future, how will we be able to do that without feeling guilty?"

Howard and I had given money away all of our married lives but never this much to one organization.

Alease explained that we merely needed to follow God's guidance. Guilt, she assured me, wasn't from God. "Just do what God tells you to do."

Alease warned that Howard and I might feel the need to try to take too much personal responsibility for Community Wholeness Venture. Instead, she advised, "The best way for us to fix it for the people we love is for us to do exactly what God tells us to do. When we do that, everybody will have what they need. God once told me that if everybody would do what he told them to do, then the resources would just move around, and everybody would have what they need.

"You are to give now because you know that financially supporting this work is on your assignment plate," Alease continued. "God will let you know if that is to change or if it is no longer yours to do. If you are called to step away financially, God will take care of that."

Alease and I began a simple phone conversation, seated in our separate homes, almost three thousand miles apart. We ended up "standing in the gap" together.

Here in the gap I could see how I could fully live into the repentance I prayed God would accept each Ash Wednesday: "[F]or the wrongs [I] have done: in [my] blindness to human need and suffering, and [my] indifference to injustice and cruelty."[5]

Mixing money and friendship was scary, but standing in the gap went beyond both. This was a spiritual step, walking hand-in-hand with God who had called Alease and me to "raise up the foundations of many generations; [we] shall be called the repairer[s] of the breach."[6]

Alease and I had shared stories of our ancestors who lived in North Carolina seven generations ago. After we remembered, we were guided to stand together in the very places that had divided us for so long. We prayed that our willingness to work in this way, with God's help, would support the work of healing breaches in the land, in our communities, our families and within ourselves.

Alease, Howard and I stepped in the gap together. We sang. We believed.

Elizabeth Tipps, age 55, 1873

Near Short Creek, North Carolina

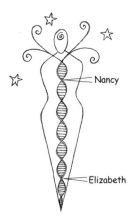

In some ways gettin' born again was the easy part. From then on, I felt truly loved—loved for the first time in my whole life—beautiful in the eyes of my Heavenly Father. But my family didn't believe I'd really changed. Given how I acted for so long, I understood why. Waitin' for them to forgive me jus' seemed like my cross to bear.

Some days was better than others.

'Specially since our money problems didn't stop when I got converted. Tenant farmin' is a hard way to live, and the best we hoped for was jus' gettin' by.

Family and friends decided to up and head out West. Our son Wilson and his family went to Texas. Forever. Hardest thing I ever did was watch them babies and grandbabies walk away like that. Musta been God holdin' me when I was wavin' goodbye, tears jus' a runnin' down my face. Look like the good Lord was showin' me how to be right on the edge of the cliff of sorrow and still see joy and hope.

David and I wanted to go to Texas too, 'cept we was old and his ma weren't well. So we stayed put.

Yesterday I was sittin' on the back porch in the afternoon sun, prayin'. Jus' as I shut my eyes, the Lord gave me a peek at our family in Texas. The grandbabies was half grown and crops 'bout ripe. They was all workin' hard, but there was a mighty good peace 'bout the place. The Lord tol' me that money problems wouldn't get them—no banks knockin' at their door. God liberated his people in Egypt, jus' like he did for mine in Texas.

I miss my family sorely. But I knew God was at work and ever'thing was gonna be jus' fine and dandy.

32

A Goddess Bursts
onto the Scene

The time between making the decision to leap and fully landing in the new had never been my favorite. I wobbled in the gap beside Alease, still unsure I was capable of trusting God to help me navigate ancestral history, money and friendship at the same time.

Seeking support, I scheduled a joint session with Candice and Rosemary. During the treatment, they suggested I take a month to listen to one God and one Goddess.

I liked the masculine and feminine balance of their invitation, yet I had no idea what Goddess I'd choose or how to listen to both the God I knew and a Goddess I knew nothing about. Goddess and God felt like one divine to me, yet my spirituality reflected a noticeable absence of the Goddess.

Rosemary asked, "What God and Goddess are calling to you right now?"

"Jesus is obviously the God," I replied. I smiled, knowing that I seamlessly moved among the three aspects of the holy trinity—God, Jesus and Holy Spirit—but wasn't sure if it sounded strange to Rosemary to call Jesus "God." She seemed unfazed.

I wasn't so certain about the Goddess. I had a faint memory of one connected to the hearth. I wasn't particularly excited about the thought of a homebody Goddess, but no one else came to mind, so I said, "Hectate is the Goddess."

Both Rosemary and Candice smiled and nodded. In our conversation that followed, it quickly became apparent that I hadn't said Hestia, the Goddess I'd imagined.

Candice told me that Hestia moved between the home and the temple, tending the sacred fires that burned in both of these hearths. In contrast, Hecate, whose name I had mispronounced as "Hectate," was goddess of the darkness at the crossroads between life and death. She reveled in the primal parts of life—fertility, childbirth, crops, death—and everything beyond the conscious realm. Hecate, Candice explained, was once revered, but later labeled evil by those who feared her feminine power.

Enjoying the sound of the name I'd mispronounced and liking a special touch that made her mine, I decided to keep experiencing the Goddess as "Hectate." She felt Texan and reminded me of generations of confident Tipps women. Nostalgic for my mother's unsentimental directness, I enjoyed Hectate's audacity.

Jesus and Hectate, I realized, embodied different aspects of the crossroads present at the heart of my life. The cross of Jesus held the intersection of the dominating cultural powers and the liberating love of God, where "the light shines in the darkness, and the darkness did not overcome it."[1] The crossroads of Hecate allowed sight in the dark, shadowy places of life, illuminating patterns and links in the mystery.

Though I'd wrestled with my understanding of Jesus during my late teens and early adulthood, Jesus had become my trusted inner guide, always close by and illuminating the path just ahead. With Hectate at his side, I felt shoved into the very places I'd been resisting.

The week after I first started listening to Hectate, I set out to Laurelwood Pub to read my newly purchased copy of *Coming Back to Life: Practices to Reconnect Our Lives, Our World.* One line jumped off the page, "Obvious parallels exist between the ways that entrenched power structures treat nature and the ways they treat women."[2] I slammed the book shut. From deep within my belly, I felt the beginnings of a primal wail. Frightened by the intensity of my visceral response, I abruptly left the pub and hurried home.

I'd never made a connection between our appalling treatment of the earth and the treatment of women, but my body knew it was true. I lay on my couch and pulled Mother's afghan over my head. No longer able to deny or avert my gaze from centuries of horrifying treatment of women and the earth, I collapsed under the weight of the disrespect, violence and degradation aimed at the bodies of women and the earth.

Many friends were victims of rape or incest, and I knew that the rate of sexual violence across the nation was tragically high. Almost universally, women disliked their bodies and were highly critical of themselves. I remembered hearing that St. John Chrysostom, author of one of my favorite prayers in the Episcopal liturgy, had also said disparaging things about women.

It didn't help to turn my thoughts to human abuse of our planet. Within the earth we had buried radioactive nuclear waste, dangerous for from ten thousand to one million years, hopeful that someone, some day would take care of it. We "tamed" rivers and polluted soil, water and air. The scientific method itself was based on Sir Francis Bacon's desire to dominate and control the natural world.

These few facts were enough to send me into a depression, but I was gripped by a more ancient fear. I remembered a story told by my great aunt Hannah Tipps, a committed Christian with an unshakable connection to the Holy Spirit. As a young woman she had taught junior high Sunday School in her small Texas town's Methodist church. She explored the power of prayer and spoke about the teens' protection by their guardian angels. She led them in prayer for the Spirit's guidance in everything from finding a lost baseball glove to handling problems with friends or family.

When some of the parents complained about her unorthodox (i.e. not Methodist) type of prayer, she was asked to resign from teaching. Hannah wondered if some people thought she was a witch.

As I contemplated my nudge to explore the depths of the feminine experience, I, too, was afraid of being labeled a witch. Intellectually, I knew that was nonsense. Viscerally, however, I was paralyzed with fear. My thoughts filled with images of ancient witch trials.

I'd lived through a few modern witch-hunts. I was born during the communist-hunt of Senator Joseph McCarthy and came into middle age in a nation on the hunt for terrorists. Fear of the "other" remained strong and pervasive in the US, but a far older fear consumed me.

Was it possible that my fright was rooted in the experiences of my female ancestors many, many generations ago and had passed on to me as concretely as my blue eyes and black hair? My feelings felt too big to be just about me. I wondered if hundreds of years of degradation of women had boiled within the anger I'd felt toward men and patriarchy in 1984 after I'd remembered what really happened with Paul's birth.

Even if rarely spoken in the moderate to liberal Methodist churches of my childhood, I had absorbed the beliefs that the body was fleshy and dangerous, pleasure was bad and alternative healing tools like essential oils and healing crystals were witchy and ineffective. I'd been taught to focus on things of the Spirit rather than things of the earth or the flesh. Yet for several years I had been following a path that welcomed the sacredness of my spirit and my female body and used gifts of the earth as well as prayer for healing and guidance.

I cowered as internalized voices roared. Even though these admonitions weren't spoken explicitly at church or home, the menacing gang roared loud and clear in my mind. Here I was again, hearing my culture's often unspoken rules about what behaviors or thoughts were good or bad or nonsense or wisdom—some that I didn't even agree with—shouting inside me. Breaking through these boundaries required strength and courage. I had neither. I needed help.

Suddenly my prayers too deep for words were answered. With the ears of my heart I heard God speak, "Nancy, you are afraid that rage will flow again as it did once before when you were forced to confront all that happened with Paul's birth. But you don't have to do it that way anymore. There is no reason to resist or prolong the process. Remember, the Spirit can be very efficient if you will open your heart and hands. Just step into this darkness, and the way will open before you."

These words rang true. I knew what to do.

Hopping up from the couch, I laughed at God's amazing ways. Now was the time to leave Nancy's fears behind for a while and playfully step into Hectate. I knew I needed bold women's music to help me step outside myself and into Hectate's shoes for a time of ritual writing. My old favorite, Helen Reddy's *All Time Greatest Hits*, seemed perfect.

Singing at the top of my lungs with fingers poised over my computer keyboard, I took a deep breath and waited. My fear and trembling disappeared as Hectate began to write.

Wednesday, July 12, 2006
Church night in the South

Dear Nancy,

Your singing sounds great. How polite of you to close the windows first. Still afraid someone will hear you and Helen singing together? Being loud still too wild for you?

It is good that Helen starts by singing "I Don't Know How to Love Him" from the *Jesus Christ Superstar* album.[3] That record was scandalous in church when you were young, remember?

Mary Magdalene, that slandered woman of long ago, speaks of her love for the wild man Jesus. She had no idea what came over her when he walked into her life. Jesus knocked your socks off too, huh? You, Mary M, and Helen sing together in perfect harmony.

Yeah, that man was different. Jesus held his masculinity in the way it was intended at creation, as part of the whole in which both masculine and feminine were valued. Damned humans had no idea how to deal with such a wild one. First they killed him; then the church guys tamed his message.

And, for the most part, the full stories about Jesus, Mary M, and all the other women never made it into the scriptures.

As Mary M quiets, Helen breaks out with another of your favorite songs, "I Am Woman."⁴ You and Helen roar well together. You belted out this song while you danced with the vacuum cleaner as a young woman back in Boise land. Funny how your wildness came out a bit when you cleaned house.

Welcome home to the fullness of your life as a woman. It took you long enough. Fifty-two years old is no spring chicken. The power of the lie is so strong it is hard for women to break through much younger. Especially strong, intelligent women like you.

Like many women of your time, you've lived out a strange combination of falling asleep and feeling invincible. You thought you could do it alone, right? At times you almost sank from the weight of your strength. You tried to play by enough of the rules that you could sustain the illusion of your independence from things as messy as sexism and patriarchy. You got a little constipated trying to hold it all in while not noticing.

Fuck invincibility and strength. They damn near drug you under a few times.

Afraid of the power of your anger, huh? Instead of stepping into the middle of your rage, you just wanted everyone to leave you alone about the big topic of gender. You and Helen wail about wanting to be left alone, but that is a lost cause.⁵

Trying to go to sleep did you no damned good. You and Sleeping Beauty took the slow-to-wake-up approach. Fifteen years one time, one and a half years another time. You were amazing—when you were betrayed or hurt or cut needlessly, you acted like nothing happened. I waited p a t i e n t l y for as long as I could, then took hold of your ovaries the first time when you FINALLY woke up that Fourth of July morning. I hung on for dear life. You had to let some of that rage out. It was building inside even as you denied its existence. Your little mind could believe anything it wanted, but I knew differently. Your rage needed to rip.

This society does its little jig, pretending everything is just peachy for everyone. You are living in an insane world. That is not the whole picture, of course. Life's beautiful, too. But it is the insane part that put you to sleep and is causing such havoc these days. Are you ready to wake up? Are you ready to open your eyes and see things as they really are?

The chains you've felt but couldn't see over the years still bind you. Your birthing body was viewed as defective and your middle-aged body is seen as passé. Cut a pregnant belly to hurry a birth and shame an aging body.

That's a shitty way to treat a woman![6]

You are terrified to go dive into the big topic of gender. Welcome. Terror that arises from within often indicates that this *is* the very place you need to go. Do you think this terror is a fluke and just happened to you? No, this is all part of the plan. The system that holds you in place is STRONG, seemingly invincible. You had an illusion of freedom—just enough freedom to keep you asleep. But the truth is that you and other women have been held captive and marginalized. Men too. Craziness like this imprisons everyone.

You'd better be angry. And at yourself too for not noticing for so long. I know it was part of the whole plan, but damn! How blind can you be?

In truth, you are wise beyond all telling of it. You just fell asleep as profoundly as Snow White did after eating the poisoned apple. You will be awakened when the fullness of God, the feminine and masculine spiral within God, kisses your own feminine strength. Waking will come when you are strong and courageous enough to walk right through the middle of the rage you feel for yourself and for all women. Even those women who believe they are as happy as clams.

Time, it is a wasting. Midnight's near, and it's hard to see the way. But I need you human women to WAKE UP NOW. You must claim your wisdom and live it in the world. If women continue to remain silent, there is little hope for this little planet.

Be furious! Let it propel you and others like you to fly into life. Do not fly into overwork, perfectionism, finger pointing—you know, the same old addictive shit. Fly into LIFE, at a life-giving pace. Do not *think* your way out of this mess. It is too far gone for that. Listen to your bodies with all of their glorious thick thighs and rounded bellies. Barbies alone won't do. We need the fullness of women of all ages, all sizes, just as you all are right now.

Oh, please! How predictable can you be? I mention thick thighs and you jump to thoughts of dieting. You and millions of others. Go ahead, forget the big topics and spend all of this emerging energy searching for the perfect figure. Whatever! Living is the best thing for your body and for the earth's body. Live big and round or tall and skinny, just *live* from your own unique body. We need YOU just as you are.

You were created with just what you need to thrive, to live fully. You were not created lacking. Quit acting like it. Believe in your greatness, your magnificence and your power. Yes, most of the current world institutions embody a distorted power, dangerous "greatness." Fuck that shit! You are talking about another kind of power. Don't be so afraid. Live. NOW.

Don't be stopped by the fact that anger scares the shit out of lots of men and women. It scares you too, remember? But that thick wall you built inside you for protection needs to come down. The world depends on it. Let the Spirit's fire burn you to a crisp. Don't be afraid. It will only burn what needs to go.

Jesus is thrilled to see you come alive again. He is definitely more patient than I am!

If you try to hold back, I'll drag this out of you. That will really hurt. So get on with it. Generations of women have your back and add their spirits to your breath.

Find that voice of yours, that WOMAN'S voice, and speak it. Living with only part of your wisdom is a luxury the world can no longer afford. None of us. Not men. Not women. Not trees or plants. Not rocks or stars. Not water or flame. Not air or animals or the cosmos.

Get off your luscious, round butt. Lordy, I have waited long enough for the essence of you to let loose in the world. Frankly, I am TIRED OF WAITING. Get on with it.

Amen, so be it, just do it, have fun along the way and all that. You are never alone. Don't forget, you have a heavenly posse leading the way.

Blessings, honey-bunchkins, Hectate

I laughed at the audacity of those words. Child's play full of crone's wisdom. Anger let loose for the sake of love and healing.

Hectate reminded me that life was more complicated than I could ever understand or control. In the face of that, I listened to my hot emotions and gargantuan dreams and found the courage to continue living in the middle of it all. Despite my resistance, despite my fears, despite my bursts of anger, I was ready to dive into what it meant for me to be a woman on this earth.

Humming along with Helen now and then helped me to remember Hectate's straight-to-the-point guidance and put a little kick in my step.

33

I Resign

Hectate kicked me out of the last vestiges of denial that I had any issues about being a woman. Now that I was ready to face the facts, I wanted to figure out how to embody the authentic feminine within me.

Be Present began its work asking black women about their lived reality. I wondered about the breadth of women's reality as understood by my friends. Curious, I asked female friends to speak of their experiences—the things they loved, the challenges they had faced and the places where they had been stopped due to their gender.

Cynthia Trenshaw, a writing buddy, responded, "Women friends can do planned ritual together to celebrate a life-passage or spontaneous ritual to celebrate the very moment we're in; we can be bawdy together one moment and be profoundly serious the next." I pictured her at her corner desk, pausing to look out over the bay to the snowcapped Olympic Mountains before she continued, "It's the women in my life who know how to BE." Cynthia and I had both been blessed by rich friendships with other women.

Others found parts of women's reality more challenging. Molly Thurston Parker, my niece, wasn't yet thirty when she started her own business. Molly explained, "I've often felt ashamed of or embarrassed by my emotional sensitivity. It saddens me to know that so many women suppress these feminine qualities of compassion and nurturing when they are exactly what our families, businesses and governments need."

Unlike Molly, it had taken me decades to understand that the conflict between being a professional and an individual with feelings wasn't just a personal struggle of mine. Women and our world suffered as a result of the culture's separation of personal relationships from work and emotions from intellect.

Lauri Leaverton, the other Texas Tart with whom I'd taken over the Portland White House, had never been one to mince words. She wrote, "I have been 'temporarily thwarted,' maybe; forced into detours, most assuredly; but I can't think of a time I've been stopped. I've been raped, beaten, spit upon, deceived, betrayed, robbed, propositioned, threatened and emptied. I don't allow the stopping. It's a pause, sometimes for years or decades, but then a deep breath and another venture, and no acceptance of permanent blockage."

I was moved by Lauri's response. Facing challenges I couldn't imagine, she inspired me to reflect on my own inner strength. I'd stalled, certainly. But I, too, had never been stopped for long.

When Howard and I joined our Beloved Community friends in March, I continued my inquiries. Over dinner and as we walked during our break time, I gravitated to the women and listened to their stories. Juanita, with her beautiful salt-and-pepper hair, a big heart and a strong connection to the Earth, shared a few books that had been helpful to her as she searched to find the feminine within the divine and nature. In middle age, she carved aside time for art and creativity as well as for grandchildren, family and work with *Street Light,* a newspaper written and sold by homeless members of her community.

When I asked Rose, her big green eyes widened as she spoke about her awakening during a Beloved Community gathering. For her, this feminine awakening involved all parts of her—body, mind and spirit—and she gained a profound sense of being known and loved by God, her Beloved.

A few weeks after we returned home from the gathering, Juanita called. She'd wakened in the middle of the night with a dream that propelled her to go to the computer and write her resignation letter. Juanita wasn't leaving something as simple as a traditional job; she was walking away from over-helping in all areas of her life. In the night's darkness, she knew she was done. She wrote the letter to inform her family.

Juanita's resignation shook me to attention. So many of my behaviors were based on old beliefs about being a woman that had sounded noble but, I'd begun to realize, had merely complicated my relationships with others and with myself. Clearly, it was time for my own resignation letter. Within a few hours of hanging up the phone with Juanita, I sat at the computer with determination and little idea of what would emerge.

April 25, 2006

I resign from the yoke of women's responsibility for almost everyone and everything.

I resign as the one who, because I am blessed with many inner gifts, is responsible for other people's mental, psychological and spiritual well-being.

I resign from the belief that others need my regular contact and care to prevent possible disasters (physical or psychological) in their lives.

I resign from the need to wear armor to keep me strong enough to shoulder this responsibility. I invite this armor to melt away. I want my back to be free to move and adjust with ease to whatever life brings.

I resign from the need to be hyper-vigilant, to see and anticipate others' needs or the outcome of absolutely anything that might happen. My eyes, inner and outer, are invited to relax and let images come to them freely. Playfully.

In essence, I resign as one of the female messiahs saddled with respon-

sibility that I could never hold. I resign from guilt arising from the inevitability of failure in accomplishing this mission.

I resign from the "good girl" sort of Christianity in which being nice is the ultimate moral virtue.

I resign from allowing imagined fears to draw a tight circumference around my life.

So many women before me have carried these burdens to their grave. Not me. I choose LIFE. A free life. A life spent listening to divine guidance on a moment-by-moment basis, falling down and getting up again.

As I choose to live on my own terms, I must also release others. I resign from my attempts to make others behave the way I think is best for them. Despite what I've thought over the years, I don't know what is right for others. When nudged, I will share and companion, but I want us all to be free.

I will show up at the sacred Table and at kitchen tables, feasting on that which brings life and leaving the rest alone.

Ironically, this way will allow me to be of more service to others than my hyper-vigilance or armor of responsibility.

I offer gratitude for the breaking of this burden that was passed on from my mother to me, as it was passed on to her from her mother and grandmothers. This legacy, shared by generations of women, is a burden dressed up as virtue.

As I stumble and dance into this new freedom, I believe, in a mysterious way I don't understand, that my resignation and new freedom spread to generations before me, around me and to those yet unborn.

It is done. Hallelujah. Help. Amen.

Nancy

Figuring out how to live after a resignation was another matter altogether. Part of me delighted at my new insights and freedom, but another part of me felt very irresponsible at the thought of stepping away from so many things I'd always assumed I was supposed to do.

How could I be a woman and be true to who I really was without those virtues that I'd clung to for so long? Would my friends really be okay without my hyper-vigilance? Would people still like me?

Stepping outside familiar patterns was scary. I held no illusions that my letter alone was enough to help me wash my hands of life-long patterns. I wanted to be part of a new legacy for women, and this felt like a critical next step.

34

Forgiveness Through Grace

After my resignation, I observed that neither the past nor present world around me had changed. My frustration with the racism of my ancestors and their culture still boiled. Knowing what I knew about the reality of Alease's and my shared history—or what Be Present called our "herstory"—I wasn't sure how to stand in the gap with Alease. I needed something more than research and information to allow me to fully participate in the partnership we both desired.

One February afternoon after a session with Candice, I knew what I needed to do.

Before I left, I told her, "I think I am supposed to go to North Carolina on a pilgrimage back to my family's North Carolina land with Alease."

Candice nodded in agreement. I shook my head, baffled at my clarity about going even though I had no idea what to do once I got there.

Within the week, I'd confirmed that Alease was willing to join me for the first part of my quest, and we both blocked off five days in mid-April for the journey. I knew I'd also return a month later to visit western North Carolina, prominent in my ancestor Jacob's military service.

Both feminine and Earth wisdom guided me. This was the first time I'd felt called to go on a spiritual pilgrimage, willing to leave with no idea of what I was supposed to do once I arrived. I needed to meet God on the land of my ancestors, trusting that transformation was possible.

I sought out Earthmothers Candice and Rosemary every week in preparation for my trip. Candice recommended I take rosemary, cajeput and black pepper essential oils for anointing the land.

Anointing the land?

"Oil from evergreen cajeput trees," she explained, "purifies and purges old rot and decay of emotion, pain, loss and fear and creates a fertile place to plant new seeds. As you step onto your ancestral land, you need some of this heavy-duty purification of the old. Rosemary will help strengthen and center you with its healing of memories, and black pepper will strengthen and fortify your cleansing."

Sacramental oils were used throughout the Bible for ritual and blessing. When Paul and Laura were young, we anointed the doorways of our home on Epiphany. Knowing that I wanted all of the spiritual and energetic support I could muster for this pilgrimage, I packed pocket-sized bottles of each of these oils, trusting I would know when and how to use them.

Friend and nature lover, Ann Linnea, came for a visit a few weeks before I left. I explained that since I'd always preferred the outdoors through a window, I was unsure what I was supposed to do once I arrived on the land of my ancestors.

Her answer was simple: "Don't try to do anything. Just look around, find a tree, and lean back against her trunk. Listen with an open heart. Then you'll know."

I began leaning against trees in my neighborhood. Breathing deeply with my back against the rough bark, something in my spirit began to settle. Rosemary had taught me to imagine releasing my emotions through the same part of my back that rested against the trunk. Against a tree, I felt a connection to nature in a way I had occasionally sensed during my visits to the rocky coast of Monterey, California.

I gathered maps of North Carolina. I wrote down the few details I knew about the location of the home of the original Tipps immigrant, Lorenz, in Salisbury, and the Dogwood Plantation of his son Jacob near Morganton. Union General Sherman had torched the courthouses that had held the titles to the land, so I had to rely on the description of the general location Mom had found during her genealogical research.

When I headed to the Portland airport to fly to North Carolina in late April 2006, I was packed, prepared and still furious at the actions of my ancestors. Anticipating being around Alease and the black women involved in her work, I recoiled at the thought of Jacob Tipps's slaveholding.

Alease and I had planned to spend the weekend in Durham before heading west to my family's land. On Sunday, I accompanied Alease to a Community Wholeness Venture core group meeting. That night, thirteen of us gathered in a rented room in a nearby church—three boys, one teenaged girl, and nine women. Twice a month, Community Wholeness Venture core group members came together for healing, support and leadership training in a circle where they were loved, touched, confronted and affirmed. Alease led the gatherings, but wisdom flowed from everyone. The young people, children or grandchildren of the women, were respected and their gifts welcomed.

For this particular meeting, the program was to be a service of anointing—a blessing given with a touch of oil—and foot washing.

"When we get our feet washed, we step out of our busy lives and into the presence of God," Alease explained to me before the others arrived. "For those few precious minutes, we can be transported to a place where everything melts away except us and God. We are in the presence of God and God gives us what we need or desire."[1]

Foot washing Community Wholeness Venture-style sounded different than my church's annual Maundy Thursday service, wherein this ritual was done in honor of Jesus washing the feet of his disciples during their last evening together.

The day's light began to fade as the ritual began. Three empty chairs stood in the middle of the room, with towels and a few bottles at their sides.

Ella, Laila and Karen, three women in Community Wholeness Venture whom I'd just met, sat at the side of the room. As part of the ministry's core group, they were learning how to strengthen their ability to hear God's guidance. Alease explained to me that God spoke to some in words, to others in pictures, to others in dreams. With practice, Alease assured me, they were learning to differentiate divine information from personal opinions or ideas. As part of their training, the women were praying to prepare themselves to hear God's message for each person whose feet were being washed.

Candles flickered around the room. Praise music played on a boom box in the corner. Conversations ceased as people prayed quietly aloud or silently. I felt my body relax into the couch.

Alease, Phyllis and Jayreza took their plastic buckets over to the sink and filled them with warm soapy water. The first to receive the anointing and foot washing were the three boys, Ella's grandsons. They sat down, removed their shoes and socks and waited quietly.

Each of the three foot washers first anointed the hands and head of the boy in front of them, stopping to whisper prayers in his ear. Soft prayers were heard in both English and in tongues, the prayer language I'd first heard thirty-five years before.

Phyllis lowered herself to the floor and began to wash Hason's feet. Soon Alease and Jayreza settled on the floor, put their hands into the warm soapy water and held Caleb and Jayleen's feet, respectively.

Phyllis began to sing as she lifted Hason's foot out of the water, cradled it gently and rubbed the soap into tiny bubbles. Time slowed to a luxurious pace as love filled the room. When the ritual was complete, the basins were taken away, cleaned and prepared for the next group of three.

I was in the third group, so while waiting, I settled into the couch and closed my eyes. My thoughts flashed to my desire to forgive my ancestors. Intellectually I knew that Jacob Tipps, like all of us, was a mixture of gift and mess. But in that moment, all I saw were my latest discoveries about the brutality on small plantations such as his, Native American slavery and massacres. I longed for a divine touch to bring the grace of forgiveness.

An image filled my mind's eye.

I soar through the sky, at one with the eagle beneath me. Wind against my face, I peer down through the tops of the Carolina pines into a large clearing. In front of a log cabin stands Jacob Tipps. His eyes scan his crops, the small slave shacks at the edge of the field and the gentle blue of the Great Smoky Mountains on the horizon.

I want to swoop down, land in the clearing and embrace him as family. But I can't. My heart clenches in anger. I turn away.

In a flash, I am back in Midland, Texas, 1965. I am a young girl, living in an all-white neighborhood, going to an all-white school and church. It hurts to see how much I don't notice. Yet I can easily see that I am so much more than my blindness. I drop to my knees and wrap my arms around my child self.

As I look up, I see my mother, Sue. She has been dead almost twenty years, but I see her full of life. She stands with a hand on one hip looking curiously around her. Despite those ways in which she is full of unacknowledged contradictions, it is easy to embrace her.

I hold her tightly for a moment. Our first hug in so long. I bend forward a little and relax into her soft body. Sighing, I glance up over her shoulder and catch sight of her father waiting just behind her. I chuckle, knowing how much Mom struggled to get her father off her back as a young woman.

Mom fades away, and I stand in front of O.R. He loved me, his only granddaughter, named after his daughter who died from polio years before. He was generous and wise. He was also sarcastic, driven and unaware of the many ways that he had used his white, male power to push his way to the top. I know that he was full of paradoxes, love and prejudice, yet I easily open my arms and embrace him in love. It is a stiff hug; hugging never came easily to him.

As our greeting ends, he fades away, leaving me in front of my great-grandfather, Arthur Tipps. Arthur, a lover of learning with only two years of formal education, who lived his life struggling as a farmer during the day and thriving as a reader at night. I open my arms and embrace him, a man I know only through stories.

As he fades, I look up to see his father, Wilson Tipps. Wilson moved from Tennessee to Texas when Arthur was two and died by the time his son was thirteen. His left hand pats my back, while his right hand hangs limply due to the gunshot wound he received during the Civil War.

The pattern repeats itself. Wilson disappears and I stand before his father David Tipps. We embrace briefly and stiffly. David and his wife Elizabeth's years of financial troubles with fourteen kids to feed had taken its toll.

As he slips away, I face John Tipps, born on the North Carolina plantation. He and his young wife, Barbara, set out to Tennessee to find their fortune. Instead, John died in the War of 1812. I embrace John as my judgment ebbs.

Jacob Tipps now stands in front of me. Grace, along with the other twelve slaves, his wife, Margaret, and their fourteen children hover in the background. My anger melts despite what I can see so clearly. We hug.

I sighed as the image faded away. My heart was newly open toward Jacob.

Opening my eyes, I looked around the room. The second group was almost finished. In the last few moments before it was my turn, I savored the glow of what I'd just undergone. I heard soft singing, gentle crying and water moving. I took a few slow breaths, grounding myself into the present moment and the room around me.

When beckoned to come, I removed my shoes and sat in the chair. Alease motioned me to put my feet into the warm water. I imagined this as the living water that Jesus promised would wash away my burdens and satisfy my thirst in a way nothing else would do. When my hands and head were anointed, I felt profound gratitude for God's sweet gift of forgiveness I'd just felt toward my ancestors.

Another image arose as Alease began to wash my feet.

I notice shards of a broken jar all around my chair. Then they disappear as suddenly as they came.

I am at the edge of a small clearing in the middle of a grove of Carolina pines. I steady myself by leaning against a tree as the power of this place saturated with years of prayer almost knocks me flat. A ring of trees in which I stand outlines a circular area that has been cleared, and the bare dirt is swept smooth. The top branches of the trees sway in the night breeze. A full moon is rising. The silence is broken by the night rustling of the animals hidden in the dark. Though I am unfamiliar with the forest at night, I am not afraid.

I hear footsteps rustling through the trees across the clearing from me. The moonlight first illuminates a woman's dress and the whites of her eyes. It isn't until she steps into the clearing that her black skin glistens in the moonlight.

Alease washing Nancy's feet

She stops a moment and stands tall, her spirit once again full and whole. This is the place where she comes to life, this place of hidden worship. She sighs, grateful to be home again.

Her hair is short and curly, cut close to her scalp. She is barefoot. Her dress, thin and worn, seems to flow as she sways side to side, moving to music only she hears. She caresses the clearing with her gaze, a place so close to the plantation in distance but a world away in the spirit. She stops abruptly when she spots me. She looks directly into my blue eyes, something not allowed in her daily life. She throws back her head and laughs, arms thrown high overhead.

I gasp; this woman before me is Grace.

Instead of the animosity and judgment I expect, she extends her hand, motions for me to come into the center of this sacred cathedral of the pines. She invites me to dance with her as she begins to sing:

> *High as de sky, wide as de sea*
> *God's hands holdin' me*
> *Holdin' me free*

She moves around the clearing, telling the story with her body as well as her voice:

> *Holdin' me in de clouds*
> *Holdin' me on de wind*

Round and round she spins, arms wrapped around her shoulders.

> *God's hands holdin' me*
> *Holdin' me free*

Grace takes my hands. We lift them together in praise, filled with love on this land where we never expected to find it. We twirl with her song, dancing with delight and awe. Releasing my hands, she runs with her arms spread wide.

> *Who can hold a spirit*
> *Dancin' like de wind*
> *Lightin' what it touches*
> *From a fire dat burns within[2]*

Grace comes back to me, and we interlace our fingers. Hers are hard and calloused, but her grip is tender. We sway together. We move apart to the edges of the clearing. Together we hold the center.

She hums for a few minutes before she begins to sing "Amazing Grace." We circle back round again and again. The presence of the Beloved, the one that passeth all understanding, dances with us.

Far from the master's church, far from my own church, we dance together in the real presence of that which is holy. I find the freedom to let my tears flow and dance my prayers, bare feet on dusty ground. Singing and swaying and praying with the Holy Spirit, our pain and my shame wash away.

> *I once was lost,*
> *but now am found;*
> *was blind, but now I see.*

Now there is room in my spirit for hope.

My tears mix with hers. Our feet are both covered with orange-brown dust. The land is healing. My broken heart is healing. Somehow, in a mysterious way that I can't begin to understand, it feels like our dance is healing wounds from Grace's life too. We whirl together, surrounded by the swaying of the tall pines. We dance as the full moon moves high in the sky and spreads her light around us.

> *'Twas grace that taught my heart to fear,*
> *and grace my fears relieved.[3]*

Our palms touch gently, arms held high. We move apart, holding each other in our gaze.

As Grace and the clearing slowly faded away, I heard Phyllis singing about the woman with an alabaster jar. Two thousand years before, Mary broke her jar of costly nard, scattering shards on the floor, and anointed the feet of Jesus. The lyrics told how Mary used her hair to spread the mixture of oil and her tears in an act of gratitude and love. As I sat with eyes closed, I settled into the paradoxes of love and broken shards, tears and dancing across the centuries from Israel to North Carolina to my own heart.

Alease lifted my feet from the water one at a time and patted them dry. She stood up and removed the basin of water. When I was ready, I walked to the couch to journal about what I had seen during my foot washing. I stopped to look outside the window. Just across the parking lot was a line of Carolina pines with the almost full moon shining overhead. Time flowed from days long gone to the present moment to generations yet unborn.

When the buckets were cleaned and all of us had closed our journals, we gathered around a table for dinner. Conversations were subdued as we ate sandwiches and digested all that had just happened.

Going from youngest to oldest, we each talked about what had been given during our foot washing. When it was my turn, I confessed that I had been stewing in anger and judgment against my ancestors for months. "But that all shifted tonight," I reported. I told them about how God opened the doorway for me to embrace my ancestors when I started with my child self and my mother and grandfather, two people whom I loved. Then I shared how Grace had invited me to a dance steeped with forgiveness.

When I was finished, Ella shared the message God had given her for me, "This is a time of new anointing for you. Soon your pain and tears about your ancestors' actions will pass. Only then will you be able to see clearly and accurately enough to tell the story that is yours to tell."

"Yes," Alease agreed. "You have an understanding that your ancestors, caught in the culture of their day, didn't have."

Laila added, "Something new and different is coming. I see a new house. And forgiveness."

Karen shared, "I was very confused when I kept hearing God say the scripture for you was I Chronicles, but then I realized that you are the chronicler of your family. The central verse for you was Chronicles 4:10. Before and after verses 9 and 10, this chapter contains a list of the descendants of Judah, the sons and the fathers of generation after generation. In the middle of the genealogy are the words, 'Jabez cried to the God of Israel, saying, 'Oh that you would bless me and enlarge my border, and that Your hand might be with me, and You would keep me from evil so it might not hurt me!'⁴ God granted Jabez's request and he offers the same to you."

I'd never liked the "prayer of Jabez." It had always sounded like a classic "American" prayer for expanded territory and personal protection. But as Karen spoke, I heard it as an affirmation. My borders had indeed stretched outward to include lands far away and times past and future. I never imagined that my world would be so broad. Like Jabez, I'd also prayed for protection against evil. Not just evil done *to* me, but evil that I might be doing with the same unconsciousness that Jacob had in his day and I had in my younger days.

One by one my ancestors embraced me. Forgiveness was given. Grace danced her forgiveness to me. I sat around a table wide enough to hold diversity of life experience, race, class, home, faith tradition, gender and age. People who had been strangers just a few hours before had become family. Lemonade and sandwiches had become Eucharist at its best. Thanks be to God.

35

Pilgrimage Back to My Ancestral Land

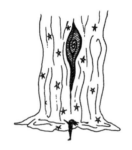

My body still vibrated with foot washing gifts of grace as Alease and I packed her car early Monday morning and headed in the direction of Salisbury. First, we were looking for the homestead of immigrant Lorenz Tipps, Jacob's father. Lack of exact locations on the map demanded a different sort of navigation, so we listened to the breezes and trusted that the Spirit would guide us.

Driving up and down country roads, Alease and I explored the area described in Mom's account of Lorenz's homesteading documents as "on Hagan Fork off Lyle Creek, tributary of the Catawba River." In that general vicinity, something faint but clear in both Alease's and my spirits indicated it was time to pull over, park the car and step out onto the land. A few fences marked off the field, but no homes lined this stretch of the road. Wandering in silence, we honored the beauty of the land and vastness of the sky. This had been Cherokee land for thousands of years. A few hundred years ago, white settlers named it Rowan County, then Lincoln County and now Catawba County. Political lines drawn in the dirt may have changed, yet the land remained whole.

Alease and I brought what felt like meager gifts—a few oils and prayer. I picked up a stick and scraped a cross in the hard, dry soil. Opening up the small bottles, I poured fragrant essential oils of tree, herb and flowering vine back into the earth. Their spicy scents rose like incense.

Over the anointed dirt, Alease and I extended our hands in blessing— hers pecan tan and mine a peachy tan. She sang of blood. I spoke of water.

Alease prayed, "Blood has saturated this land. History tried to shove these bloodstains under the grass. We know they are still here."

She leaned her head back and began to sing, "Nothing can for sin atone; nothing but the blood of Jesus."[1] As the last notes of the hymn faded away, she was silent for a few minutes. "Today a new blood is offered, poured freely into this blood-soaked land. This is birthing blood, cleansing blood flowing from Immanuel's veins."

I added my prayer: "Come living waters, come to this country soaked with generations of tears. Wash the land and satisfy our deepest thirst."[2]

When the anointing was complete and a rock left to mark the spot, we returned to the car and drove away. The reality of both of our ancestors' experiences remained unchanged, yet I felt lighter.

We stopped in town to break bread together and share stories sparked by the morning. Then, we headed west to track down the land that once was Jacob and Margaret Tipps's Dogwood Plantation.

After the Revolutionary War, Lorenz's son Jacob moved westward a few miles to Burke and Caldwell Counties to make his fortune. He staked his claim, worked the land and received the title to six hundred and forty acres. Jacob and Margaret had fourteen children and thirteen African slaves.

"Near the Morganton-Lenoir airport" was as much as we knew. Alease and I drove up and down the roads near the airport. Old Amherst Road wound its way to a new subdivision. We turned around and drove halfway back down the road. Once again, we both agreed when it felt like we had arrived at the right place, and we stopped the car. Stepping out, we walked through a break in the trees onto to the edge of a pasture. Ancient mountains had eons ago eroded into the blue hills that lined the far side of the field, while Jacob's plantation home and slave shacks had long since disintegrated.

Sitting on the ground, I picked up a rock. Once again I scored the hard earth and poured out the anointing oils as Alease and I prayed. Under Alease's gentle guidance I was able to release my skepticism and pray in tongues. Just as I had been led to the prayer languages of silence, intercession, liturgy and journaling, here in North Carolina I found my way home to the prayer that had so warmed my heart in Texas thirty-five years before. My words that poured into that land may have sounded like gibberish, but they were saturated with Spirit.

As my prayer grew silent, I stood and walked over to a white pine that might have shaded my family members when they lived here. Through her prickly bark, a warm tingling soothed my back, just behind my heart. Memories flooded back of leaning against the Mimosa tree in Abilene and elm in Midland—I'd been leaning against trees all my life but hadn't noticed it before. I imagined living water coursing through my body and out this very spot, washing away my burden. Grateful for my foot washing's illumination of the shadow and clarity within us all, I'd found healing of my shame and anger at Jacob. The sin of racism and slave-owning remained, but compassion flowed freely in me and out into the tree. Gazing at the smoky mountains, Alease stood at my side praying softly.

A white pick-up truck whizzing down the road startled me. Through the dust I saw a white-skinned man at the wheel, gun on a rack behind his head. When he caught sight of us, he did a double take. I assumed he wondered what we were up to.

Actually, it wasn't a bad question. What in the world were we up to?

We were there on a sacred pilgrimage, not to our spiritual holy land in Israel but to our ancestral land. Standing here in the gap together we felt the hallowed ground under our feet and prayed that healing would move forward and back through the generations.

The next day we headed for our respective homes. Alease dropped me off at the Charlotte airport to fly back to Portland, and she completed the drive to Durham. Through this shared pilgrimage, I had been given a way to honor my ancestors without forgetting that they also owned slaves. The land and our prayers wove the stories of Alease's and my families, their joy and woe, into a single fabric.

As I pondered our journey during the flight back home, I noticed a shift in me. For months I'd been stuck in outrage and shame, unable to stop being mad or take any action. Back in one of my ancestral homelands, I'd been given the gift of perspective and healing. Once I'd been able to let it go, I was ready to move forward.

I'd barely unpacked when I heard that Ann Linnea was going to offer a mini Women's Quest outside Boone, North Carolina, in early June. Howard and I had already scheduled a trip to Europe in mid June, so I decided to fly back for the second half of my ancestral pilgrimage before attending the Quest and meeting up with Howard at the Washington, DC, airport. Alease was busy for this next step of my journey, so I'd be traveling solo.

Preparing for my Women's Quest, I realized that I was going to sleep outside, alone, on the land. I'd long loved solitude and retreat, but always indoors. I wondered what this adventure would bring.

Armed with a backpack full of camping supplies and clothes for time on the road and my Europe trip, I flew to southwestern North Carolina. I arrived on the eightieth anniversary of my mother's birth, grateful that her genealogical work had paved the way for my journey.

I planned first to crisscross Rutherford's Trace, the route General Rutherford followed when he led two thousand North Carolina militia soldiers, including Jacob Tipps, against the Cherokee. The soldiers had burned Nikwasi (now Franklin), Tlanusi-yi (now Murphy) and thirty-four other towns.

I drove into Murphy as a few locals prepared for their Memorial Day ceremony. The rest of the town was closed. On a downtown street was a black-and-white North Carolina historical sign:

De Soto
In 1540 an expedition of Spaniards

led by De Soto,
first Europeans to explore this area,
passed near here.

Omitted was the fact that De Soto's expedition began the long and tragic campaign of destruction of the Native Americans at the hands of Spanish, French and English settlers.

I drove out of town and headed east on Route 64. Turning left onto Mission Road near the site of the old Baptist Mission, I stopped to buy an ear of roasted corn from a roadside stand at the edge of lush green hills.

What must it have been like for the white settlers after arduous travels over sea and land to arrive on this rich soil and start a new life?

What must it have been like for native peoples who had lived here for thousands of years to be ripped from their homeland to far-off Oklahoma?

I drove past a huge gold-painted metal cross, stuck like a sword into the hillside. That seemed like an appropriate image as the cross and sword had so often been intertwined.

Somewhere between Murphy and Haynesville, I pulled over to the side of the road and parked the car. Heading for a clump of trees, I passed an ignored, bullet-riddled "No Dumping" sign right in front of an old couch and a dilapidated washing machine. Not fifty feet off the road, I stood among trees beside a trickling brook.

I leaned against a northern red oak tree. Offering fragrant oils onto the fallen leaves resting on the tree's roots, I also poured out my grief at the actions of soldiers who had marched across the land.

I ended my brief ritual by praying, "Help us to honestly face this gash, this breach in the land and in our lives. Give us the courage to see history in all of its stark truth and to find a different way into the future, one that honors all of life and its diversity."

I turned and walked to the car.

Down the road, I stopped in Franklin, a town built on the ashes of Nikwasi. The Franklin Historical Museum's earliest artifacts were from 1817, the year white-skinned settlers claimed this land. Before I left, I asked for directions to the "mound," a flat-topped low hill that once supported the long house, a sacred Cherokee gathering place.

The thirty-foot high grassy mound of earth looked out of place at the edge of the business district. The Hot Spot gas station filled the corner across the street, and carpets were sold next door. In the middle of it all was one of the few Cherokee mounds still in existence. When the Cherokees first established Nikwasi, they gathered the dirt, brought it to the center of their village and carefully packed it into this mound. A long house, home of the tribal council's ever-burning sacred fire, was built on its flat top. Was this sacred building burned both times the white settlers destroyed the town, in 1761 and again in 1776?

I acted on impulse, not meaning to be disrespectful. I didn't stop to read the guidebook that reported the tribe's request that tourists refrain from climbing the mound. Instead, I heard an inexorable call to connect with the land and offer her fragrant oils and healing prayers.

I removed my shoes and climbed, spiraling my way to the top. Once there, I lay on my back, looked up at the hot sky and listened. When it felt like time, I sat up and offered healing oils to the mound. I felt as if the Cherokee would have understood the intimate connection between plants and humans, spirit and physical human/leafy bodies, and recognized the multitude of ways that gifts were exchanged in both directions. Words seemed extraneous in this place saturated with ancient prayers. When I felt complete, I slowly retraced my steps down the mound and back to the car.

Driving around the area, I soon found an inn on top of a hill right outside Franklin. I was the only one staying for the night in this stately old building with its impressive wrap-around front porch. My room had a high bed angled in the corner between large windows on both sides. The cooling breezes of dusk smelled like a storm was brewing as I drifted off to sleep and was transported back to the Cherokee mound.

The heat of the afternoon sun on my back fades into the heat of the fire at my feet. I sit beside a sacred fire atop the Nikwasi mound. One moment I feel alone here, exposed on all sides to anyone who passes by. The next moment the earth rumbles slowly and I begin to feel the presence of others. Slowly this gathering grows from across the ages, reaching to the highest heavens from deep within the earth.

All arrive as the final rays of the sun fade and the moon rises. The Cherokee council house that once sat firmly on this mound is long gone, so the stars form our roof. The town of Franklin has slipped away, and the ancient forest surrounds us. The sacred fire flares up and flickers its welcome, warming us sitting at its edge. The grassy mound supports us. We meet in the dark of night, this unlikely council from across the ages.

There are six of us sitting on logs at the fire's edge. My ancestors Lorenz and Jacob Tipps, sit next to Grace. Dragging Canoe, one of the Cherokee who used to live on his ancestral land that became North Carolina, finds himself next to Jesus of Nazareth. I complete the circle. But we humans are only a small part of this council.

Mockingbird watches from the low branch of a rhododendron bush. Usually quiet at night, she sings her story into the circle. Sitting on an oak branch is Owl, unseen but watching us carefully, asking, "Who, Who?" Raja, my grey tabby cat who died a few years ago, stretches out at my feet. The leaves of the plants rustle as they reach toward the fire. Far under the earth beneath us the rocks and minerals form a foundation for our council. The night stars twinkle brilliantly above our heads.

We gather together to listen carefully to what is said in many different languages and ways. Our specific experience on this land gives each of us a unique perspective. Now, from a place beyond time, we have much to say. And we have much to learn.

Raja gets up and meanders over to rub his fur against Grace's leg. She smiles and reaches over to scratch him behind the ears. He slowly, luxuriously, moves his way around the circle. In our Klamath Falls home he used to mark his territory, peeing here or there around the house to claim his space. Here there is no need for marking territory. Tonight all share this land.

A bit confused, I awoke back into my rented room, before the diverse council had spoken. What wisdom would they say to us today? Pondering my question, I loaded the car in the early morning light and headed due north of Morganton to Jefferson, North Carolina, situated near Tennessee and Virginia.

Through PeerSpirit, Ann Linnea typically led groups of people on weeklong treks into the wilderness of the West, but this four-day quest into North Carolina would give us a taste of the longer experience. Here on the land of my ancestors, I hoped that sleeping outside on our Earth—a planet that was around billions of years before humans did anything—would help give me the bigger perspective.

One of the dozen women questers, a North Carolina native, owned the farm where we camped. She was the fifth generation of her family to live on the land. Her great-great grandfather had bought it in 1830, about the time my family left North Carolina for neighboring Tennessee. Forestland surrounded mown grass fields. At night, the fireflies flitted about.

On our first day together, we explored the rolling green hills and the forest under a sky that fluctuated between light blue and dark rain clouds. When we came together in a circle at dusk, Ann said, "If one becomes utterly still, Earth speaks in language we can understand."

I was learning to listen. I'd only been camping a few times in my life and was beginning to enjoy being outside.

Late afternoon of our second day, we gathered around a campfire. One by one, each of us stood for a blessing before being sent off for twenty-four hours alone. When Ann called my name, I put on my backpack and headed into the woods at the edge of the field where we'd spent our first day together. Past white oaks, yellow poplars and ground cedar, I found a camping spot. Darkness was only a few hours off, and it smelled like rain. I hurried to set up my tent, finishing just as the drops began to fall.

Lying in the darkness, I wondered what the rain would have said at the council of my dreams.

A gentle beating of water on leaves outside my tent soon becomes the pattering of drops on the trees around the council. Rain begins to fall steadily from the sky, one puffy white cloud in an otherwise clear expanse. I laugh. For the past week I have been hurrying around trying to avoid the rain in North Carolina. Hurry to put up my tent before the rain starts, hurry to take it down so it stays dry, wait to drive until after the storm passes. I was acting as if rain was some sort of enemy. Now, sitting around this council fire, the rain again finds me. This time I relax back and let the drops splash on my warm skin, a welcome relief from the heat.

A drop of rain begins to speak, "The water that flows through your veins, bathes your tissues, flows over the earth, and falls from the sky is the same water that was present in Life's birthing. Water that was. Water that is. Water that always will be."

Dawn brought sunshine and summer warmth. The day unfolded without the normal breaks of mealtime since I was fasting on this portion of the quest. I tied a string between two trees, and began to knot the ends of cloth squares I'd brought with me. All during my trip I'd written prayers on the cloth so I could string the pieces up here at my campsite. Underneath the small, flapping prayer flags I laid maple and oak leaves and pine needles alongside a heart-shaped rattle and a few stones from home.

I was too afraid of getting lost to walk far from my campground. Lying on the ground, leaning against a tree or napping on my sleeping bag, I let my mind wander. I enjoyed the forest's beauty.

As evening signaled the approaching end of my time alone, I sat leaning against a tree and poured cajuput, rosemary and black pepper oil into the earth. From Salisbury to Morgantown to Franklin to this farm, I'd been on a pilgrimage carrying a spiritual offering of three oils, prayer and presence to this land where my ancestors had lived seven and eight generations ago. It mattered where I stood.

Here in the forest, I knew that I had changed along the way. My anger and judgment were replaced by compassion, allowing me to focus on making changes in my own life rather than resenting behaviors of people long dead. I was grateful to have spent this time in the place of my ancestors, fearing that otherwise I might have been stuck in my head trying to figure it all out.

Before I rose to return to base camp, I began to sing my favorite Taize chant, "O, Lord hear my prayer."[3] I wanted the internal shift I had undergone to reverberate into the land. When my spirit was filled with music and longing, I slowly slipped back into silence. The forest herself seemed to join me. The wind was still. Billowy clouds covered the sun.

Suddenly the wind blew through the leaves at the top of the canopy. Slowly, slowly the wind worked her way down to the ground, finally rustling fallen dry leaves at the forest floor. A tree creaked in the background.

Sitting on the ground, I was grateful to be on this land so close to where my ancestors had lived so many years before. Last month when Alease and I traveled together, we'd stood firmly in the gap together believing that we created something new. Now, on June 4, 2006, at Abundance Summit, North Carolina, I sat in sacred council with Spirit, nature and ancestors with unfathomable wisdom all around.

By the time our quest had ended, I was refreshed and ready for a few days of driving to sort through my North Carolina memories.

The next leg of my journey was a short stop at Sharon and Bill Gerred's home in Washington, DC. When I arrived, as was our custom, we visited late into the night. I woke early the next morning and slipped out onto their back porch with a steaming cup of coffee. Off to my left, I noticed a spider weaving a web on the fence. I was transported back to Franklin, North Carolina.

> *A spider swings down in the midst of the Nikwasi council, momentarily stopping the construction of her web in the branches overhead. When the thread grows still, she speaks saying, "I love to go into the dark spaces, into the shadows. It is safe in the dark. Just follow me. I will show you how to weave all of life, masculine and feminine, past and future, sadness and grief, light and dark into a glorious and strong web. My body holds the symbol of infinity, and my work shows the way there. Do not let your fear keep you away from the dark within or without." She scurries up the thread back to her weaving.*

To be home with friends who lived so far away. To be from a family with a strong pioneering spirit who also owned slaves. Life was indeed filled with paradox. I said good-bye to the Gerreds and headed to the airport to begin the final leg of my journey to Europe, the old country.

Howard and I flew to London before heading south to Lyndhurst, England, where he was attending a conference on eco-architecture. While he was in class, I explored the town and the woods and wrote about my recent quests.

Lying in bed in the light of the full moon, I was reassured to remember that I'd watched the same moon from my own window in Portland, the woods of North Carolina and inner city Washington. What would the moon say to those of us gathered at the council?

> *All is held together by a dance of attraction. This includes my round body, the rocks, the earth and each of your bodies. There is a pull within our atoms, our molecules and your living cells that keeps us all dancing together. In that way, in a mystery beyond all telling, this entire universe is held together by attraction. You can call it gravity if you prefer. Call it whatever you want.*
> *In truth, we are held together by Love.*

It was hard to remember where I was on the earth and in time. Luckily, Howard was there to help me navigate the flight to Italy where we met Paul and Laura. We all explored Rome then Florence in the middle of a heat wave.

Our final European stop was Tübingen, Germany, where Laura's freshman year roommate was studying for the year. This college town was near the "old world" home of Lorenz Tipps. Leaving the family behind for an afternoon, I took two trains and headed for his hometown of Billigheim, near Landau in the Pfalz region. The landscape around Landau looked remarkably like North Carolina. Lorenz had traveled a long way to find land that looked like home.

In Billigheim, churches, buildings and homes built before Lorenz left this land in 1738 still stood strong, unlike the settler's homes in North Carolina. I followed my instincts and sat in a park in the middle of town, beside the Queich River, with anointing oils in hand.

Lorenz had left behind a country torn apart by wars over church leadership and political power. He had left a place where leaders killed more women accused of witchcraft than anywhere else on the European continent. How had all of that German violence affected his family in the "new world"?

Two hundred years after Lorenz immigrated, his ancestral homeland was scarred by racial hatred and spilled blood of the Holocaust. The German Nazis tried to wipe out the Jews. The US settlers tried to wipe out the Native Americans. Unfortunately, the end of these wars merely left wounds and gashes unhealed. Violence continued to break out around the world. Was this cycle destined to continue forever?

I sighed and leaned back against a great maple tree. When I closed my eyes I heard Lorenz speak to us at the council.

> *In the old country, things were chaotic. War after war after war. Women called witches and burned for the 'good of the community.' Including my grandmother. After she died, we never spoke her name again.*
> *Death and fear, it seemed, were everywhere.*
> *I was bitter. Hard to farm in blood soaked fields.*
> *I was fed up! I left. It was hard to leave Mutter and my kleine Schwester Catharina, but I shook the dust off my feet and sailed away.*

This German legacy of wars and hatred was unconsciously brought across the ocean with the settlers. A new land, revolution, or the birth of a country hadn't been enough to change this violent inheritance. I believed that these gashes had to be addressed in another way—one powerful enough to end this deadly cycle and begin the possibility of new life.

With that end in mind, I made my simple offering of anointing oils and silent prayers. The scents of sharp pepper, savory rosemary and the faint camphorous aroma of cajeput mixed with the freshly mown grass and dusty dry leaves. I stood, looked around one last time and returned to the trains, then planes, that would take me home again.

Our human history with race, as with class and gender, had been harsh and divisive. But I refused to believe that fracture was inevitable, even though it continued today. I was beginning to trust my meager offerings and prayers to send out ripples through my life and through the generations to come. I clung to the reminder of Jesus that we were all neighbors. I also found solace in Be Present's clarity that when we were willing to do something different in the present moment, history/herstory changed. Anointing the land was one part of the change; waking up to how race, class and gender played out in my thinking and actions, and then adapting my behavior, was another.

Margaret Tipps, age 35, 1808

Tipps Dogwood Plantation, North Carolina

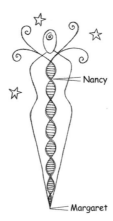

Today, on the second day of this New Year, my life changed forever.

I almost wept with relief when I looked through my kitchen window and saw the two of 'em riding towards the house in our wagon. Jacob looked so proud holding the reins, with a wide-eyed woman squatting in the wagon bed behind him. God heard the cry of my heart and finally gave me my very own slave!

I left the half-made kuchen on the counter and wiped the flour off my hands. I paused just a moment to offer a prayer of thanks. Then I stood up tall, pushed a few grey hairs back into my bun, smoothed out my calico dress, threw a warm shawl over my shoulders and stepped out onto the porch.

She came just before my patience collapsed into exhaustion. Finally. I am free.

Her skin is black as night and hair short. Her dress is thin and ragged, but I can tell she is strong.

Her name is Grace. And grace she is to me. Amazing grace.

I set up a mat for her in the small room off the pantry. Showed her where the cooking, cleaning and gardening things are. She takes orders and doesn't appear to be a dummkopf like some of them.

I can't stop praising God for his care of us. First the gift of this land, open and available, waiting for us. Then for the children and the love that still kindles between Jacob and me. And, finally, for the gift of these slaves.

Gelobt sei Gott who heard my weary cry and brought us Grace.

Grace, age 19, 1808

From Grey's Plantation to Tipps's Plantation

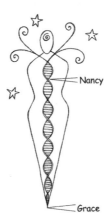

Year after year
workin' in Missus Grey kitchen
cookin', cleanin' and hollad at
dawn to dusk

De only thing I looks forward to
was de moonlight hours
with muh man
Clarence

Two nights ago
arms 'round him
heart warm
body tinglin'
legs round his
muh body brimmin' full

Master Grey busts in
jerk me away
laughin'
threw me and a rag dress
into de back of de wagon

Before dawn, bouncin' away
freezin' inside and out

Snatched
like a wild lightin' storm
rippin' grain from shaft 'fore its time
tears flow'n but silent as a mouse
scared de whip
would shred muh heart even more

To a strange farm
down de road a piece
with brother and sister strangers
poked, prodded
sold

Wanted to up and die
in de strange wagon
bouncin'
bruisin'
muh heart broken

Finally spent
I sat up and looks 'round.
der they was
from muh dream
blue mountains
Spirit smoke

Lawd
Why dis a'way?

In de middle of a
busted heart
Lawd's peace
warmed muh bones

Moment muh feet touched
her kitchen floor
muh toes was hot
Lawd done already been here

Wonder if she feels it too?

Home in dis place of
bondage
wonder where I'll be a plantin' muh seeds
of grace
in de garden?
over de hot stove?
in de white chiles?
in muh own chiles?
in de bathin' river?
heap of questions

Lookin' in de
pale blue eyes
of de lady
I sees generations of our families
she looks in muh eyes
and sees muh strong back

Which of us can see?
Which of us is free?
de good Lawd
is crazy as a coot

Who would have thought
muh heart could
be broken
and flamin'
between dawn and de settin' sun?

36

Women Speak

I'd left at sunrise to fly from Portland to Lubbock, Texas, in January 2007 to celebrate the ninetieth birthday of Great Uncle Red Tipps. His twin brother, Chunk, was to attend but at the last minute became too ill to travel from his home in Utah. Red, his wife, Hannah, and Shelby, the granddaughter whom they were raising, were my closest relatives remaining in Texas. The extended family celebrated with the mix of honoring and ribbing, storytelling and feasting that I'd always associated with O.R., Red and the Tipps family.

On the way to the airport for my flight back home, I asked Aunt Martha, "Tell me something good about Texas."

As soon as the words were out of my mouth, I realized that my disgust with Texas was alive and well. Apparently, little had shifted since Kate Lillis's innocent question, "Where were you born?" As much as I'd been trying to stop cutting out parts of myself, clearly I still hadn't come to terms with my native state.

Instantly, I knew. Just as I had returned to North Carolina the previous spring and summer, I needed to take a pilgrimage to the Texas lands of my younger years. I set the date to coincide with my fifty-third birthday in May.

Considering another trip to Texas and confronting my feelings about the state, I was grumpy. I lamented in my journal, page after page, hoping to purge my system of its gloomy criticism of everything I didn't like about Texas:

- *Huge churches too often full of cultural Christianity*
- *Pride, arrogance of things Texan*
- *Barrenness of the land*
- *Worship of sports*
- *Fear that Texan friendliness covered judgment and racism*
- *Texas history and the treatment of Native Americans and Mexicans*

It didn't help to get it out on paper.

The next month, just as the camellias were blooming in Portland, I returned to Candice and Rosemary for help. Through healing sessions with both women, I slowed down enough to begin to see my next steps. One Thursday just before I left Candice's office, she made a suggestion: "Why don't you listen to your female ancestors and see if they have anything to tell you about their lives that might help you today?"

I nodded and thanked her, all the while thinking, "But they're all dead. And how can I listen to my ancestors when I have trouble hearing myself?"

Talking about my ancestors stirred up memories of my grandmothers. I remembered both of them more by their silence than their personalities or actions. Troubled by that fact, I often wished I'd known them better to find out whether they were truly bland or if I just didn't know enough about them.

I couldn't sleep that night, realizing that my grandmothers weren't the only ones whose voices were quiet; I'd silenced myself more times than I wanted to admit. Words sometimes got lost as I tried to figure out when I should say what was on my mind and how to say it gently, respectfully. On that February night, it dawned on me that every woman I knew had silenced herself, often for a man. Not just push-over women, every woman.

Having once awakened to the ways I had silenced myself, I now realized how much I had silenced, or ignored, my grandmothers. Why?

I'd written my resignation letter and sometimes was able to live it. What sort of things might my grandmothers have wished they could have walked away from?

Grandpa Mathys seemed so comfortable around my brother and me. We walked through his garden, went to the county fair with him to see his prize-winning dahlias and visited with him over breakfast. By contrast, Grandma Mathys faded into the background. She aged faster than he did and eventually slipped into senility without me ever knowing what she had learned or valued.

During childhood visits to Wichita Falls, my grandmother Mano (Ruth Tipps) cooked, sewed or sat quietly at the edges of the conversation. She'd read to me in the evenings. But mostly, I worked hard to behave myself so as to avoid her sharp reprimand. By contrast, O.R. was bigger than life whether he was quoting poetry or pontificating on just about anything. Always a little on edge in his presence, I nevertheless enjoyed his attention.

What had happened in them or in me that made my grandmothers seem dim in my childhood memories? Why had I found my grandfathers so much more compelling?

Had the opportunities open to women in their day been too limited for the power of their intellect and the desires of their hearts, or did I believe that "women's work" was boring and not worth noticing?

I wondered if patriarchy had affected my grandmothers even more profoundly than it had affected me. Were my grandmothers sad? Did they have wisdom they wanted to share with me, had I only been interested? Was it possible that my grandmothers and their ancestors would be willing to speak to me now?

Thirty-five years after Ann Mathys's death and twenty-two years after Ruth Tipps's death, I was ready to listen. As the tulip tree outside my window was in full bloom, glorious even in the rain, I snuggled under the blue afghan Mom had knitted for me and read through her genealogical writing about both families. I contacted Milwaukee Downer and University of Wisconsin archives to get information about Ann's college days. I rummaged through boxes in the basement and located a notebook that held Ruth's hand-written, condensed short stories for her storytelling club.

I called Aunt Martha to see if she remembered anything about her mother, Ruth, and she shared a few stories I hadn't heard. A few weeks later Martha called back. She'd remembered a story about Ruth and her brother, Hope, transforming a chicken carcass into a feast for a visiting preacher one Sunday afternoon. I loved knowing that the woman I'd thought was boring had once been a young girl mischievously cooking up a prank.

I emailed my Mathys cousins. One of them, Jim, replied with a few of his memories. "I remember one funny story when I had long hair and Grandma [Ann] was giving me a ride home, which at this point in her life was a scary thing. We saw some hippies hitchhiking. They were longhaired and looked a lot like me. Grandma said, 'Now where are their parents to let them look like that and hitchhike? That is just a disgrace.'" Jim had grown up in the same town as our Mathys grandparents and had lively memories of both of them.

I'd already listened to Hectate, and she'd spoken her mind without hesitation. Would I hear anything if I listened to my grandmothers by sitting at the computer and waiting expectantly?

I decided to start with Ruth. As the candles flickered, I lay on the couch and breathed deeply. Quieting the voices telling me that this was a crazy thing to do, I prayed to follow Ruth's guidance as I typed.

Her story flowed easily. Ruth had lots to say. Some stories I knew; some took twists and turns. She was more complex than I'd imagined, and Ruth insisted her stories be included in my book.

The following week, just as the azaleas were bursting into color, I prepared to hear Ann's story. The University of Wisconsin archivist had found and sent me a copy of her master's thesis and a variety of school

and alumni articles that mentioned her
activities. My Mathys family memora-
bilia box held a tattered, cloth covered
theme book filled with handwritten
instructions for dozens of different
dances.

With the facts and family stories
in mind, I returned to the couch to
pray, releasing any remaining skepticism about this process. Ann spoke
and was resolute that I have her dance
book close at hand. She told her story
using dance and playful metaphors for
various parts of her life. I was excited
when she spoke of her love dance with

Ruth

John as the Tango—one that held
the power of their connection even if, as I suspected, they'd never really
tangoed. Lively and confident, she defied my memories of her.

A few weeks later Mom appeared. While my grandmothers wanted
to tell me several parts of their life story, Sue only had one new story

Ann

Sue

she wanted to tell me. Despite the fact that she had no problem speaking her mind when she was alive, Mom was a quieter ancestor than my grandmothers.

After listening to these three women, I played with the stories of my remaining Tipps women ancestors. Mom had gleaned and recorded details of their lives from family stories and legal records, but my primary source was prayerful listening. Of my long line of female ancestors, Elizabeth, Barbara and Margaret wanted to be included in my book.

The last woman to share her story was Grace, a slave of Margaret and Jacob Tipps.

Neither the veil of death nor the passing of years had silenced these women's voices.

Editing and re-editing their stories involved experiments with dialects. While I dickered with exact words these ancestors may have used, their central messages held strong.

I had so much fun imagining the lives of my ancestors that I wondered what my own story would be if I listened to my young self in the same way. Silenced parts of me began to bubble up in the language of myth and wanted to speak, too.

I lay on my couch and asked, "Who am I? What is my story?"

I hopped up to my computer and began to write.

Once upon a time, long, long ago, a wild girl was born onto this planet. She was made of flesh and blood all right, but she was also made of fire and water.

I laughed. Maybe blasting through life with the power of a steam locomotive wasn't the worst thing in the world. My myth continued.

Men drilled through the earth's crust, through the hard shale and into the gas-filled rock. Black oil and bubbly gas burst through the earth's surface, into the wild girl's feet. Scorching, fiery black gold, red blood and shimmering gas bursting with the power of the Spirit shot through her from toe to head.

The Beverly Hillbillies TV show of my childhood had called oil "Texas tea," and here it was flowing right through me. In this story, being born on Texas soil sounded mighty fine. No wonder I'd struggled with feeling boiling mad—the miracle was that I hadn't burnt to a crisp.

Luckily, however, as the earth's flaming blood pumped into her veins, cool water fell into her eyes from the heavens above. This same water once filled the ancient seas. These rains filled her body, mixing with the earth's oily blood in her veins. It was not a gentle mixing as steam poured out of her ears.

Maybe that's why I was drawn to soaking in the tub when I needed to center myself. Or part of the reason Community Wholeness Venture's foot washing was so powerful for me. And why I loved the process of anointing the land with a different sort of oil and imagined it combining with the living water of Jesus.

As the story unfolded, I was born looking a little different than most folks. I had beautiful eyes—eight of them. Eyes on the bottom of my feet, palms of my hands, over my heart, on my forehead and the two regular ones on my face. Though others may have thought this strange, my myth-self was clear.

She knew that once upon a time everyone in the worldly kingdom was born with lots of eyes like she had, but as things got civilized around here most folks thought it primitive to have so much sight. The doctor, for example, was concerned.

No wonder my eyeballs had been getting so tired all spring. I'd been trying to do all of my seeing through only two of my eight eyes! I loved seeing how my personality showed up on the computer screen.

It wasn't long before everyone knew that this eight-eyed steam girl was a Texan through and through: a wild, independent, bold seeker filled with courage, adventure and creativity.

Clearly she wasn't ashamed of any part of herself—steam, eight-eyes or being a native Texan. Why should I be?

Even so, the story unfolded, and her parents and the neighbors got concerned about this strange little girl. She needed taming. They found a cowboy to lasso in her six odd-eyeballs and tied them securely behind her two face-eyeballs.

Soon she forgot about the other six eyes she was born with, and tried to just see what she saw in the flesh, so to speak. That feat required an amazing amount of creativity and ignored a canyon load of wisdom.

Yet once the extra eyes were taken care of, her uncontrolled steaminess became a problem. Her folks found a beautiful skein of yarn from grandma's knitting box and began to wrap her up, for her own good of course, to contain the steamy outbursts.

Although the eight-eyed steam girl and I were one in the same, my story sometimes felt heavy and overwhelming. Her story, on the other hand, felt lighthearted. I was amazed at the difference a little shift of perspective and a dash of play could make.

My myth also alerted me that the time had come for me to begin to release my resentment of Dr. Lock and my oft-repeated litany of disappointments, betrayals and regrets. Looking back at my life through the lens of myth had opened up unexpected possibilities.

I also realized that some parts of myself that I'd tried so hard to change were the very parts that gave me character. Within myth, my quirks and foibles spiced up my life rather than spoiling it.

Grandmothers spoke across the generations. My mother surprised me with the rest of a story I'd heard only in part. My mythic self appeared in my/her steamy, eight-eyed glory. All of the women shared their experiences traveling from despair to hope. Each in her own voice. Each in her own way. I'd never had so much fun.

Barbara Tipps, age 31, 1826

Near Short Creek, North Carolina

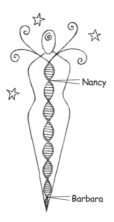

Jus' like before, ever'body left. Sheets cleaned. Blood washed away. Rebecca suckin' at my breast. She's beautiful. She's a gift.

Gift sure was painful to git though. Felt good at the beginnin', then hurt. Good now.

When I first knowed I was pregnant nine months ago, I cried myself to sleep. And I dreamed.

> *I was at a barn dance at Conner's place. I was pregnant, but nobody knew. People, lots of people, filled the barn with laughter and do-se-doing. I slipped out unnoticed, ran down to the river and collapsed, sobbing on the rocks at the water's edge.*
>
> *A woman, dark as night, walked out of the trees and headed towards me. Her left hand gently stroked the neck of a black panther. She was calm, but my heart almost pounded out of my chest. I sat still, barely breathing, as the woman and animal approached me.*
>
> *They stopped at my side. The woman looked me directly in the eye. Slowly she reached out for me. I hesitated, then slipped my hand into hers. Silently, she led me to the*

river and the three of us stepped into the fast-flowing water. Wrapping my skirt tightly around me, I took that first step.

All the while, the panther's golden eyes remained fixed on me. I knew the animal was trying to tell me something. I had no idea what.

The river flowed quickly by, but we could easily stand up in the chest-deep water. The panther dove under water behind me and abruptly knocked my feet out from under me. I would have screamed but the woman held me firmly, placing a hand on my back and guiding me to float. I relaxed and soon was fully supported by the water and her firm hand.

I sighed and closed my eyes. The panther came up close to me, opposite the woman. Slowly, gently she began to lick the tears off my cheeks with her scratchy tongue. Her breath was hot and smelled faintly of jasmine.

The woman began to sing in a language I didn't understand. It sounded like prayer. My heavy heart seemed washed of its burden, and I was filled with grace.

The panther dove under the water again and sharply bumped my upper back.

I woke up sittin' in the middle of my bed, scared and pregnant. My heart was poundin'. I got up, wrapped a shawl 'round me and went out to my rockin' chair on the front porch to catch my breath. The moonlight warmed my soul. After my dream, I was still scared, but I jus' knowed everythin' was gonna be okay.

I never told who the daddy was. Nobody ask, and I wasn't sayin'. I jus' kept goin' 'round to the church, to the fields, to town. Kept my back straight. Kept my head high. Kept gittin' rounder and bigger. Thought to myself, I'm not ashamed, and I'm not gonna act like I was.

This was my six time birthin'. It was easy labor. Lily and Sophia came to help. Rebecca was born on the same bed where she was made.

She's beautiful, sleepin' in the moonlight. Rebecca's my angel sent by God.

37

Pilgrimage Back Home

As May neared, I finalized plans for my trip to my birthplace. With my female ancestors and the eight-eyed steam girl to help me, I began my preparation by recalling aspects of my Texas childhood. Starting with Texas wisdom, Tipps-style, I wrote down family proverbs:

- *To whom much is given, much is required.*
- *We Tipps girls really are smarter than everyone else.*
- *Save the battles for the ones worth fighting.*
- *A realistic twenty-one year old man is a fool, but an idealistic forty year old is an even bigger fool.*
- *Step up to the licking post and take your licks.*

Curious to find images of my childhood in Texas, I searched through old slides and photos. One picture captured four-year-old me beaming in my new Christmas dress beside a tiny tree in my Nursery Street front yard. Nostalgic for my first house, I wrote the current homeowners to ask if I could drop by during my visit.

Filled with images and axioms, I turned my attention to the other things I wanted to take with me on this pilgrimage. Once again I packed my favorite land anointing oils—cajeput, rosemary and black pepper—my journal and computer, traveling music and a few rocks and crystals.

I flew back to Lubbock to begin this journey. After a good steak dinner and conversation with Great Uncle Red, Hannah and Shelby, I slipped into bed. Despite my fatigue, I couldn't fall asleep. I'd tried to force myself to love Texas again, but nothing had shifted. Hours later, about two in the morning, God spoke, "You keep trying to stretch your heart wide enough to hold more of life's paradoxes—including Texas. That isn't necessary. The human heart was created as wide as the universe."

I'd spent years trying to stretch the edges of my neighborhood and, more recently, the boundaries of my heart. I wanted more room for God and my global family within its chambers. As God's words flowed through me, my struggle subsided, and I relaxed in the same way I had years before when I received the reassurance that I wasn't a fraud in the Church. Even though I couldn't yet fully embrace my Texan roots, I knew that all was well.

I fell asleep.

Bright and early the next morning I headed north, successfully outrunning a West Texas-sized thunderstorm. I turned up the radio and sang along. I had more "refined" tastes in music when I'd lived here, but country and gospel felt right for this trip.

Spring was my favorite season everywhere, especially in Texas. Wildflowers filled the road-side fields: Black-eyed Susans, dune bluebonnets and red and yellow Indian blankets. The grass around the highway was a brilliant green from all of the rain that had fallen the past few months.

As the odometer climbed, the landscape changed. Flat prairie was left behind as the road rose onto the caliche caprock. The dirt's hue changed from tan-colored to orange to dark brown and back to orange. Grasses, mesquite, sage. I thought I spied mountains in the distance but soon realized they were only clouds. I remembered that this was big sky country, broken only by mammoth clouds that billowed, stormed or blew away.

I stopped in downtown Quitaque, Texas, my mother's birthplace. The street was torn up for road construction. I slipped into the Sportsman Bar and Grill for a burger and fries. While eating, I overheard locals talking about a nearby oil spill. This was oil country, but I presumed this wasn't oil from a geyser's blow or tanker spill, but rather a leaking gas station or ranch tank.

Stopping at the Quitaque cemetery on the outskirts of town, I visited the graves of my great grandparents, Allie and Arthur, and their daughter Martha. I remembered stopping in this cemetery during our 1991 Tipps Family reunion, and I could almost see family members, many now dead, milling around. I sat on the grass wondering if I'd feel something or hear something from the three generations of family who had lived in this part of the country. All I felt was the morning breeze and a delicate sense that God and my ancestors were glad I'd returned.

A few miles down the road at the Briscoe county seat, I toured the Silverton jail in the corner of the county courthouse grounds, where twenty-six year old O.R. Tipps was elected county judge in 1926, shortly after Mom was born. A few years later my preschool-aged mother sometimes joined her father at the courthouse and slipped over to the tiny jail to visit the prisoners while he worked in the courtroom. I felt O.R.'s love of justice and search for the truth and Mom's curiosity about people bubbling through my personality. Our three styles were very different, but we had much in common. Excited to be in the same place where Mom and O.R. had once walked, I dropped anointing oils around the grounds. The oils seemed to bridge across the years, creating a connection between us that was deeper than our separation.

When my mother's family left Silverton in the summer of 1933, they headed to Wichita Falls. Before I drove there myself, I stopped for a few days at the ranch in Roberts County. My grandfather and his business partner, Charles Christie, had owned a twelve thousand acre cattle ranch near Miami, Texas.

I had scant memories of my one visit to the ranch. Forty odd years later, I was back, greeted by Newell Rankin, the ranch manager.

Things had changed. In the late 1960s and 1970s a few far-flung oil jacks pumped away. Oil and gas exploration had grown over the intervening years, skyrocketing in the five years before my pilgrimage.

Knowing this, I'd expected to see barren, dry land scarred with oil and gas wells, but Newell explained that they were in another part of the ranch. As far as I could see in any direction from the guesthouse were fields of grass ending at the horizon. Only a few windmills and one drilling platform were visible off in the distance, surrounded by grazing cattle.

"Be careful of the rattlesnakes warming themselves on the porch steps," Newell warned as I carried my bags into the house.

Fear of snakes had long fueled my childhood dislike of the outdoors. In recent years I had been intrigued with one Native American understanding of a snake's "medicine" as transmutation of poison into something life-giving.[1] As I anointed the land around the house, I offered my respect to the snakes, while asking that they stay away during my visit.

Newell had moved to the ranch the year I left Texas. He knew every rolling hill and gully like the back of his hand. The following morning he drove me all around the ranch, through the grassy hills, to flat landings paved with caliche rock cement that surrounded the wells and holding tanks. Trucks drained these tanks, holding either oil or condensate and water that remained after the pumping process. Gas, the primary petroleum component under this land, was transported via underground pipelines.

Petroleum was part of my family legacy. My childhood was financed by Dad's wages from Shell Oil Company. College, financial gifts throughout my adult years and my financial inheritance had been primarily funded from natural gas and oil that had collected for millennia under this ranch.

Oil and gas were fruit from the depths, natural resources of the earth. My Portland home was heated by natural gas and my rental car powered by oil. Humans had always used the earth's resources for their needs, and the use of fossil fuels was no exception.

But our national and global energy use had skyrocketed, and petroleum currently generated eighty-five percent of the world's ever-growing energy use. As the fields were depleted, more extreme measures of extraction were being used. Oil and gas wells, including those on the ranch, were beginning to use hydraulic fracturing, called fracking, where water, chemicals and sand were pumped under pressure to break open subterranean caverns and release trapped fuels. The effect of this practice on earthquakes, water contamination and pollution was not yet clear.

Standing on the drilling platforms, I couldn't escape the fact that my wealth flowed through oil and gas production. Sometimes I laughed at the irony that Howard and I were working toward a new paradigm of living gently on the earth while fossil fuels were the sources of our wealth. Sometimes I wanted to cry. Either way, the truth remained. There were no easy answers.

I'd stopped at the ranch to come to terms with this fact and to offer simple rituals on this land. I prayed that Howard's and my work in the world, funded by this resource, would act like snake medicine and help transmute the poisons of the overuse of fossil fuels into something that would serve the life of future generations. Taking the flow of natural resource from far under the earth's crust into our bank accounts, then aligning that money with our hearts and Spirit were central to this transmutation. Howard and I had worked to move the obstacles of our stupid thinking to keep our financial decisions in line with this intent. Grateful to be on my family's land of cows and petroleum fields, I offered prayers and a different sort of oil from the earth's surface to the bustling oil fields and the pastoral ranch house.

On the eve of my birthday, I drove out of the Texas panhandle on the road to Wichita Falls. When I arrived, I checked into a motel. The next morning, my fifty-third birthday, I drove to the Nursery Street house my parents had built fifty-five years before. My preschool memories and 1950s photographs showed short, thin saplings in the front yard. Now, under a towering Texas ash tree, I walked from my rental car to the front porch. The house was white, just like it had been when I'd lived there. The current owner welcomed me in for a cup of coffee. When I remarked that the living room walls were the same soft green as in my old photographs, she told me that her husband had randomly chosen that color the year before. My bedroom was now a teenager's room, and off limits for my tour. The kitchen had been expanded and remodeled and looked nothing like I remembered. In the backyard, the little red boat was history. Empty lots all around were long ago filled with houses.

After our visit and tour, the current owners headed out for a family reunion, and I returned to my hotel. A few hours later, I drove back to my old home. I wanted to offer prayers and anointing oils without having to explain my actions to strangers.

Nancy on Nursery Street, 1956

I started in the alley at the back of the house, trying to remember where my little red boat sandbox and playhouse had once stood. As I wandered around the corner back to Nursery Street, I could almost see newlyweds Mom and Dad, arms around each other, admiring their brand new home. The scene of my daydream shifted forward two years, as Dad slowly turned their 1950 Chevy into the driveway and parked in the carport. He hurried out and went around to open the passenger door. Gingerly, Mom stepped out with newborn me in her arms. Finally, I saw myself at four years old, proudly showing the world my new felt Christmas skirt Mom had carefully sewed for me. I was beautiful and I knew it.

With memories dancing in my head, I offered a prayer of gratitude for the gift of life and shook out a few drops of cajeput, rosemary and black pepper oil. Standing on the same land that held me for the first six years of my life, a few wandering parts of my spirit came home again. The exuberant me that I'd silenced as a little girl was beginning to feel at home in my skin again. My young obsession with being nice was fading, leaving room for my kind and honest self instead. And the girl who had once risked everything, even her balance, to touch the sacred in a dream returned with my brave willingness to reach out for what I wanted.

I saw eight-eyed steam girl me at the helm of her little red boat docked in the backyard. For a time, they tamed me. But the Nancy who'd returned to Texas was beginning to delight, rather than recoil, at her diverse sight and unpredictable outbursts. Looking at my life myth as I stood at the edge of my former backyard, I saw how profoundly my culture had believed that too much sight or spurting was too much for a girl. Here on Nursery Street, I returned home to myself.

Knit together in my mother's womb in this place over half a century ago, I was becoming the woman I was created to be. I knew I couldn't be part of a diverse world unless I first came home to accept who I was— Texan, white skinned, "American," Christian, wealthy woman. No need to cut out parts of myself to be acceptable. I felt welcomed.

O.R. Tipps, age 65, 1965

Wichita Falls, Texas

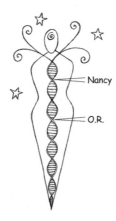

Once, in an attempt to avoid paying more taxes than I needed to, I received my earnings from an oil financing deal in the form of a working cattle ranch. I spent enjoyable hours after work at my law practice writing letters and making phone calls to buy calves and sell fattened cattle, working out the details of ranching with the assistance of ranch manager, Mr. Earyl Smyth, who lived and worked on the ranch near Miami, Texas. My Monday through Saturday workdays, and many nights, were full of law, oil financing and ranching.

Sometimes it was good to exchange my desk chair in the law office for a horse on the ranch. As Badger Clark used to say,

> *When my feet is in the stirrups*
> *And my hawse is on the bust,*
> *With his hoofs a-flashin' lightnin'*
> *From a cloud of golden dust,*
> *And the bawlin' of the cattle*
> *Is a-comin' down the wind*
> *Then a finer life than ridin'*
> *Would be mighty hard to find.[1]*

In 1956, I decided that three full-time jobs was too much. I resigned from active law practice. I kept my office, however, for work relating to the ranch.

Cattle grazed on the grasses that covered the arid Robert's County ranch land from the time they were born or purchased until they were ready for slaughter. That whole process took three to five years. In the back of my mind, now that I have more time, I wondered if there wasn't a more efficient way to fatten the cattle for slaughter. It made sense to me that if we could streamline the automobile industry, we could do the same with the cattle industry. That time will come, probably soon.

In looking back over the years, I am very grateful for the kind of life I have lived thus far. Some of it has been hard, but never boring.

"Back Porch at the Ranch" by Sue

38

Pilgrimage in Place

No sooner had I unpacked, than Candice suggested I undertake yet another pilgrimage.

"It's time to bless the land where you live," she suggested. "You have been transplanted here, as have many others around you. Look for others who want to join you in this work."

On my walks through the neighborhood, I wondered where to start. I knew this prayer needed to flow out from my home to the Rosegate Condominium community of twenty households. But I wasn't used to asking neighbors to join me in prayer, much less blessing the land.

I trusted that if God wanted me to be praying with neighbors, God would have to arrange that. Until then, I prayed for my neighborhood by myself. I hoped those of us who lived here would set down strong roots as we formed a simple community, snug in homes we loved, extending forgiveness to each other in our inevitable disagreements.

Unknown to me, a conflict had emerged between neighbors. Anger flared. Feelings were hurt. Accusations and assumptions flowed.

When a tearful, distraught neighbor came to my living room looking for support, I was ready with my invitation. "Would you like to gather with me, and others if they're interested, to pray about this?" I asked.

She brightened at the prospect and said, "Yes, definitely."

The next evening, I walked outside to visit with her and another neighbor. As I grew close enough to hear their conversation, I realized that they were speaking of their despair at the divisive spirit that seemed so threatening in our community. I extended my invitation to prayer to the neighbor, and our group now included three women—two Christians and one Jew.

Soon another resident asked to talk to me privately. In my living room, she shared her angst about the neighborhood conflict and wondered if I would be interested in joining her in prayer for this community. I told her it was already happening, and we walked outside to the courtyard and joined the others to plan our first prayer gathering.

Within minutes another neighbor stopped by. "You all looked so inviting when I looked outside that I wanted to come offer my greetings even though I can't stay," she said.

When I invited her to the prayer gathering, she was also excited to participate.

The following day, as an official emergency board meeting was being held about the issue, the five of us gathered under the tulip tree—an unofficial emergency prayer gathering. We had just stepped into the gap of discord that was growing in this small piece of land and offered our prayers for healing. Before we closed, we agreed to continue praying each day, each in our own way. Some included Rosegate in their morning quiet time. Some committed to pray prayers from their synagogue/church's liturgy. Others prayed while they walked. I promised to walk around our neighborhood, strengthening a protective spiritual hedge around our bigger community—sometimes using words, other times oils or leaning against trees.

Before going to bed that night, I sat alone on the couch in the light of a small candle, awed by the power of what had just happened. Each of us had felt the Spirit's nudge to reach out for prayer and personal support. We came together organically without preplanning or organization. While my other pilgrimages had required weeks of time, travel and money, this one required only a willingness to say "Yes" when need and neighbors came knocking. Grace had permeated my neighborhood, even during discord.

Grateful, I blew out the candle and headed to bed. Within a few weeks, the crisis at Rosegate passed without escalating. Nevertheless, the five of us continued to meet monthly, confident that our loving prayers were our gift to our community. Every time we gathered, we blessed each household, one at a time, before turning our prayers to our wonderful aging buildings and the leadership given by the volunteer condo board.

After so many years of struggling and trying to make things happen, I was comforted that faithfulness and listening within were the only things required. God, working behind the scenes, did the rest. Our hearts, our community and the land under our homes were blessed.

39

Grandfathers

As glad as I was to be home, another trip loomed on the horizon. During those few weeks of "home time," I picked up a book that a friend recommended when I was grappling with my Texas origins: China Galland's *Love Cemetery*. Heading out to sit in the sun on a courtyard chair, I began to read. Galland, born and raised in East Texas, learned that an unmarked slave cemetery was tucked at the edge of her ancestral land near Marshall, Texas. That sparked her quest to help protect and restore one of the area's slave cemeteries—Love Cemetery—and to share the challenges she faced in the process.[1]

Intrigued that another white, Southern woman was writing about her personal and ancestral legacy, I couldn't put the book down. In those pages I met Reda Rackley, yet another white, Southern woman. Reda was also a Kontomble Diviner in the Dagara tradition of West Africa. Galland hoped that Rackley could offer rituals to honor the African Americans buried in the abandoned cemetery.

Curious to know more about Reda Rackley and her practice of anointing the land, I checked out her webpage. Discovering that she lived near Monterey, California, where I was visiting the following week, I called to make an appointment to see her. Rose Feerick and Sharon Pavelda, Beloved Community friends living in the San Francisco Bay area, decided to join me.

We drove into the Carmel Valley mid-afternoon on July 17, 2006. Reda Rackley greeted us with a warm smile, and exuded softness and ease. Like me, she was in her fifties. When we stepped into her home, the wall of windows made it appear that the outdoor trees, plants and rocks were part of her living room. Though we'd just met and I was unsure about the details of Reda's work, I felt fully grounded and settled in my body, not nervous at all.

Sipping cups of tea, Rose, Sharon and I sat in Reda's ritual room. She explained that she would soon step into her small shrine and ask the ancestors for guidance for each of us through Kontomble, a wild, nature spirit that spoke the language of the indigenous soul and bridged the gap between the living and the ancestors. Kontomble, Reda told us, would speak through her in what sounded like a high-pitched language of sounds, which Reda would then translate for us.

Just before we started, Reda mentioned that today was the anniversary of her mother's death. I thought of my own parents. Caught in traveler's time, I'd forgotten the significance of July seventeenth—Dad would have been eighty-five on this day. This time with Reda and the ancestors felt like a fitting way to honor his birthday.

African masks, drums, animal skins and cloths decorated the walls of the room that held the ancestor shrine. Rose, Sharon and I settled into chairs while Reda stepped into a cloth covered, closet-like space and began to ring her bell and shake her rattle as she prayed in English. Once she completed her invocation, the ringing and rattling continued as Kontomble spoke her strange-sounding language, first to Rose and Sharon.

When that language quieted, Reda explained what had been said. Kontomble spoke, sometimes unprompted and sometimes answering specific questions, with breaks for Reda to translate for us.

When it was my turn, I listened carefully to hear what would be offered to guide the next steps of my inquiry into the big topics. I was startled to hear that the focus was on my Mathys family rather than the Tipps. Before I could say anything, Kontomble began to speak again. Soon Reda translated saying, "Your ancestors forced slaves to pave the earth with red bricks. You have come to wash the red bricks through the point of your pen, using ink instead of blood."

Kontomble spoke again, over bell and rattle. Reda told me, "Ask your father to sing a blessing song for you."

When Kontomble was done speaking to each of us, Reda closed with a prayer and silence. Reda came out of the shrine and sat with us to answer questions.

I spoke up first. "It didn't make any sense about my Mathys ancestors and slaves. My grandfather came to Green Bay, Wisconsin, as a baby in 1892. His family had nothing to do with slavery."

Reda was silent for a few minutes. "Where did he come from?"

"Belgium."

"What do you know about Belgian history?"

Very little.

"Weren't Rwanda and Burundi once Belgian colonies?" Rose asked.

Oh my.

I knew that African colonization involved brutality and racism, especially in these two countries. No part of my ancestral legacy, it seemed, was free from oppression. Was that part of everyone's family history if they went back enough generations?

When I returned home, I dove into accounts of the Belgian domination of Africa. The story I uncovered was gruesome. In 1885 Belgian King Leopold "founded" the land he called the Congo Free State (later Rwanda and Burundi) as his own private colony. Booker T. Washington wrote an article, "Cruelty in the Congo Country," where he reported, "There was never anything in American slavery that could be compared to the barbarous conditions existing today [1904] in the Congo Free State."[2] In 1908 King Leopold turned the colony over to Belgium. During the years of Leopold's rule, the population of the Congo declined from an estimated twenty-five million to less than nine million.

Further research revealed that some of the hostilities that erupted in the 1994 Rwanda massacres were the fruit of policies established during the years Belgium ruled that country. After reading page after page of atrocities at the hand of Belgium and its King, I uncovered one final fact—Belgium produced the greatest variety of bricks in the world. Metaphorically at least, Belgium had laid a red brick road washed with the blood of slaves. Was it possible that the ink in my pen could help wash away this horrible legacy?

I hoped so.

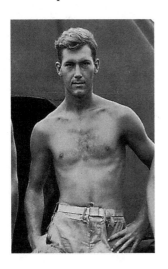

Ed   *O.R.*

Eager to leave this grim history behind, I turned my focus on Reda's instruction for me to listen for my father's song. Dad had blessed me the day before he died with six simple words—"I wish you the very best." Was there more he had to say six years later?

I returned to my couch for prayer, and then sat at the computer to listen for Dad's voice. He spoke in verses and gently insisted that his words be included in my ever-growing book.

As I strolled my neighborhood in the summer sun and warmth, I wondered whether my grandfathers also wanted to speak. Every time I stopped to admire Portland's blue hydrangeas, hot pink fuchsias and bright dahlias, I thought of Grandpa Mathys's flowers. Our neighborhood farmers

John

market sold fresh vegetables straight from nearby gardens. Had some of the plants been grown from seeds that had their roots in his company? I didn't eat as much beef as I used to, but I also couldn't eat a grilled steak without remembering O.R.'s ranch and backyard barbeque.

O.R. announced that he'd already told his story in the 1965 letter he wrote to his daughters, Mom and Martha. Growing up, I hadn't always agreed with O.R.'s demands, but this time I was glad to include excerpts adapted from his letter in my book.

Grandpa Mathys was only too happy to speak. From his birth in St. Joris Weert, Belgium, to his death in Monterey, California, John Mathys shared snapshots of his life with me.

My parents and grandparents apparently weren't satisfied being stuck in past memories. They wanted me to see life through their eyes. Although once they'd shared their stories, they had no desire to answer my big questions directly. They left that to me. I hoped that listening to my ancestors would give me some hints as I lived with the questions, trusting that one day I would live my way into answers.

Grace, age 61, 1850

Tipps Dogwood Plantation, North Carolina

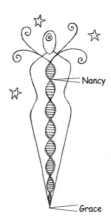

De wind do it
warsh over me
de Spirit do it
blow in me
wind and Spirit both
blessin' me

De earth do it
holds me
de Magnolia tree
cover me

De only home I ever had
was wit' de Lawd
livin' in muh heart
de dirt under muh feet

Ain't dat funny
muh home as big as eternity
whiles muh body ain't free

40

Standing in the Gap

On January 1, 2009, I shot out of bed at 1:04 a.m., grabbing a dirty shirt off the floor to catch our cat's vomit in its folds, thereby saving the upholstery of the bedroom chair.

From there I went to the bathroom and emptied a smelly litter box.

A few minutes later I was up again, catching cat vomit in a towel rather than on our rug.

My first acts of the New Year. I certainly hoped things would improve.

By 3:00 a.m. both cats were snoring gently, and I was too. But Howard was tossing and turning and finally woke me up to talk.

Just before going to bed the night before, he'd checked our financial reports. Our stocks were down again. That trend had been happening for months, but it hadn't worried him since our family natural gas and oil income had remained high. But by mid-autumn that income had begun to plummet, and it was now one-third of the amount it had been just a few months before. Howard's fears were raging, and he wanted to talk.

"What if we don't have enough to be safe in these uncertain times?

Have we given too much away? Do we need to hold onto our money until things get back to normal?"

I asked sleepily, "Why the hell did you look at those reports just before coming to bed?"

Even in the midnight darkness, I believed that we had enough. But hearing Howard's fears, I realized that our income was now equal to the amount we'd planned to give away in 2009.

Others seemed able to stick with fiscal logic: When times get tough, give away less. But I had a harder time separating what was best for our family from the needs of the organizations we supported financially. In my eyes, the future of the world for my children and grandchildren was intimately related to the mission of these groups. How could I balance what felt like "enough" for me with what felt like "enough" to support amazing people doing crucial work for our world?

Now I was scared.

I hoped our ever-changing gas and oil royalty income would suddenly shoot up again so we could avoid decreasing our donations. Unfortunately, that would also mean high natural gas prices for home use, and many were already struggling to make ends meet without that added cost. No matter what I wanted, the checks kept getting smaller.

For months, I feared that our monthly donation to Community Wholeness Venture would soon need to decrease, but I was afraid to tell Alease. I knew she would honor our decision, but I also knew the impact it would have on salaries and ministry costs. During each call, I'd vaguely bring up the possibility that our donation might need to decrease and then quickly change the topic. Finally, I could wait no longer. Our donation needed to decrease beginning the following month.

In the middle of our next phone conversation, I blurted it out. Neither of us spoke for a few moments, and the call soon ended.

Alease called back the next day. She began, "I'm calling because I want to deal with the silence that happened on yesterday's phone call. I don't want that silence or this situation to become a wall between us. We are standing in the gap together to 'repair the wall and stand in the breach,' not to construct new walls or gaps between us!"

I was grateful that she'd beat me to the call. I'd had no idea what to say.

Alease continued, "I got silent because it just caught me off guard. It just came out of nowhere; we weren't even talking about money, then whamo-bamo. Also, I could tell that you were uncomfortable, and I didn't want to make that worse for you. I was at a loss for words."

I understood.

Here in the gap, I stood close enough to Alease to know that money was very tight for Community Wholeness Venture. I was uncomfortable with the fact that our decreasing donations would make the ministry's cash flow even tighter.

Howard and I had made a commitment to give in relationship to our income. When it increased, our giving increased and vice versa. Yet before we made the final decision, Howard and I prayerfully listened to make sure that we weren't guided to step outside our plan and donate from our savings. The clarity remained that we needed to decrease the donation amount.

Despite that clarity, despite our respect for Alease and the work of Community Wholeness Venture, I still felt guilty: We could have given from our savings.

Trapped in my distress, I hadn't wanted to tell Alease about it. I put it off. Then I blurted it out in our difficult conversation.

In my guilt that we had more than enough and that Community Wholeness Venture didn't have enough, I forgot what I knew about Alease and the spiritual sight of her ministry. From the very beginning, Alease had reminded us if we followed God's guidance, we would know how to respond. We had done that, but I hadn't fully trusted what we'd heard. In addition, I had slipped into wanting to fix the ministry's financial need, something Alease had warned me specifically not to do.

Alease felt the sharp hit of my actions that flowed from my anxiety. Because of who she was, she decided to call me rather than walk away angry at my behavior or believe that I was just like all of those centuries of wealthy, white folks acting disrespectful. Though I lost sight of Alease, she never lost sight of me.

It would have been easier to keep friendships and money separate and to remain blind to the complexity of how money moved in this world. That, however, would have required me to live in a narrow world.

Alease said, "God gave me a song to teach me about the work of relationships. It's not just a song to be sung; it is a song to be lived." She began to sing about the choice between building up walls to keep others out or loving with the love of God. Only the latter, her song proclaimed, was filled with grace and resulted in transformation.

I laughed. How did I get to a place where, in the middle of a potentially difficult financial conversation, my friend sang to me about love, dismantling my wall of discomfort? I'd stepped into a holy mystery right in the middle of a difficult financial reality, and I was half terrified and half awed.

I knew I had been born for such a moment as this. Partnership had always been close to my heart. I longed for it, found it, lost it and found it again. Here with Alease and Community Wholeness Venture, I had stepped into intimacy in the middle of the gaps that had too long separated people. In the gap together I'd blown it, but our commitment—hers to speak and mine to keep aligning my behavior and my values—held us firm. The good Lord had strange ways and kept offering me opportunities that brought up conflicting feelings—"holy shit" and "thank God"—in the same moment.

I preferred friendship within these gaps, even when it hurt my heart. "Heart to heart and breast to breast, that's how God's power flows."[1] I wanted God's power to flow through my life, building a world that served us all.

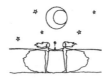

41

Pilgrimage Inside

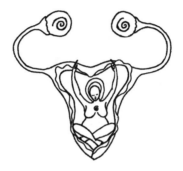

Stepping into the gap with Alease was a leap off the firm ground I'd grown accustomed to in our giving. I'd already broken so-called "healthy boundaries" between donor and recipient and between my private money and the commonwealth, but this leap with Alease was full of more unknowns. Searching for alternative models of interdependence, I wondered if women's wisdom could teach me new paradigm skills for standing with Alease.

In fall 2009 Laura was living at home again as she navigated a difficult transition between college graduation and finding a job. I sat at my computer wondering where to turn for ideas when Laura passed by with her dirty clothes. Wondering if she might shed light on my pondering, I called her into my office and started to ask about her experience as a woman. She interrupted me to announce, "Girls are backstabbing bitches."

I knew Laura had felt betrayed by her girlfriends during her senior year in college, yet I was unprepared for the starkness of her words. She had always been a rudder for her girlfriends, supporting them through thick and thin. I'd assumed she enjoyed being a woman.

"Do you think women are born that way?" I asked.

"Oh no," she replied, then continued, "we're expected to hate everything about ourselves, to be insecure about everything. It's in the culture and on the media. All girls my age are literally miserable. Therefore, we beat up our bodies or make other girls unhappy. Most girls are insecure in this world, and the way we deal with it is to point out everyone else's flaws."

Laura headed downstairs to do her laundry while I stayed at my computer, stunned. Her words pointed to a more insidious discontent than just the difficulty of her own life events. The consequences of patriarchy had already passed into another generation of women.

Shaken by Laura's words, I searched for distraction in my email. One stood out from the rest. Reda Rackley, the woman who had spoken to me about my Belgian ancestors, had sent out an invitation. She and her friend Claudia Wood were offering nine months of bi-monthly conference calls for "Sisters of the Crossroads" interested in gathering "with other women to explore the feminine mysteries, reset the truth and erase the lies that have been written on the walls of our wombs."[1]

"Support Her" by Sue

Laura had just articulated very clearly the destructive lies written on the walls of her feminine psyche and body. I was also struggling to release parts of my own cultural training, the rancid fruit of centuries of patriarchy. I was ready to reset the truth in a circle of other women, even if we gathered via the telephone.

The email continued,

> Mami Wata, Mother of the Waters—grabbed hold of my leg and pulled me to the bottom of her sandy waters, she said, "child no more waitin—the waitin is over—you go tell your sisters time to get up now, time to walk down that muddy road like they got sparkling jewels between their thighs and eyes. The waiting is over – no time left to debate whether women should be true to the Old One that has patiently waited—when you betray yourself you betray the Ancient Feminine. [Reda and Claudia] have carved a map of beauty and ritual—your tears, laughter and offerings will be left at the crossroads of creation, it is time to put on your high heels, your high head, and travel deep into the promises you made before you were born.[2]

Immediately I knew I wanted to journey with other sisters away from backstabbing and into our fullness as women—for me, for Laura and for the generations who followed us.

Nine women, varying in age from twenty-five to sixty, living all across the county, responded to this summons. We met on the phone eighteen times over the next nine months, with a planned pilgrimage to Jamaica as the culmination of our time together. The coldness of a conference call warmed with the power of what we shared—the demands of mothering young children, the complex issues that arose with our grown children, aging parents, surgeries, threats of foreclosure.

We explored taking charge and letting go, learning lessons and ranting about life's unfairness. Still, gratitude with grace emerged in the midst of it all. We listened, cried, laughed, prayed and spoke the truth of our lives. Ancient stories were shared alongside accounts about what happened last week. Rituals and simple acts packed with Spirit opened doors along the way.

Late that fall, I shared with these sisters of the crossroads that I'd just discovered a local "sister." Browsing through Powell's Books, I came across Tami Lynn Kent's, *Wild Feminine: Finding Power, Spirit, & Joy in the Root of the Female Body*. Kent was a Portland physical therapist.

In the pages of her book, I found another alternative to backstabbing, self-hating bitches. Tami Kent wove a tapestry of stories, information and rituals for honoring our feminine bodies, our womanly natures, Spirit and our ancestral legacies. Naturally connected to Spirit and my mind, I considered myself less fluent in the language of my body. Through her book and then one-on-one healing sessions, Tami pointed the way for me to find power, spirit and joy within my flesh-and-blood pelvic bowl.[3] Her way of working with the pelvic bowl incorporated the embodiment of energetic and ancestral patterns enhancing what I already knew about the intricacies of human muscles and movement. My ability to feel energy moving through my body was becoming just as perceptible as my belly muscles contracting and relaxing.

Since working with Rosemary and Candice, I'd focused mostly on moving my attention from my head—and thinking—down to my heart, softening and letting the energy flow from there out into the world. Tami's work reminded me that I'd overlooked the root of my feminine body. Whenever I shifted my attention down to my pelvis, I also tapped into my feminine intuition.

The Sisters of the Crossroads shared books and resources, just as we shared stories. We were grateful for all women who knew that the time of waiting was over and were stepping into their own wisdom.

As winter turned to spring, Reda and Claudia reissued the second part of their invitation: Come to Jamaica for five days, the land where Mami Wata called our circle together, for an initiation into the feminine mysteries.

I had no idea what the feminine mysteries were. No matter, as this island, surrounded by the feminine waters of the ocean, called to me. I wanted to go with Reda and Claudia as my guides. Though only four of us Sisters were able to come, we carried the power of the work of all of the women we'd journeyed with over the nine months of phone conversations.

Jamaica held the memories of the ancient medicine of Africa, the birthplace of all humanity and the ancestral homeland of most black-skinned Jamaicans. Music, dance, celebration and longing permeated this little island. The land held towering silk cotton trees, lush vegetation and limestone caves surrounded by turquoise waters. Jamaica knew heartbreak and domination, as well as liberation and joy. This time I traveled to a land not my own, and the pilgrimage was to the ground of my own being.

In late June 2010, I boarded the red-eye in Portland, landed in Houston for breakfast and was in Montego Bay, Jamaica by lunchtime. As soon as I stepped out of the airport doors, I spotted Reda. Claudia and Lawrence and I were meeting in-the-flesh for the first time. Claudia was tall, tan and eager to welcome us to this island she now called home. Lawrence was a petite Parisian who lived in San Francisco. We climbed into the car with Marlin, our Jamaican driver, a man with a broad smile and a gentle spirit.

Although I was sleep deprived, the sights and sounds along the coastal road to Negril kept me awake. We drove through bustling towns filled with people and brightly painted one-story buildings. The poverty wasn't as extreme as I'd seen in Haiti, but the villages contrasted starkly with the nearby huge, walled-in resorts, which drank up huge amounts of natural resources while giving little back to Jamaica. I relaxed when we drove past white sand beaches and the ocean on the right side of the road and hills covered with trees, grasses and flowers on the left.

Lawrence and I shared a cabin in small, locally owned Villas Sur Mer, a set of simple yet elegant cottages with a beautiful courtyard swimming pool. Our schedule was generous with time to settle in, so I unpacked in my bedroom and headed to the pool with a glass of rum. My red-eye fatigue began to fade.

By dinnertime I was ready to visit with the three other women. We savored Jamaican jerk chicken from Claudia's favorite vendor down the street.

Over dessert, I laughed at Reda's audacity when she broke into a topic I'd always thought was unspeakable, and said, "Tell me about your initiation into womanhood through the first time you had sex."

The other women answered first, sharing stories laced with disappointment. Then they looked at me, waiting for my answer.

I wanted to be telling a different story, as I was damn tired of mine. My initiation into the feminine mysteries through the first time I had sex was an initiation into a culturally-affirmed feminine swindle: losing myself in relationship with a man. Rather than this initiation being a freely offered invitation accepted with a definite "yes" and followed by pleasure, mine had been wrapped up in low self-image, taking care of others, picking up responsibility that wasn't mine and forgetting to ask myself what I wanted. I was scarred by my initiation and the wound was still tender.

Over the years I'd understood that my response wasn't due to personal stupidity. Around the dining table in Jamaica and from women friends over the years, I'd heard many variations on the theme of being snatched into sexual encounters without a clear personal decision.

When I read the Sisters of the Crossroads invitation, my heart leapt at the notion that the time of betraying myself and the Ancient Feminine One was over, and that I could now walk like I had a "sparkling jewel between my thighs and my eyes." I wanted to shake off the vestiges of the destructive ways the media and culture had taught me to be a woman.

As I told the women about my college experience, suddenly I saw an option I hadn't considered thirty-six years before. Instead of staying trapped in mental loops of worry, I could have stopped to sense what I wanted for myself. If I had done that, I might have reacted with gratitude for the magnificence of my own sexual body, walked away from Al and reignited my relationship with Howard.

Churning up these memories made it hard to fall asleep that night. The power of my experience held alongside the experience of too many other women only confirmed the urgency that the time of patient waiting must end. Our daughters and granddaughters, as well as our sons and grandsons, deserved another way to be women and men in this culture.

After an hour of tossing and turning, trying to figure out what I could do to change a system that felt so pervasive, I remembered that thinking and fearful loops in my head would get me nowhere. I pulled my attention down into my pelvis and remembered that I was in Jamaica to reclaim the feminine mysteries through prayerful ritual and a loving and supportive community, the only things powerful enough to turn the tide toward a thriving life for us all, women and men.

I slipped into a peaceful sleep for the rest of the night.

After a good breakfast, we prepared for our first ritual that afternoon. I journaled and rested. When it was almost time, I checked in with my feminine wisdom to see if I was to put on any of my small, traveling collection of essential oils. I put cajeput on the top of my head, my third eye and heart. I wanted to remove any obstacles to my connection to Spirit, my sight and my heart. This pilgrimage was about shifting the energy within me rather than the land.

Lawrence awaited her turn in the cabin as I followed Reda and Claudia out of our villa, through the gardens, down curving steps and past a rusted iron gate. We stepped into a tall cave that opened out to the ocean. On the flat stone floor, in the middle of the cave, Reda and Claudia had set up a massage table surrounded by flower petals. Deck chairs were pushed to the side under a showerhead set into the rock wall.

I was invited to go to the ocean-side edge of the cave and stand in silence for a few minutes. I remembered Reda saying that each of our toes represented a generation of grandmothers who were with us as we walked this earth. Splashed with a fine spray of the crashing ocean waves, I calculated that ten toes, or ten generations of my grandmothers, included two-thousand forty six women.

Reda and Claudia escorted me to the massage table and invited me to lie down on my belly. Soon they were both massaging me, in a soft rhythm that was unique to each one and yet bound together. Feeling their gentle touch, and remembering Candice and Rosemary when they used to give me a joint treatment, caused every cell in my body to shimmer in gratitude for the extravagance of all I had been given on this journey of life. All of my regrets fell away. As they anointed my back, arms and legs with oil, it felt like old, broken shards fell out of me. As the ritual massage progressed, these shards turned to sparkling dust and blew out over the ocean. This ritual was sensuous, filled with love—grandmotherly love, funny and potent. Under Reda and Claudia's hands, I felt kneaded back together in my body and spirit, filling in the holes I'd cut into myself.

Afterwards, they invited me to lie on the table for a few minutes, absorbing all that had been given. Once I dressed, Claudia and Reda offered a blessing. I climbed up the steps alone and returned to my room, retreating under the covers in bed, letting the oil, images and love seep into me.

The following day we played, walking over short waterfalls in a fast moving river, exploring the island and sharing stories. My favorite stop was at a towering, grandmother silk cotton tree, with tall strong ribs of roots splaying out from the trunk.

On our next to last day, I spent the morning resting in preparation for our initiation into the feminine mysteries. Claudia told Lawrence and me to wear something we could easily remove, so I tied my flaming orange sarong around me like a strapless dress. The four of us retraced our steps down into the limestone cave. The tide was in, and waves crashed at the edge. The afternoon was hot, but the shade in the cavern was comfortable. We sat with our backs to the ocean, facing the ritual space prepared for us—a circle outlined by flickering candles and flower petals.

Lawrence stepped into the circle first. I sat quietly beside Reda and Claudia. Claudia invited Lawrence to ritually claim the inner gifts that had emerged for her during the week. Lawrence was quiet for a few moments. Then her voice arose from the depths of her belly. When Lawrence was finished, Claudia and Reda rinsed her off under the showerhead and gave her a new dress.

When it was my turn, I stood and waited for instructions. Reda told me, "You have long held your tongue folded back into your throat, silencing your own language and your song. Step into the circle to speak or sing or dance with your grandmothers in the fullness of who you are."

I took a slow breath and moved my attention down to my heart and pelvis, waiting to be guided from there. I felt the presence of Grace and grandmothers, Ann and Ruth, and I began to dance. I started singing in tongues, softly then with gusto. My prayer language song was saturated with excitement.

I spun with the oceans, the cave, the grandmothers and the sisters sitting at the edge of the circle. Swirling under and above and inside it all was the divine, a God who was bigger than any dogma or church or gender. In the middle of the dance, I took off my sarong and danced naked. I was twirling my way back to the bare bones of who I was born to be. That little girl who had twirled around inviting her dad to dance was alive and well within me. The person I was born to be was rising again after a long slumber.

When I was finished, Claudia guided me under the warm shower. After I dried off, she gave me a new dress—a little sundress with sequins and fiery swirls. Here, I wasn't too much. My silence had been broken. Unlike the time Nurse Gina and bare patient Nancy were scolded, no one told me I should be ashamed of myself for being naked. I was fully received—by myself and by my sisters, here at the crossroads.

It seemed that my little red boat had sailed to Jamaica to pick me up, now a full-grown woman, inviting me to step in as the captain. I wished I could invite Laura into my boat, but she needed to find her own and in her own way. Nevertheless, I knew that we Sisters of the Crossroads had opened up some new pathways to make things easier for her and the next generation of women.

Something happened to me in Jamaica the summer of 2010. The wild feminine part of me had wandered far off, but that summer she finally came home again.

My pilgrimages had brought me full circle. I was becoming more at home within my own skin and with my global family. Wildness was not to be feared, as I'd always thought, but was a return to our natural, untamed selves. "Mami Wata, Mother of the Waters—grabbed hold of my leg and pulled me to the bottom of her sandy waters," and, in the waters and caves of Jamaica, I danced my way back toward the woman I was born to be.

Ann Mathys

Heaven

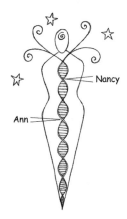

I loved my son Ed, but I never liked his wife very much.

Sue was just so plain, so uncultured in her manners and dress, so brassy.

Sue was also free. John enjoyed her curiosity, just like he used to love mine. Let me be clear, I never wanted Sue's style—she was so Southern—yet I wanted a return to the freedom I felt as a young dancer in the ivory towers. Sue reminded me of something I didn't have anymore, so I shrank back from her and, consequently, from her daughter, Nancy. Nancy tried to be nice, but I know she felt the distance between us.

In the years that followed, I slid out of my mind. When it was time, John moved me into a home for old folks. It was hard to locate even an inch of me that resembled who I was when I first twirled around Lake Michigan as a young girl. Yet sometimes, in moments almost too short to notice, I was free inside. For a second or two, I floated and swirled like a ballerina in my imagination.

On June 1, 1972, when John said good-bye, we both knew it was the end. I felt the tremble of a faded Tango when he leaned over to kiss my cheek before he turned and walked out the nursing home door. Just after he stepped into our home a few minutes later, he dropped to the kitchen floor where years before we had waltzed between bites of pickled pig's feet and date bars.

Luckily it took me only thirty-two days to join him in the great by-and-by.

John and I are now free to Tango on the clouds, tap on the stars, and turn cartwheels on the moon. Whenever we stop to catch our breath, we sprinkle stardust over our grandchildren, great-grandchildren, and great-great grandchildren. Sue and Ed, O.R. and Ruth often join us in the sparkle tossing.

Ann, circa 1915

42

Called to Return

I hated to leave friendships or walk away from organizations. I too often assumed that circumstances leading to breaking a relationship were my fault, or at least could have been prevented if I'd only done more.

Sometimes the leavings were for good and sometimes for just a season.

When I returned home from Jamaica, I was ready to revisit two institutions I'd left three years earlier. Now that my feminine core was stronger, I was ready to ease back in to the aspects of both church and medicine that aligned with my values.

I'd taken a sabbatical from attending church while I followed God's leading into the feminine spirituality that I missed in my Christian tradition. During those few years away, I learned how to listen to the voice of the divine singing through my body, intuition and nature.

For most of my adult life, I'd struggled to find language for addressing the sacred that encompassed the masculine and feminine balance I knew experientially. Ironically, as much as I wanted to address the divine as "Mother" or imagine Goddess rather than God, my prayers naturally were addressed to "Gracious God" or "Lord." I was not confused, though, as the God I knew was feminine as much as masculine. In my heart, in my pelvic bowl, through my intuition and in the trees, the divine reverberated ever outward, encompassing a wholeness larger than words or gender.

During my church sabbatical, Jesus stayed at my side. I'd never felt the need to toss out the baby—Jesus, God and the Spirit—with the bathwater—the patriarchal ecclesiastical traditions. While I wanted to forever leave behind my childhood indoctrination into niceness, obedience without listening inwardly and a second-class status for women, I was as much Christian as I was a native Texan. And the stream of the Christian tradition that most fed my spirit was the incarnational—focusing on "making present and visible the realm of the invisible spirit."[1]

In worship this was done through simple acts of sacrament such as Eucharist, anointing with oil and ancient prayers in traditional or modern words that we prayed week after week. I experienced this repetition as a way of letting the vibration work its way down to the core of my cells. Despite my struggles with the church as institution, the Episcopal church as community gathering place reminded me who I was and *whose* I was. I was ready to return for weekly worship, knowing that my presence there was a critical piece of my spiritual path.

On a Sunday in September, I walked around the block to the red doors of St. Michael and All Angels Episcopal Church and slipped into a pew where decorated sunlight poured through the stained glass windows. I closed my eyes in prayer and was flooded with gratitude. Running my fingers along the wooden pew, I felt my body settle as my spirit rose with the organ prelude. The congregation stood to sing, "All creatures of our God and King"[2] and I knew I was home.

My relationship with the "healthcare" system was more estranged than my relationship with the church, and so returning to Western medicine was more complicated.

I couldn't abide my old belief that doctors always knew what was best for my health or that my most effective medicine necessarily came from a pharmacy. Yet I wanted the scientific and technological expertise I could access through a medical doctor. Now that I felt stronger within, I was ready to practice listening inwardly to my body and spirit while also hearing a physician's recommendation.

The difficulty was that many of the pillars of the Western medical system didn't make sense to me. In my experience, illness wasn't always an indicator that something was wrong. Similarly, the dark night of the soul[a] wasn't a loss of faith—even though it often felt that way—but rather a clearing out for a huge leap of faith.

I believed that human life was innately full of adventure and danger, falling apart and being reborn. Denying that or trying to fix those paradoxes made no sense to me. What I had grown to believe was this: We are not locked into a battle against illness; we are engaged in a partnership with the fullness of who we are, housed in a body born for healing.

I stepped back into aspects of medical care in ways that honored what I'd learned about my own medicine. My first line of wellness support, though, came through essential oils, vibrational essences, massage, Feldenkrais, acupuncture and other "alternative" forms of healing.

In addition, I visited a homeopathic physician who was originally an MD. She no longer practiced Western medicine, but she was familiar with both systems of healing. I also sought out a primary care naturopathic physician whom I trusted.

That fall, when I had a skin problem, my homeopathic physician recommended that I make an appointment with a dermatologist. I listened to his diagnosis – I had ringworm on my neck – and was grateful for his expertise. Before I filled the prescription, however, I checked out options. I decided to try a natural healing method—apple cider vinegar soaked cloths on my neck, cod liver oil spread over the infection and tea tree oil. Had my ringworm not cleared up within a few weeks, I would have filled the prescription.

This new approach required me to take an extraordinary amount of personal responsibility for my own health. It was scary, but I could no longer blindly accept the Western medical perspective. At the same time,

I wanted to be able to grow past my fear and distress about that system, so all forms of healing would be available to me.

In all major US institutions—religious, medical, legal, educational, economic and governmental—I experienced a set of assumptions that were vigorously affirmed by most people but were often in conflict with my values. Saying "no" when acquiescence was the polite or expected response made my "nice girl" self very uncomfortable.

My childhood dream about church as the Leaning Tower of Pisa continued to show me how to live into my own fullness while residing in the US at the bridging of the twentieth and twenty-first centuries. When I'd first returned to this dream at the Academy for Spiritual Formation, I assumed that my work was either to push the tower, or institution, over so the essence could be freed to rise again or to try my hardest to push it upright, hoping that reform would be enough. I tried both ways with all of the familial strength and gumption I had inherited but only ended up sweaty and frustrated. I discovered that wasn't my work to do.

Instead, my work was to dance inside and outside the doors of institutions, clinging tightly to the essential truths.

Dancing was fun, and it required much. I had to show up with my full self, using every one of my eight eyeballs to see clearly where to step. I had to wake from my slumber and see the diversity of the world, not reacting from past experiences or assumptions but living in the present moment and its vast possibilities for movement. To honor what I had learned, I had to be light on my feet as well as stand solidly, even when the foundations of life as I had always known them crumbled around me.

The delightful little caveat was that I didn't have to do it flawlessly—no part of creation abided by uniform perfection. I just had to dance. God, always, and my friends, usually, were there to help. I could live my experiments striving to create the future I wanted to leave for our world's children and grandchildren.

I'd begun to live with new questions. What does it mean for me to walk as the Spirit guides, even if institutional riptides try to pull me in the other direction? What does it mean to hear the song in a conch shell, while the cultural loud speakers blast away?

I didn't yet know the answers, but I had begun a life of pilgrimage and good journeys rose before me. As my grandfather John reminded me, "Next year's harvest looms with great promise."[b]

43

Prayer for the Beginning and the End

My life has been a spiritual journey lived in my flesh-and-blood body, walking on planet Earth in the Milky Way galaxy in both the twentieth and twenty-first centuries. Looking back, I see the patterns and threads that have woven through my fifty-eight years, around the globe and across time.

My life didn't begin with my birth, nor will it end with my death. Ancestors prepared the way. Generations yet unborn will reap the benefits and shoulder the damage of my choices today. My family tree is planted deeply in this earth, and its branches reach out over the land and across time. The further back I trace my family, the more I see that all of our family trees are intertwined. Eventually all of our branches arch back toward Africa, the motherland of humankind.

My story turned out to be much bigger than I'd imagined as a little girl in Wichita Falls, Texas. My grandmother Ruth, who held me soon after my birth, reminded me of the transformative power of a good, big story, in which the edges of life were limited only by my imagination.

Barbara, my great-great-great-great grandmother, taught me that I needed to break a few rules to be given new life. She gave me the courage to step beyond some of the implicit and primarily unspoken regulations of my culture.

Great-great-great grandmother Elizabeth showed me how anger could mutate from a healthy emotion into an automatic response to life's difficulties. Yet hardened as she was, Elizabeth found the healing power of God's love. It didn't solve her daily problems, but it gave her perspective and guidance that made all the difference.

Margaret, my great-great-great-great-great grandmother, broke down my assumptions about people who participated in behaviors I found appalling. She didn't show up as either the enlightened woman trapped in her culture—as I'd wanted—or as a thoroughly bad woman. Margaret's confidence in her worldview reminded me of the importance of holding my assumptions lightly, willing to change if I woke up and saw something I'd never noticed before.

Grandfather O.R. held firm to the importance of hard work, duty and determination. Sue, his daughter and my mother, also excelled at these virtues, but she never forgot the power of creativity and the arts. Sue also discovered that living up to the family motto of "Tipps girls are smarter than everyone else" had a dangerous edge for us women. I hear her warning me not to try to be twice as good in order to be considered equal, but rather just to be me.

Grandfather John spent his life close to the land and the plants that grew therein. Though my conscious connection with the gardens and trees went underground for a few decades, he reminded me that a deep connection to the earth was part of my inheritance.

My father, Ed, taught me the power of letting go, even though it took him almost a lifetime to learn the art of release. Dad taught me that it was never too late to learn new tricks or right old wrongs.

Hectate, never one to mince words, demanded that I get off my ass and begin to do what was mine to do. Doing it with attitude, and a few well-placed swear words, definitely helps!

The ever-changing moon that spoke on the evening Laura was born softened my experience of time. She shed light on the benefits of trusting the waxing and waning of life.

The eight-eyed steam girl gave me a mythical glimpse of my unique creation and personality. She illuminated the starkness of the silencing and taming of my little girl self. Her playful story softens the edges of my life and helps me to sail through it all in my own little red boat.

The circle of wisdom I'd first dreamed about in Franklin, North Carolina, held more voices than I'd ever imagined. Now I know that when I make decisions about how to live my life, I need to listen to the voices of the animals and plants, water and moon, ancestors and descendants, and to myself. The power of the sacred fire that burned in the longhouse on Nikwasi's mound may have been snuffed out by men in Jacob's troop, but it still burns brightly in the Spirit.

Grace. You asked me to dance and you never left. Thank you for your gift of grace flowing across the generations.

I am eternally grateful that my neighborhood expands around the world and that the edges of my life stretch across the generations. I invite you, dear reader, to stand in the gap with me; together we who are alive today have the power to change the world. The need is urgent. This quest is not child's play. If we don't change, personally and globally, we will leave a poisoned legacy for generations to come.

It doesn't have to be hard, although sometimes it will be. It can be joyful, though sometimes it won't feel like that. Jesus spoke to this paradox when he talked about losing our lives to gain them. On the other side of things falling apart is new life. We merely have to wake up and keep growing as our clarity expands. Grandmother Ann taught me that the dance of life is not always a straight line. Take one step forward. And then the following step to the right. And two steps backward before heading forward again.

We are not alone. Grace abounds at every turn.

Godspeed, my friends, fellow pilgrims on the path and dancers outside
the lines. Ann and I will twirl together forever, weaving beauty across
the rips in the fabric of life in the best ways we know how. In this dance,
those willing to be cracked wide open will find that our differences add
to the grace of our movement. Will you join us?

Prayer is, for me, the perfect place to begin and end. I offer the prayer
I wrote for daily use when I first began this exploration in 2005. I've
adapted it so we can pray together:

> The Spirit of the Lord is upon us,
> because the Spirit has anointed us to bring good news
> to the poor and to the rich.
> The Spirit has sent us to proclaim release to the captives,
> recovery of sight to the blind,
> to set free the oppressed and oppressors
> within and without,
> and to proclaim Jubilee;
> a time of Sabbath, restoration and celebration.[1]
>
> Gracious God,
> Please let us lay aside everything that we think we know
> about ourselves,
> each other,
> about Life,
> and about you, God,
> for an open mind, open heart and open eyes and ears
> so that we can experience anew, with freshness and clarity,
> Your hand in our lives and throughout the world.
>
> Give us the courage to stand in Your Light
> to see what is real, within and without,
> and to be open to divine surprises of transformation
> throughout our days and nights.

We honor the Divine hand which pours this new wine into our lives.
Give us courage to continue on this path,
relinquishing illusions of control
as we take this Pilgrimage of Life.

Amen. So be it. Help. Thank you.

Epilogue

Dear Grace,

It will be years before you walk on this planet Earth, but the same stardust and DNA swirls through our bodies. You were the last thing on my mind when I began to write this book. Then one day you introduced yourself as my granddaughter from seven generations in the future and, as if your life depended on it, encouraged me to keep diving deeper.

It's hard to know how to speak in ways you will understand a few hundred years from now. Just as when I read Biblical texts written two thousand years ago, when you read my words, things will be different. What I can say for certain is that I wrote from the truest place I knew and hope that my words will translate across time and space.

This journey has been full of Graces and grace. One Grace was a slave of our ancestors, Jacob and Margaret Tipps, seven generations before me. I don't know the details of her life, but I discovered that living on a small plantation in the eighteen hundreds, she likely experienced brutality. Yet this Grace reached out to me and showed me that life is much bigger than I'd ever imagined. She refused to let me drift off to sleep again. You, young Grace, were right by her side.

My generation carries the responsibility to live our lives in such a way that yours is left with possibilities rather than the remains of today's physical and spiritual toxins. I don't want you to be born onto a planet split apart between those who have access to money and power and those who don't. I don't want you to struggle against a patriarchal undertow to find your own voice. I don't want you to have to live among people who believe that the color of one's skin is an indicator of value. Instead, I long for you to be the person you were created to be, living in communities with others embodying their own fullness.

This book is my gift to further that end.

Walking on this Earth between Grace and Grace, I am Nancy Ann Mathys Thurston. In Hebrew, both Nancy and Ann mean grace. In a world filled with grace and Grace, anything is possible. I pray that my story will be intertwined with the stories of many, forming a web strong enough to beautifully support generations yet unborn.

Thanks be to God.

Blessings,

Nancy

Grace's Family Tree

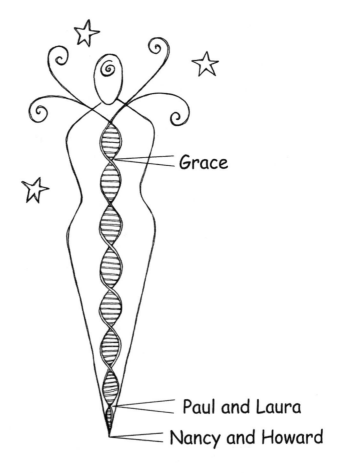

Notes

Introduction

1. Joanna Macy, "The Great Turning," http://www.joannamacy.net/thegreatturning.html.

1. This Little World of Mine

1. "City of Wichita Falls, Texas City Motto," last modified January 2011, http://www.wichitafallstx.gov/.

2. Michael Horowitz, "House Size Matters (A Lot)," August 8, 2006, http://www.bsr-vt.org/Articles/House%20Size%20Matters%20-%20M%20Horowitz%208-8-06.pdf.

2. Grandparents Set the Table

1. Edward L. Bernays, "The Engineering of Consent," Annals of the American Academy of Political and Social Science (1947): 113, in *The Engineering of Consent,* ed. Edward L. Bernays and Howard Walden Cutler (Oklahoma: University of Oklahoma Press, 1955).

2. "Central Intelligence Agency: Guatemala 1954," accessed April 26, 2011, http://www.conservapedia.com/Central_Intelligence_Agency.

3. Jesus Went Before Us

1. Elisha A. Hoffman, *Leaning on the Everlasting Arms: The Glad Evangel for Revival, Camp, and Evangelistic Meetings* (Georgia: A. J. Showalter & Company, 1887).

4. Land of the Free

1. George H. Gallup, *The Gallup Poll: Public Opinion 1935-1971, Volume 3* (New York: Random House, 1972), survey #662-K.

2. Jo Freeman, "How 'Sex' Got Into Title VII: Persistent Opportunism as a Maker of Public Policy," Women, Law, and Public Policy, http://uic.edu/orgs/cwluherstory/jofreeman/lawandpolicy/titlevii.htm.

3. Nancy L. Cohen, "How the Sexual Revolution Changed America Forever," February 5, 2012, http://www.alternet.org/books/153969/how_the_sexual_revolution_changed_america_forever?page=5.

4. Poppy Goodin, "Voice of Justice: Mr. James Bradford," Lee High School scholarship essay, March 1, 1999, 6, http://www.utexas.edu/world/barbarajordan/scholar/1998.html.

5. Goodin, "Voice of Justice."

Ruth Tipps, 1925
1. Thomas Hood, "Ruth," in *The Oxford Book of English Verse: 1250-1900*, ed. Arthur Quiller-Couch, accessed May 4th, 2012, http://toplovepoems.com/poem_ruth.php.

5. Budding Love
1. O.R. Tipps, letter to the author.
2. Nancy Mathys (Thurston), "Letter to the Editor," Twelve Fifteen, June 2, 1968, 12.
3. "Group of Girls Puff Cigarettes as a Gesture of 'Freedom'," New York Times, April 1, 1929.
4. "Very Personally Yours," (Wisconsin: Kimberly-Clark Corporation, 1961), 13.

6. Stranger Prayer
1. Christian Classics Ethereal Library, "I Felt My Heart Strangely Warmed," in Journal of John Wesley, Chapter 2, http://www.ccel.org/ccel/wesley/journal.vi.ii.xvi.html.
2. The United Methodist Hymnal: Book of United Methodist Worship (Nashville: The United Methodist Publishing House, 1989), 34.
3. Ibid.
4. John 1:1-5.

7. Upperclassman
1. Howard Thurston, handwritten notes to the author with little illustrations on the side, 1970-1972.
2. Walter D. Nims, "Precious and Few," LP, Caesar's Music Library/Emerald City Music, 1970.

Ann Cahoon (Mathys), 1913
1. Annie (Ann) Rowland Cahoon (Mathys), "Moral Training Through Leadership of Play and Games," (Master of Science Thesis, University of Wisconsin, 1915), 23.

   Ann's original words: "Another important factor is the amount of real happiness given by games. This is an important factor in character building and refers to both boys and girls."

a. All of the dances mentioned or described in Ann's chapters were hand-written in the lesson plan notebook she used in the college dance classes she taught sometime between 1915 and 1917.

8. A Completely Free Woman
1. 1 Timothy 2:11-12.
2. Galatians 3:28.
3. "Equal Credit Opportunity Act," 1974, http://www.cardreport.com/laws/ecoa.html.

O.R. Tipps, 1933

    a. Paraphrased from a letter O.R. Tipps wrote in 1965 to his two daughters, Sue and Martha, reflecting back over his life.

11. Birthing Myself

    1. Morton Kelsey, *Other Side of Silence: Guide to Christian Meditation*, revised, (New Jersey: Paulist Press, 1997).

    2. Don McClannen, Ministry of Money Newsletter (1982): 20.

    3. Luke 3:11.

    4. Matthew 6:24.

    5. Carol Gilligan, *In a Different Voice: Psychological Theory and Women's Development* (Cambridge: Harvard University Press, 1982).

    6. Suzanne Arms, *Immaculate Deception: A New Look at Women and Childbirth in America* (Boston: Houghton Mifflin, 1975).

    7. National Organization for Women, "The National Organization for Women's 1966 Statement of Purpose," http://www.now.org/history/purpos66.html.

13. Moving to the Frozen Edge of the Earth

    1. Chris Olson's words about Nancy, 1989.

    2. Shel Silverstein, "Boa Constrictor," on Peter, Paul and Mommy, BMI, Tro-Hollis Music, Inc., 1969.

    3. Anne Wilson Schaef, *Women's Reality: An Emerging Female System* (New York: HarperOne, 1992).

Ann Mathys, 1924

    1. Ann Cahoon (Mathys), "Moral Training Through Leadership of Play and Games," 24.

14. The Flight Inside

    1. "The Academy for Spiritual Formation," http://www.upperroom.org/academy/.

    2. See "Jesus Went Before Us" for the first telling of this dream.

    3. Kings 2: 12-15.

    4. Ephesians 3:20b.

    5. Jonathan Kozol, *Rachel and Her Children: Homeless Families in America* (New York: Three Rivers Press, 2006).

15. My World Stretches Outward

    1. Kathleen Norris, *Dakota: A Spiritual Geography* (Boston: Houghton Mifflin Harcourt, 1993).

    2. Paul Farmer, *Uses of Haiti* (Monroe: Common Courage Press, 1994), 61.

    3. Farmer, *Uses of Haiti*.

    4. Peter Menzel, *The Material World* (San Francisco: Sierra Club Books, 1994), 156.

5. Etty Hillesum, *An Interrupted Life and Letters From Westerbork* (New York: Metropolitan Books, 1983) 96.

6. Hillesum, *An Interrupted Life*, 97.

Ruth Tipps, 1979

1. Amy Morris Lillie, "Land of the Pilgrim's Pride," in *The Book of Three Festivals: Stories for Christmas, Easter, Thanksgiving* (New York: EP Dutton, 1948).

2. Rumer Godden, *The Kitchen Madonna* (New York: The Viking Press, Inc., 1967).

3. Ann Shelley, "How the Woman Got Her Ring: A Too-True Story, with Abject Apologies to Kipling," The Husk (1933): 13(1), 5-8.

16. It Was True

1. Randall Mullins, "Contemplation and the Powers: Government Agencies Found Guilty of Conspiracy in the Assassination of Martin Luther King, Jr.," Contemplation and Non-Violence (2001): 12, 1-2.

2. King Center, "Full Trial Transcript," http://www.thekingcenter.com/tkc/trial. html.

3. Martin Luther King Jr., "Beyond Vietnam: A Time to Break Silence," (delivered April, 1967 at Manhattan's Riverside Church), http://www. commondreams.org/views04/0115-13.htm.

17. Letting Go into Death

1. "A Service of Death and Resurrection," in *The United Methodist Hymnal* (Tennessee: The United Methodist Publishing House, 1969), 871.

2. For further reading on Kennedy's death, see *JFK and the Unspeakable: Why He Died and Why It Matters* by James W. Douglass (New York: Touchstone, 2010).

18. Being Present

1. April Lang and Shelly Peiken, "Dream in Color," perf. by Regina Belle on Passion, Columbia, 1993.

a. The phrases in quotes come from the Be Present, Inc. vision statement, which is printed below. See http://www.bepresent.org/history for further information about Be Present, Inc.

We are a diverse network of people willing to risk being different with one another, our families, communities, workplaces and organizations.

We are committed to a process that builds personal and community well-being on the strength of self-knowledge rather than on the distress of oppression.

Because we believe that enduring progressive change begins

with and is sustained by persistent personal growth, we
bring to people a model for personal and organizational
effectiveness which replaces silence with information,
assumptions with a diversity of insights, and powerlessness
with a sense of personal responsibility.

19. Rolling in the Dough

    1.   Zaid Jilani, "How Unequal We Are: The Top Five Facts You Should Know About the Wealthiest One Percent of Americans," ThinkProgress Economy, October 3, 2011, http://thinkprogress.org/economy/2011/10/03/334156/top-five-wealthiest-one-percent/.

20. Playing with Dynamite

    1.   George W. Bush, "Statement from Camp David," September 16, 2001, http://www.presidency.ucsb.edu/mediaplay.php?id=63199&admin=43.

    2.   Sharon Gerred, "A Beloved Community Gathering Reflection," given at a Beloved Community gathering, 2001.

    3.   Annie Dillard, *Teaching a Stone to Talk: Expeditions and Encounters* (New York: HarperCollins Publishers, 1982), 52.

    4.   Dillard, *Teaching a Stone to Talk: Expeditions and Encounters,* 52.

    5.   Jeremiah 20: 7-13.

    6.   Nancy Thurston, "Economic Injustice: Fire Burning in the Bones," in *Preaching as Prophetic Calling: Sermons that Work XII*, ed. Roger Alling and David J. Schlafer (Pennsylvania: Morehouse Publishing, 2004), 50-51.

    7.   Elizabeth Blackwell, *Pioneer Work in Opening the Medical Profession to Women* (New York: Longmans, Green and Company, 1895), 21.

22. Whites Only in a World of Many Colors

    1.   George Lipsitz, *The Possessive Investment in Whiteness: How White People Profit from Identity Politics* (Philadelphia: Temple University Press, 1988).

    2.   Be Present, Inc., "Be Present Empowerment Model®," http://www.bepresent.org/empowermentmodel.

23. Called to Leave

    1.   "Ash Wednesday Liturgy," in *The Book of Common Prayer* (New York: Seabury Press, 1979), 267-268.

    2.   Abraham J. Heschel, *The Prophets: An Introduction, Volume I* (New York: Harper & Row, Harper Torchbooks, 1962).

    3.   Heschel, *The Prophets,* 3.

    4.   Heschel, *The Prophets,* 16.

    5.   Jeremiah 20:9.

24. Front Page News

    1.   Dana Tims, "Tax Cuts in Oregon, High Income," The Oregonian, August 1, 2003, A10.

Sue Mathys, 1976

    a.   This chapter is primarily in Sue's own words, with my adaptations.

25. Two Texas Tarts Take Over the White House

    1.   Mars Bonfire, "Born to be Wild," perf. by Steppenwolf on Easy Rider, LP, ABC-Dunhill Records, 1969.

    2.   Joe Darion and Mitch Leigh, "The Impossible Dream," perf. by Simon Gilbert on Man of LaMancha, LP, 1965.

    3.   Tony Hatch, "Downtown," perf. by Petula Clark on Downtown, LP, Pye Studios, 1964.

26. Following the Trail

    1.   Soulshock, Kenneth Karlin, Alex Cantrell, Philip "Silky" White, "Leave (Get Out)," perf. by JoJo on JoJo, CD, Da Family and Blackground, 2004.

    2.   Asa Packer Mansion, "From Farmer to Coal and Railroad Magnate," accessed April 26, 2011, http://www.galenfrysinger.com/asa_packer_mansion_jim_thorpe_pa.htm.

    3.   Estate of Jim Thorpe, "Jim Thorpe: The Word's Greatest Athlete," accessed April 16, 2012, http://www.cmgww.com/sports/thorpe/index.html.

    4.   Alexander McCall Smith, The No. 1 Ladies' Detective Agency (New York: Anchor Books, 1999), 17.

    5.   Robert F. Kennedy Jr., from a speech given at Omega Institute's "Living a Fearless Life" conference, quoted in More Than Money (2004): 37, 31.

    6.   Barbara Landis, "Carlisle Indian Industrial School History: Pratt, Ft. Mason Prisoners and Hampton", 1996, http://www.carlisleindianschool.org.

    7.   Landis, "Carlisle Indian Industrial School History."

27. A Diverse Portfolio

    1.   "Portfolio 21 Investments," last updated April 14, 2011, http://www.portfolio21.com/index.php.

28. Womanly Arts

    1.   Brian Froud and Jessica Macbeth, The Faeries' Oracle (New York: Simon & Schuster, 2000).

    2.   Jamie Sams and David Carson, Medicine Cards (New York: St. Martin's Press, 1988).

    3.   Froud and Macbeth, Faeries' Oracle, "Card 29: Ta'Om the Poet," 109-111.

    4.   Froud and Macbeth, Faeries' Oracle, "Card 42: Myk the Myomancer," 135-136.

    5.   Froud and Macbeth, Faeries' Oracle, "Card 12: The Singer of the Challis," 72-74.

    6.   Sams and Carson, Medicine Cards, "Card 7: Skunk," 65-67.

29. The Trail Leads Back Home

    1.   Alan Gallay, "Forgotten Story of Indian Slavery," Race and History News and Views, August 3, 2003, http://www.raceandhistory.com/cgi-bin/forum/webbbs_config.pl/noframes/read/1362.

2. O.R. Tipps, letter to his daughters, June 25, 1965.

3. Tipps, 1965.

30. Money Made Howard Stupid Home

1. Anne Wilson Schaef, *When Society Becomes an Addict* (New York: HarperCollins, 1987).

2. Edward L. Bernays, *Propaganda* (Brooklyn: Ig Publishing, 2005, first pub. 1928), 37.

3. "Harvest Time Mission Statement," http://www.harvesttime.cc/.

Ann Mathys, 1957

1. Ann C. Mathys, article submitted to the "First Person Editor," Reader's Digest, February 27, 1957.

31. Did My People Survive Slavery?

1. Bernice Johnson Reagon, "I Remember, I Believe," on Sacred Ground, CD, Songtalk Publishing Co., 1995.

2. Martin Luther King Jr., "Beyond Vietnam: A Time to Break Silence," (delivered April, 1967 at Manhattan's Riverside Church), http://www.commondreams.org/views04/0115-13.htm.

3. Community Wholeness Venture, "Home Page Mission Statement," accessed April 19, 2012, http://communitywholenessventure.org/.

4. Ezekiel 22:29-30.

5. "Ash Wednesday Liturgy," in *The Book of Common Prayer* (New York: Seabury Press, 1979), 267-268.

6. Isaiah 58:12.

a. Jim Crow referred to a series of rigid segregation laws and etiquette rules enacted against people with black skin from 1877 to the mid 1960s in the majority of US states, including my current home state of Oregon. In many areas, widespread violence and lynching reinforced these laws.

32. A Goddess Bursts onto the Scene

1. John 1:5.

2. Joanna Macy and Molly Young Brown, *Coming Back to Life: Practices to Reconnect Our Lives, Our World* (Stony Creek: New Society Publishers, 1998), 48.

3. Lloyd Webber and Tim Rice, "I Don't Know How to Love Him," from Jesus Christ Superstar, perf. by Helen Reddy on Helen Reddy: All Time Greatest Hits, CD, 1995.

4. Ready, Helen and Ray Burton, "I Am Woman," perf. by Helen Reddy on Helen Reddy: All Time Greatest Hits, CD, 1995.

5. Linda Laurie, "Leave Me Alone (Ruby Red Dress)," perf. by Helen Reddy on Helen Reddy: All Time Greatest Hits, CD, 1995.

6. Harriet Schock, "Ain't No Way to Treat a Lady," perf. by Helen Reddy on Helen Reddy: All Time Greatest Hits, CD, 1995.

34. Forgiveness Through Grace

1. Alease Bess, "Footwashing," manuscript draft (unpublished), October 19, 2010.
2. Alease Bess, "Grace," song lyrics (unpublished), 2007.
3. John Newton, "Amazing Grace," in *Olney Hymns*, 1779, accessed May 4, 2012, http://www.ccel.org/ccel/newton/olneyhymns.toc.html.
4. Chronicles 4:10.

35. Pilgrimage Back to My Ancestral Land

1. Robert Lowry, "Nothing but the Blood," in *Gospel Music* (New York: Biglow & Main, 1876), http://www.hymntime.com/tch/htm/n/b/t/nbtblood.htm.
2. Paraphrase of Isaiah 55:1, John 4:10, and John 7:38.
3. Jacques Berthier, "O Lord, Hear My Prayer, Ateliers et Presses de Taize," on Songs of Taize: O Lord, Hear My Prayer and My Soul is at Rest, Volume I, CD, Kingway Music, 1999.

37. Pilgrimage Back Home

1. Jamie Sams and David Carson, *Medicine Cards* (New York: St. Martin's Press, 1988), 61.

O.R. Tipps, 1965

1. Badger Clark, "Ridin'," in *Sun and Saddle Leather* (Boston: The Gorham Press, 1922).
   This was one of O.R.'s favorite books, and one of many poems he quoted regularly.

39. Grandfathers

1. China Galland, *Love Cemetery: Unburying the Secret History of Slaves* (New York: HarperOne, 2007).
2. "The Booker T. Washington Papers," University of Illinois Press (1904): 8, 85, http://www.historycooperative.org/btw/Vol.8/html/85.html.

40. Standing in the Gap

1. Alease Bess, "Heart to Heart," song lyrics (unpublished), 1996.

41. Pilgrimage Inside

1. Reda Rackley and Claudia Wood, email to author, 2010.
2. Rackley and Wood, 2010.
3. Tami Lynn Kent, *Wild Feminine: Finding Power, Spirit & Joy in the Root of the Female Body* (Portland: Tami Kent, LLC, 2008).

42. Called to Return

1. Richard J. Foster, *Streams of Living Water: Celebrating the Great Traditions of the Christian Faith* (New York: HarperCollins, 1998), 237.

2. William Draper, trans., "All Creatures of our God and King," in *The Episcopal Church Hymnal: 1982* (New York: Viking Penguin, Inc., 1988).

a. The phrase "dark night of the soul" was the title of a poem by St. John of the Cross, which explored the portion of the spiritual journey that involved the soul's deepening relationship with God, specifically in regard to the purification of the senses and spirit. Though the "dark night" feels like a time of separation from God, in reality it is a powerful movement towards spiritual maturity and union with God.

b. See John Mathys, 1914.

43. Prayer for the Beginning and the End

1. Adapted from Luke 4:18-19.

Books for the Pilgrimage

These are a few of the many books that have been sustenance for my journey through the big topics. As I look back over the list, I notice diversity—fiction and nonfiction, adult and children's literature, female and male authors. I also notice that most of the authors are white, so I'm now committing to consciously expand my list with books by authors of races and cultures other than my own. Any recommendations?

Bess, Alease. Stepping Off the World: The Miraculous Ministry and Mystery of Foot Washing (due to be published late 2012).

Baldwin, Christina. Storycatcher: Making Sense of Our Lives through the Power and Practice of Story (California: New World Library, 2005).

Bourgeault, Cynthia. The Wisdom Jesus: Transforming Heart and Mind—A New Perspective on Christ and His Message (Massachusetts: Shambhala, 2008).

Carlson, Nancy. I Like Me! (New York: Viking Penguin, Inc., 1988).

Cogan, Priscilla. Winona's Web: A Novel of Discovery (Massachusetts: Two Canoes Press, 2010).

Collins, Chuck and Felice Yeskel with United for a Fair Economy. Economic Apartheid in America: A Primer on Economic Inequality & Insecurity (New York: The New Press, 2000).

DiPucchio, Kelly. Grace for President (New York: Hyperion, 2008).

Douglass, James W. JFK and the Unspeakable: Why He Died and Why It Matters (New York: Touchstone, 2010).

Feldenkrais, Moshe. The Potent Self: A Study of Spontaneity and Compulsion (California: Frog Books, 2002).

Flinders, Carol Lee. Enduring Lives: Portraits of Women and Faith in Action (New York: Tarcher, 2006).

Franquemont, Sharon. You Already Know What to Do: 10 Invitations to the Intuitive Life. (New York: Tarcher/Putnam, 1999).

Galland, China. Love Cemetery: Unburying the Secret History of Slaves (New York: HarperOne, 2007).

Garson, Barbara. Money Makes the World Go Around: One Investor Tracks Her Cash Through the Global Economy, from Brooklyn to Bangkok and Back (New York: Penguin Group, 2001).

Greenwood, Michael T., PhD and Peter Nunn, PhD. Paradox and Healing: Medicine, Mythology and Transformation (California: New Century Press, 1994).

Hafiz, trans. Daniel Ladinsky. The Gift (New York: Penguin Compass, 1999).

Hall, Edward T. The Dance of Life: The Other Dimension of Time (Maine: Anchor, 1984).

Hillesum, Etty. An Interrupted Life and Letters From Westerbork (New York: Metropolitan Books, 1983).

Hillman, Anne. The Dancing Animal Woman: A Celebration of Life (Vermont: Bramble Books, 1994).

---. Awakening the Energies of Love: Discovering Fire for the Second Time (Vermont: Bramble Books, 2008).

Jensen, Derrick. A Language Older Than Words (Vermont: Chelsea Green, 2004).

---. The Culture of Make Believe (Vermont: Chelsea Green, 2004).

Kallos, Stephanie. Broken for You (New York: Grove Press, 2004).

Kelly, Marjorie. The Divine Right of Capital: Dethroning the Corporate Aristocracy (California: Berrett-Koehler Publishers, Inc., 2001).

Kent, Tami Lynn. Wild Feminine: Finding Power, Spirit & Joy in the Root of the Female Body (Portland: Tami Kent, LLC, 2008).

Kidd, Sue Monk. The Secret Life of Bees (New York: Penguin Group, 2002). *I also love several of her other books:* When the Heart Waits: Spiritual Direction for Life's Sacred Questions; The Dance of the Dissident Daughter; and Traveling with Pomegranates: A Mother and Daughter Journey to the Sacred Places of Greece, Turkey, and France *(the latter written with her daughter, Ann Kidd Taylor).*

King Jr., Martin Luther. "Beyond Vietnam: A Time to Break Silence" (Speech delivered at Riverside Church, New York City, April 4, 1967) http://www.americanrhetoric.com/speeches/mlkatimetobreaksilence.htm.

Kingsolver, Barbara. The Poisonwood Bible: A Novel (New York: Harper Perennial Modern Classics, 2008).

Leddy, Mary Jo. Radical Gratitude (New York: Orbis Books, 2002).

L'Engle, Madeleine. The Other Side of the Sun (Illinois: Harold Shaw Publishers, 1971). *I've read most of her books and love them all.*

Le Guin, Ursula K. A Wizard of Earthsea (New York: Bantam Dell, 2004). *Reading all of the books in the "Earthsea Cycle" is time well spent.*

Leondar-Wright, Betsy. Class Matters: Cross-Class Alliance Building for Middle-Class Activists (British Columbia: New Society Publishers, 2005).

Linnea, Ann and Lyanda Lynn Haupt. Keepers of the Trees: A Guide to Re-Greening North America (New York: Skyhorse Publishing, 2010).

Lipsitz, George. The Possessive Investment in Whiteness: How White People Profit from Identity Politics (Philadelphia: Temple University Press, 1988).

Macy, Joanna and Molly Young Brown. Coming Back to Life: Practices to Reconnect Our Lives, Our World (Stony Creek: New Society Publishers, 1998).

Maitri, Sandra. The Spiritual Dimension of the Enneagram: Nine Faces of the Soul (New York: Tarcher, 2001).

May, Gerald G. The Awakened Heart: Opening Yourself to the Love You Need (New York: HarperOne, 1993).

Norris, Kathleen. Dakota: A Spiritual Geography (Boston: Houghton Mifflin Harcourt, 1993).

Pepper, William F. An Act of State: The Execution of Martin Luther King (New York: Verso, 2003).

Pinkola Estés, Clarissa, PhD. Women Who Run with the Wolves: Myths and Stories of the Wild Woman Archetype (New York: Ballantine Books, 1996).

---. Untie the Strong Woman: Blessed Mother's Immaculate Love for the Wild Soul (Colorado: Sounds True, Inc., 2011).

Plass, Adrian. The Sacred Diary of Adrian Plass, Aged 37 ¾ (Michigan: Zondervan, 2005).

Riso, Don Richard and Russ Hudson. The Wisdom of the Enneagram: The Complete Guide to Psychological and Spiritual Growth for the Nine Personality Types (New York: Bantam Dell, 1999).

Rohr, Richard. Jesus' Plan for a New World: The Sermon on the Mount (St. Anthony Messenger Press, 1996).

Rolheiser, Ronald. The Holy Longing: The Search for a Christian Spirituality (New York: The Doubleday Religious Publishing Group, 1999).

Sams, Jamie. The Thirteen Original Clan Mothers: Your Sacred Path to Discovering the Gifts, Talents, and Abilities of the Feminine through the Ancient Teachings of the Sisterhood (New York: HarperCollins, 1994).

Singh, Kathleen Dowling. Grace in Dying: How We Are Transformed Spiritually As We Die (New York: HarperCollins Publishers, 1998).

Swimme, Brian, PhD. The Universe is a Green Dragon: A Cosmic Creation Story (Vermont: Bear & Company, 1984).

Tolle, Eckhart. The Power of Now: A Guide to Spiritual Enlightenment (California: New World Library, 2004).

Tutu, Desmond. No Future Without Forgiveness (New York: Doubleday, 1999).

Twain, Mark. The War Prayer (New York: Harper Colophon, 1984).

Violi, Jen. Putting Makeup on Dead People (New York: Hyperion Books, 2011).

Volf, Miroslav. Exclusion & Embrace: A Theological Exploration of Identity, Otherness, and Reconciliation (Tennessee: Abingdon Press, 1996).

Weed, Susan S. New Menopausal Years: The Wise Woman Way – Alternative Approaches for Women 30-90 (New York: Ash Tree Publishing, 2011).

Wink, Walter. The Powers That Be: Theology for a New Millennium (New York: Three Rivers Press, 1999).

Zinn, Howard. A People's History of the United States: 1942-Present (New York: HarperCollins Publishers, 2003).

Art Among Words

Why? by Sue

I am my mother's daughter.

I grew up not only with art hanging on the walls but also silk-screened Christmas cards drying on the dining room floor, sketches on bits of paper around the house and half-finished stitcheries folded up beside Mom's living room chair.

When Mom was alive, it wasn't easy for me to be artistically creative. Despite her encouragement, I never felt like I measured up to her talent. Since her death, I've still felt her encouragement, but I've let go of the need to measure up. Now I find myself regularly making all kinds of art. Over the years I have sewed, macraméd a guitar strap for Howard and an owl for our wall and penned letters. In writing this book, I've often stopped to do line drawings, as well as collage or additional creative work with my ideas in media other than writing.

Shortly after I began writing *Big Topics at Midnight*, I read Derrick Jenson's *A Language Older Than Words*. His combination of words and art, two languages dear to my heart, let me know that it was possible to have drawings in an adult book. Given that the essence of my journey was exploring diversity, it only made sense to create a book that looked like a cornucopia.

I met artist Khara Scott-Bey at a Be Present training and asked if she'd be willing to do some drawings for a book I was writing. To my delight, she was. Khara intuitively knew which nugget to pull from each chapter for the accompanying illustration. She also designed my "family tree"—an exquisite woman filled with a DNA spiral, the miraculous strand that connects me to my ancestors and descendants.

In addition, I included a few photographs of Mom's art—stitcheries, woodcuts and a couple of silkscreen prints. I loved how some of her pieces dovetailed with my writing.

For me, exploring big topics required many doorways: verbal, visual and more. I hope the drawings and pictures in this book bring you as much delight as they've given me.

Sue   *Khara*   *Nancy*

My Creative Support Team

I wrote this book. But I didn't walk alone.

Three people in particular supported my creative process and made this book what it is. Christina Baldwin, co-founder of PeerSpirit and teacher of the workshop "The Self as the Source of the Story," called together writers circles that held me in the early phases of the work. Christina told me that there was a book in my story and "held the rim" to support my writing during these past seven years.

Jen Violi moved to Portland just in the nick of time. After I'd thought I was finished with the book for the second time, only to realize that I needed a whole new structure, Jen stepped onto the scene. Copies of the manuscript have gone back and forth between us hundreds of times over the last two years. Jen knew how to call forth my best writing, send me back to dive deeper and make the suggestions that honored my voice.

Khara Scott-Bey made her appearance during this final year of the book's gestation, first to listen and then to draw an image for each chapter. Most of the time, her first idea perfectly captured the spirit of the chapter.

I highly recommend each of these women and invite you to check out their work.

Christina Baldwin: Writer, Wanderer, Teacher on the Trail of Community and Story

Christina was a founder of the journal writing movement in the late 1970s. For over twenty years she has taught a classic memoir seminar that has helped amateur and avocational writers deepen their practice from private pleasure to published books. She is a global pioneer in personal writing and circle process—connecting these passions through the art of *storycatching*, creating respectful spaces for speaking and listening, writing and reading. Her company, co-founded with Ann Linnea in 1994, is PeerSpirit. Her best known titles include, *Life's Companion, Journal Writing as Spiritual Practice, Storycatcher, Making Sense of our Lives through the Power and Practice of Story*, and *The Circle Way, A Leader in Every Chair* (with Linnea). www.peerspirit.com

Jen Violi: Writer and Book Midwife

Jen Violi, author of *Putting Makeup on Dead People*, creates her life amidst the green and caffeine in Portland, Oregon. Also, she's a book midwife, helping writers bring forth the books they were meant to write. So why not coach or editor? Book writing is personal and life-changing, and what Jen offers honors that. Side effects can include back pain, weird food cravings and big feelings, so Jen's work with writers includes healthy supplements of compassion, reverence and pickles, as needed. www.jenvioli.com.

Khara Scott-Bey: Artist, Expressive Art Therapist

Native Ohioan Khara Scott-Bey currently resides in Berkeley, California, where she received her MA in Expressive Arts Therapy at the California Institute of Integral Studies. Her work as a therapist is rooted in her work as an activist and artist. Khara's approach is grounded in social justice work, Womanist Psychology, Jungian theory, and Person Centered practices. She is a practitioner of Generative Somatics and a Be Present workshop facilitator. Currently Khara is an assistant teacher for Generative Somatics, has a budding private practice and works as a domestic violence advocate for GLIDE's women's center in San Francisco. For more information on Khara and her modalities, visit www.livetobecome.com or check out her online store at www.livetobecome.etsy.com.

The Gift Flows

Big Topics at Midnight: A Texas Girl Wakes Up to Race, Class, Gender and Herself was a gift that gushed into my life. Working on this book guided, delighted and most of all awakened me. I felt privileged to be invited by Spirit to walk this journey of waking up, and every step of the way I was lavishly supported by Spirit, people and the Earth. I don't want this gift to stop with me.

My family wealth came through a fruit of the earth held deep underground—natural gas. Receiving money from petrochemicals whose use and overuse has harmed our planet troubled me, so Howard and I committed to transmuting the environmental damage into gift and letting the wealth move. In part, we allowed the money to flow into our family to support our material needs while we did the work of our hearts. In part, we also allowed the money to flow into the transformational work of organizations.

As this book takes off and makes millions (why not dream big?), I bring the same awareness and commitment to the movement and sharing of wealth and gift. To that end, ten percent of the proceeds from the sale of this book will be invested in three non-profits dear to my heart: Be Present, Inc., Harvest Time, and Community Wholeness Venture.

All three organizations walk their talk. Their values and missions inform and enliven their programs, planning, organizational structures, finances, creativity and human resource policies. Each plays a critical role in the movement toward sustainable social change and spiritual transformation needed by our world today.

Largely due to the vision and mentoring of these three organizations, I have come home to myself and to the world around me. Each has offered me its own unique set of tools, perspective and flavor that has nourished my spirit and illuminated the path. Within the middle of all three, I am on holy ground.

Be Present, Inc. believes that in order to create peace and justice for all people, we are all responsible for examining the impact of race, gender, class, power, homophobia, and more, on the effectiveness of our relationships and social movements. We develop sustainable leadership for social justice through teaching the Be Present Empowerment Model®, providing training and systems of support, building a national network of activists, and fostering active partnerships with other nonprofits engaged in strengthening the capacity of individuals, families, schools, communities, and organizations to thrive and change the world.

www.bepresent.org

Community Wholeness Venture (CWV) is changing the world, one heart, one mind, one life at a time. Our exciting challenge is this: for systemic change to occur, people must learn to negotiate and maximize many differences in culture, values, religion, abilities, understandings, and more. CWV is founded upon the premise that the only way to change what is outside of us is to change what is inside of us. We are building leaders from the inside out. We need individuals to step forward into divine destiny and to skillfully use biblical principles and spiritual gifts to change the world by changing lives.

www.communitywholenessventure.org

Harvest Time invites Christians of wealth to come together in circles to engage with money as a doorway to spiritual transformation at the personal, communal and systemic levels. Through small group retreats, personal spiritual companionship and written reflections, Harvest Time offers inspiration, encouragement and challenge to people of wealth who desire to align their faith and their financial resources. Rooted in the Christian tradition, Harvest Time welcomes people of all faiths who feel called to join our circles and journey along the path of Spirit in the service of love, joy and justice.

www.harvesttime.cc

Index

About Nancy

Nancy Thurston has always been drawn toward healing work. After three academic degrees and a career in physical therapy, she turned to spiritual formation, particularly through bringing money into alignment with her heart. With a desire for cross-class conversation, she found her own experience was woefully inadequate for understanding the issues that emerged in relationships across differences in financial access as well as differences in skin color and gender.

Nancy participated in the two-year Academy for Spiritual Formation, trained as a Bible study teacher and studied the art of spiritual direction. She has been a licensed lay preacher in the Episcopal church and an Associate with the Sisters of the Presentation of the Blessed Virgin Mary in Fargo, North Dakota. Nancy has co-facilitated trainings through Journey Into Freedom and Be Present, Inc. and is currently board president of Harvest Time. For Be Present, Nancy serves as both co-chair of the Board of Directors' Vision Based Social Change Fundraising Committee and a member of their Capacity Building Campaign Team.

Through writing, leadership and philanthropy, Nancy continues to work for healing across the generations and around the globe—always starting with herself. *Big Topics at Midnight: A Texas Girl Wakes Up to Race, Class, Gender and Herself* is her first book. She and her husband, Howard, live in Portland, Oregon, and have two adult children.

www.nancymthurston.com